Sacred Engagements

Sacred Engagements

Interfaith Marriage, Religious Toleration,
and the British Novel, 1750–1820

ALISON CONWAY

Johns Hopkins University Press
Baltimore

© 2023 Johns Hopkins University Press
All rights reserved. Published 2023
Printed in the United States of America on acid-free paper
2 4 6 8 9 7 5 3 1

Johns Hopkins University Press
2715 North Charles Street
Baltimore, Maryland 21218
www.press.jhu.edu

Library of Congress Cataloging-in-Publication Data

Names: Conway, Alison, author.
Title: Sacred engagements : interfaith marriage, religious toleration, and the British novel, 1750–1820 / Alison Conway.
Description: Baltimore : Johns Hopkins University Press, 2023. | Includes bibliographical references and index.
Identifiers: LCCN 2022010130 | ISBN 9781421445144 (hardcover : acid-free paper) | ISBN 9781421445151 (paperback) | ISBN 9781421445168 (ebook)
Subjects: LCSH: English fiction—18th century—History and criticism. | English fiction—19th century—History and criticism. | Interfaith marriage in literature. | Religious tolerance in literature. | Women in literature. | Richardson, Samuel, 1689-1761. History of Sir Charles Grandison. | Brooke, Frances, 1724?-1789. History of Emily Montague. | Inchbald, Mrs., 1753-1821. Simple story. | Edgeworth, Maria, 1768-1849. Harrington. | Religion and politics—Great Britain—History. | LCGFT: Literary criticism.
Classification: LCC PR858.M36 C66 2023 | DDC 823/.6093543—dc23/eng/20220722
LC record available at https://lccn.loc.gov/2022010130

A catalog record for this book is available from the British Library.

Illustrations © The Trustees of the British Museum. All rights reserved.

Special discounts are available for bulk purchases of this book. For more information, please contact Special Sales at specialsales@jh.edu.

For Cathy

CONTENTS

List of Illustrations ix
Acknowledgments xi

Introduction: Novel Intimacies 1

1 Religious Toleration and Interfaith Marriage, 1640–1720 18

2 *Sir Charles Grandison*'s Religious Disturbances 47

3 Frances Brooke's Civil Disputes 82

4 Elizabeth Inchbald among the Cisalpines 110

5 Maria Edgeworth's Jewish Enlightenment 137

Conclusion: *Mansfield Park* Closes Its Gates 163

Notes 171
Bibliography 195
Index 215

ILLUSTRATIONS

Anon., *An extravaganza or young Solomon besieging Fitzhubbub* (1786)   16
William Hogarth, *The Harlot's Progress* (1732)   51
Anon., *The Jerusalem Infirmary* (c. 1750)   52
Louis Philippe Boitard, *The Grand Conference or the Jew Predominant* (1753)   55
Anon., *Vox Populi Vox Dei, or The Jew Act Repealed* (1753)   59
John Dixon, *The Oracle* (1774)   93
Thomas Rowlandson, *Transplanting of Teeth* (1787)   147

ACKNOWLEDGMENTS

This book was written under difficult circumstances: the dismantling of homes and community, a death in the family, and COVID-19. I have never been more grateful for the generosity of friends and colleagues. During the first summer of the pandemic, Toni Bowers, Shawn Maurer, Helen Thompson, Betty Schellenberg, Mary Helen McMurran, Susan Manly, and Pam Perkins provided incisive commentary on chapter drafts. Cathy Gallagher and Tita Chico helped me frame the book's central questions. Rebecca Probert answered many questions concerning marriage practices in the long eighteenth century. In the final round of edits, Elizabeth Kraft was my *Grandison* champion, and I'm happy that this study references a new edition of the novel, published by Cambridge University Press, thanks to her. Peter Sabor tracked down obscure Richardson references whose full citations I had forgotten to note. A special thanks to Devoney Looser and George Justice, who provided support and help at just the right moment.

I have long felt lucky to have homes in both the Canadian and the American Societies for Eighteenth-Century Studies, and I want to thank those who provided feedback in conference sessions, and over coffee, lunch, and dinner, for their attention and engagement. A 2012 Huntington Library fellowship allowed for a deep dive into the archives. That summer I was fortunate enough to be at the Huntington with Steve Pincus, who organized lunches where readers could present their work. Steve's enthusiasm was, and remains, infectious. My thanks to the Huntington's staff for making visits to the library enjoyable, always. The Social Sciences and Humanities Research Council of Canada provided funding support for this project. A Gale and Graham Wright award, administered by the University of Western Ontario, and start-up funds at my new institutional home at the University of British Columbia, Okanagan, also provided support. I'm grateful for the careful work of research assistants Emily Sugerman and Mathieu Aubin. Catherine Goldstead, at Johns Hopkins University Press, guided the project to submission; my thanks to her and to Carrie Watterson for their fine editorial skills.

My colleagues in the English Department at the University of Western Ontario, Anne Schuurman, Kate Stanley, and Jonathan Boulter, reminded me, on a daily basis, why literary studies matter. My new colleagues in UBCO's gender and women's studies program, Ilya Parkins, Sue Frohlick, and Heather Latimer, have supported me with dog walks and dinners, and I thank them for their friendship and feminist acumen. For her kindness, Katherine Binhammer can't be thanked enough. For cheering me on in dark times, my thanks to Jamie Zeppa. My father's work as a historian of modern Germany taught me early the dangers of xenophobia and anti-Semitism. My mother's deep and abiding Christian faith has shown me the importance of supporting women's religious independence. For my parents' love and support, I thank them. My immediate family members have me close at hand, and I'm glad my children developed a sardonic wit as they matured into adults. For thirty-one years, Bryce Traister has been by my side, and I'm grateful every day for his understanding.

As I approach the final years of my career, I want to thank the PhD supervisor who made it possible. When I took a graduate seminar with Cathy Gallagher in 1989 (Women Writers before Jane Austen), I could not have known how profoundly she would shape my life and work. From dissertation to this book, she has strength-tested my ideas and shared her own. The joy Cathy brings to her readings of the novel and to the world at large has served as a lifeline, every time I've needed one. This book is dedicated to her.

A portion of chapter 2 was originally published as "*Sir Charles Grandison* and the Sexual Politics of Toleration" in *Lumen: Selected Proceedings from the Canadian Society for Eighteenth-Century Studies* 30 (2011): 1–20. A few sentences and paragraphs from the book first appeared in "'Uncommon Sentiments': Religious Freedom and the Marriage Plot in Charlotte Lennox's *Henrietta*," *Tulsa Studies in Women's Literature* 34, no. 2 (Fall 2015): 231–48; and "'Unequally Yoked': Defoe and the Challenge of Mixed Marriage," in *Reflections on Sentiment: Essays in Honor of George Starr*, edited by Alessa Johns (Newark: University of Delaware Press, 2016), 11–28.

Sacred Engagements

INTRODUCTION

Novel Intimacies

> Be ye not unequally yoked together with unbelievers: for what fellowship hath righteousness with unrighteousness? And what communion hath light with darkness?
>
> —*2 Corinthians 6:14*

When I began this project, I looked forward to using "unequally yoked" in my book title—that is, until I entered the words into the search engine of World-Cat, where they appear in nearly two dozen titles published between 1891 and 2019. A review of publications since 2010 reveals an even split between works of fiction, including a trilogy in an African American Christian romance series, and self-help titles such as *Unequally Yoked: Staying Committed to Jesus and Your Unbelieving Spouse* (2018). A tag line of a 2010 DVD, *Unequally Yoked*, asks, "Who will Trina Mills choose? The man who has won her heart or the man that shares her faith?" The contest between religious duty and romantic love provides rich soil for exegesis. We can read allegorically, watching Trina choose between the secular world and the church. We can map Trina's religious interiority: will her faith hold her heart steady? And we can hope that Trina's Christian example might serve as a beacon for her romantic love interest, bringing him onto the right path.

As a reader of eighteenth-century literature, I look back to Daniel Defoe for an early rendering of the questions raised by Trina's dilemma. In his 1722 conduct manual, *Religious Courtship*, Defoe tells the story of three sisters choosing marriage partners after the death of their mother. On her death bed, their mother makes them promise, "1 *Never to marry any man, whatever his person or fortune be, that did not, at least, profess to be a* Religious Man. *2 Never to marry any man, how religious soever he may seem to be, if he was not of the same principles and opinion regarding religion as themselves.*"[1] One of the sisters describes the promise they have made to their mother, as well as the injunctions themselves, as "very sacred engagements."[2] Choosing a marriage partner wisely honors a family's religious commitments. To marry an outsider is to compromise the integrity of the family's boundaries. Conjugal love is rooted in religious sameness, and the spouses foster, in their mutual regard, the faith that binds their larger Christian community.

But, as is so often the case in Defoe's writing, the conduct book goes on to challenge the prohibitions it lays down. The stories it tells about marriage complicate the idea that religious sameness can be secured between spouses, once and for all, by either pre- or postmarital declarations. Instead, we read of spouses whose commitments wax and wane, who convert from one Christian denomination to another, who fall into unbelief before converting to belief again. *All* marriages, we discover, have the potential to take on a "mixed" quality as they unfold. Religious consensus among family members involves a complex set of negotiations that involve the larger community. Peaceful coexistence depends on that community's ability to develop narratives that ameliorate the pain of marital strife caused by religious difference.[3]

In this book, I argue that the conversation about interfaith marriage that unfolds in prose fiction between 1750 and 1820 advances the novel's thinking on the subject of religious toleration and the role it plays in community formation.[4] Interfaith marriage models an ethics of sociability capable of sustaining the religious pluralism that was written into English law by the Toleration Act of 1689, expanding the legal framework to encompass a new cultural sensibility. In Mary Collyer's 1755 novel, *Felicia to Charlotte*, Felicia narrates an exchange between her husband and a Protestant father charged with bullying his daughter, who was raised in the Catholic faith by her now deceased mother: "Lucius artfully introduced the subject of religious liberty, which he proved to be the birthright of every reasonable being. He made use of the most convincing arguments. He quoted the incomparable Mr. Locke's piece on this subject; a work, which he assured us, was of more value than a Peruvian mine."[5] Lucius's familiarity with John Locke's *Letter Concerning Toleration* (1689) signals his status as a civil gentleman, whose "artful" and "convincing" rhetoric invites others to join his conversational circle. He persuades the father to relent in his persecution and, by doing so, models a paternal governance that advocates for gentler modes of rule than that of patriarchal compulsion. As Susan Staves has observed, Lucius represents "a new kind of masculine hero," one whose sensibility exemplifies the philosophical ideals of the British Enlightenment, a sensibility contrasted, in this novel, to that of a zealous Calvinist, Prudella, whose public displays of religiosity veil her sexual corruption.[6]

Novelists reflecting on toleration and marriage had Locke in view, but marriage practices in local communities also shaped the conversations they undertook. Precise numbers are difficult to determine, but religious minorities were few throughout the eighteenth century. The number of Jews, for instance, rose from five hundred in 1680 to twenty-five thousand in 1800—a dramatic increase—but they continued to represent less than 1 percent of the overall population.[7] Catholics, similarly, hovered around 1 percent of the English population throughout the period. Protestant Dissent varied, with numbers among Quakers and Presbyterians dropping while others (Congregationalists and Baptists) rose with the evangelical turn in the 1760s; but, again, Dissenters were less than 10 percent of the total population before 1800.[8] Despite these small numbers, interfaith marriage remained a cultural preoccupation, and, as a practice, we see a steady increase in rates of these marriages.[9] In his study of late seventeenth-century Lancashire Catholics, Michael Galgano notes that "the high proportion of mixed marriages stood in marked contrast with the early part of the [seventeenth] century when such actions signified apostasy."[10] A hundred years later, "in the north-east, mixed marriages were almost as common as those between two Roman Catholics."[11] Among Protestant sects, the dearth of suitable partners in small communities meant that interfaith marriages were common among Quakers, Baptists, and Congregationalists.[12] As David J. Hall notes of the Quakers, "It is difficult to see how it could have been otherwise, given the small numbers in the Society relative to any particular community."[13] The meeting minutes of the Rothwell Congregational Church acknowledge, in 1691, that church members might find themselves involved with members of other local denominations: "It was unanimously agreed that our brethren and sisters should chiefly endeavor to marry among themselves or else them that are Church Members, but if a brother or sister should be inclined towards any that are not members of a Church in a Gospell order, that then they at first should make it known to the officers, or any of them, and they to the Church; that soe the Church may be satisfied ere they proceed to entangle one another's affections."[14] In October 1698 the same church notes that "messengers . . . sent to admonish sister Sarah Uffington a 2d. time brought for answer which was to this effect, that if the church would provide for an honest man she would possibly renounce the company of the carnall man, but she thought there were but few honest men in the Church."[15] Sarah Uffington's complaint concerning the lack of "honest" men in her congregation underscores how communities had to weigh competing claims—the desire for uniformity against the individual worthiness of a prospective marriage partner. Edward H. Milligan documents the various compromises recorded in Quaker meeting minutes when the community was confronted by someone who had married "out": "Sometimes monthly meetings satisfied their consciences by securing an apology in terms which did not actually express regret for the marriage. . . . [M]any of those who were disowned were, after a decent lapse, reinstated."[16] Clearly practical considerations overrode cultural prohibitions, however much congregations and communities encouraged their young people to marry "in."

I need to pause, here, to introduce the terms guiding my study of marriage in the long eighteenth century. The term "interfaith" does not appear in the *OED* until the twentieth century, when it is used to distinguish marriages that cross faith and denomination divides from other kinds of mixed unions, including those of race and ethnicity.[17] In the seventeenth and eighteenth centuries, the term "mixed marriage" describes interfaith unions, most commonly, but I use the contemporary term to avoid the connotation of "interracial" that "mixed" has acquired.[18] These categories of intermarriage are not, of course, discrete now; nor were they in the eighteenth century, and their overlap informs this study, most immediately with regard to its investigation of Jewish-Christian marriages in England. In her study of British marriage practices, Rebecca Probert has observed that a tolerance for the distinctiveness of Jewish marriage, which was exempted from the regulations of the Hardwicke Marriage Act of 1753, did not translate into an acceptance of Jews as part of English society in the eighteenth century: "The virulent reaction to the contemporaneous Jewish Naturalization Bill illustrates that there was a profound difference between accepting their distinctiveness and accepting them as English citizens."[19] Although the racial category of the "semite" would not appear for another hundred years, it is clear that a racial logic governs English attitudes toward Jews in the eighteenth century.[20] English anti-Semitism shows us how categories of race evolved before they were given their contemporary forms by modern science and the nation-state. "The category of race was co-constituted with religion," notes Nasar Meer.[21] My readings of the question of Judaism and the marriage plot show how questions of religious belief and the problem of conversion are also questions about the racial purity of the nation's marriages, organized around the principle of "one flesh." As British Protestantism gained its hegemonic status at home and abroad, a broad range of subjects, including Italian Catholics, came to be associated with "blackness" and, by extension, impurity.[22] And as the scope of imperialism and the trade in enslaved peoples expanded, the imbrication of religious, ethnic, and racial categories became even more pronounced. Frances Brooke's account of marriage between French Canadian men and Indigenous women in *The History of Emily Montague*, for instance, is not only about the power of non-Christian spiritual practices in relation to British subjects, but also the possibilities afforded by mixed-race unions.[23]

My focus, however, remains on the practice and representation of intermarriage we now call "interfaith," as a way of delineating the novel's response to debates about toleration and marriage regulation in eighteenth-century Britain, which referenced Catholics, Protestant Dissenters, and Jews. Christian/Muslim and Christian/Hindu marriage plots began to appear in eighteenth-century narratives and would take hold of the cultural imagination in the nineteenth century with the consolidation of the British Empire.[24] But my primary concern is the novel's engagement with an evolving legal and political theory of religious toleration in Britain. As Rebecca Probert notes, "religious minorities, such as Hindus and Muslims," registered "not at all in the case law."[25] Nor do I attend to international marriages, such as those that appear in Charlotte Smith's novels, or to the allegories of an England-Ireland union imagined by Sydney Morgan.[26] My focus is on the unsettling feelings created by difference *within* the nation—the moment when the familiar becomes *unheimlich*, when the advent of religious pluralism threatened to place a stranger in the marriage bed.[27] By the beginning of the nineteenth century, those "strangers" would include new arrivals in the British Isles, and "home" would include the colonies. In a 2006 essay on Charlotte Smith's *Desmond*, Anne K. Mellor asks, "Where would one locate a new interracial, international, interfaith community? Certainly not in England."[28] The eighteenth-century novels I examine here outline an alternative story, and I hope future studies will build on the foundation this book lays down, using it as a starting point from which to trace the cultural histories of marginalized communities as they are recounted by the novel.

In addition to attending to how alterity was projected onto the religious minorities studied here as part of a long history of domestic racism, it is also important to keep in view how the category of "whiteness" evolved in relation to toleration discourse. In a recent essay on *Paradise Lost*, Daniel Shore notes how Milton's poem inscribes concepts of racial difference "into the division between the universality of persons who enjoy liberty and those excluded from that pseudo-universality."[29] Shore draws on the work of Charles W. Mills, who argues that "liberalism . . . has historically been predominantly a racial liberalism, in which conceptions of personhood and resulting schedules of rights, duties, and government responsibilities have all been racialized."[30] Mills acknowledges his indebtedness to Carole Pateman's account of patriarchal liberalism, and my work brings these two critiques into conversation. The interfaith marriage plot, I argue, reveals the connection between liberal understandings of sexual difference and its theory of religious toleration. Religious toleration, in the public sphere, depends on politeness and civility—modes that bracket the interrogation of conviction and sincerity in others. Religion's strong feelings, I suggest, are relegated to the private sphere; family religious uniformity serves as the bedrock for toleration in the public sphere. That uniformity, however, depends on women's willingness to subordinate their own religious freedom to the regulation of their husbands. Here, Locke's social theory comes into play, whereby women "naturally" submit to their husband's authority. At the same time, the masculine subject must continuously prove not only his patriarchal authority in the home but also his status as an English gentleman in public. In her reading of Locke, Teresa Bejan argues that the model of civility that he promotes reflects an "unabashedly elite and elitist standard"—one firmly anchored in a white social imaginary.[31]

In making this argument, I contribute a cultural piece to the larger puzzle of secularism's evolution in the West. Following Talal Asad and other postcolonial critics, I understand secularism not as the retreat of religion from the public sphere, but as a reconfiguration of Protestant Christian epistemologies. Secularism, Asad argues, "is an enactment by which a political medium (representation of citizenship) redefines and transcends particular and differentiating practices of the self that are articulated through class, gender, and religion."[32] This enactment is gendered, racialized, and faith specific; it is the white male Protestant subject who advances secularism's agenda in the nineteenth century. In a 2013 essay, Joan Wallach Scott shows how the private/public opposition that underpins secularism "rests on a vision of sexual difference that legitimates the political and social inequality of women."[33] In the Christian West, Scott argues, the "feminization of belief" produced a fear of female religiosity that "threatened to disrupt or undermine the rational pursuits that constitute politics."[34] This fear persists today in Western accounts of Muslim women and the debates around the hijab that invariably attend discussions of their faith, Scott observes.

This book studies the moment before secularism's emergence in the mid-nineteenth century.[35] In considering secularism's prehistory in the eighteenth-century novel, we see what we might call a "counterfactual" toleration history, one that makes *explicit* the gendered division of affective labor that shapes political philosophy and that refuses the conflation of toleration and secularism. I follow Scott's line of investigation by showing how toleration moves the work of religious belief into the home to better protect the formal practices of civility in the public sphere. Masculine religiosity defines itself by its self-restraint, its ability to maintain a polite difference from "zeal." Women's strong religious feelings, cultivated in the home, do not threaten the political, as in Scott's account, but sustain it by creating family uniformity. But when women's religious obligations set them at odds with their love objects, as they do in the instance of the interfaith marriage plot, those obligations challenge conjugal imperatives.

The interfaith marriage plot explores the contradiction that emerges when women are obliged to relinquish their conscience to confirm the authority of men. To relinquish conscience to another is to violate a central tenet of liberal toleration theory. In focusing their attention on this contradiction, narratives that represent interfaith unions interrupt the more commonplace marriage plot of the eighteenth-century novel. By now we are familiar with the conventions governing this plot: its efforts to unite like-minded individuals, its advocacy for women's moral authority, and its concern for the social advancement of the middling ranks.[36] Feminist critics have identified the novel's contribution to the evolution of modern liberalism, including its naturalization of women's subordination in marriage.[37] Interfaith marriage counters the novel's alignment of marriage with the privatization of religious feeling and, by doing so, effectively politicizes marriage.

In advancing this argument, I write against the more familiar critical narrative—that women's emancipation from religious strictures creates the conditions for modern feminism.[38] Susan Stanford Friedman has described religion as "the elephant in the room" of feminist intersectionality: "Why has intersectionality as a theoretical concept and methodology in queer/feminist studies left out religion as a constitutive part of identity?" The problem, she suggests, is that intersectional theory rests on theories of power that do not sufficiently account for women's religious activism.[39] Scholars of eighteenth-century cultural history have provided rich accounts of women's religious thought but, for the most part, these accounts have remained isolated from readings of the canonical texts of prose fiction.[40] This book studies women's religious activism to underscore the central role played by the novel in shaping cultural understandings of gender in relation to an emergent religious pluralism.

The secularization thesis has long dominated histories of the novel. It associates the rise of the woman author with a move away from questions of faith and religious community, part of a larger trajectory that leads to the disappearance of religion from the public sphere. So, for instance, Lisa O'Connell describes a shift from political and religious controversy in the novels of Samuel Richardson and Henry Fielding to the "heroine-focussed secular narratives" of Jane Austen and Frances Burney.[41] Justin Neuman has shown how literary critics' reliance on the secularization thesis prevents them from seeing how fiction provides a window onto an expansive range of religious experiences. Were we to account for "the embodied and communal aspects of religiosity" in our readings of the novel, he suggests, a very different picture of faith and its vicissitudes would appear.[42]

To read the eighteenth-century novel from a postsecular vantage point is, by my account, to attend to how prose fiction shapes cultural understandings of the seventeenth century's legacy—religious pluralism—both in relation to the statecraft of religious toleration and to long-standing practices of communal coexistence.[43] By "postsecular" I mean two things: first, a historical claim about the toleration debate, one that foregrounds the importance of seventeenth-century religious thought to Enlightenment discourse, complicating the faith/reason opposition maintained by secular epistemologies; and second, a way of reading, one that brings "secular" and "religious" into dialogue with each other through an interpretation of narrative hermeneutics. The eighteenth century, read through this postsecular lens, both advances and critiques modernity's habits of mind and of life, complicating its normative discourses even as they are formed. In their accounts of religious toleration and interfaith marriage, eighteenth-century authors confront the facts of ongoing conflict—conflict that came to a head in the Gordon Riots of 1780—and its resemblance to the religious violence of the seventeenth century. As they advance the project of modern marriage, they echo John Milton's account of divorce, forged during a civil war.

Novels that take up these questions start with interfaith marriage to highlight the competing obligations—communal, familial, and conjugal—that shape a religious life. The eighteenth-century realist novel frames the questions surrounding interfaith marriage as hermeneutic challenges: In a world divided among Quakers, Baptists, Congregationalists, Presbyterians, Anglicans, Catholics, and Jews, how does one "read" another person's faith? Which of the stories that individuals tell about faith prove more or less reliable? How do conflicting stories challenge the possibility of a stable cultural norms? Narrative questions thus become central to navigating the problem of religious pluralism and, more particularly, to identifying the rights of religious minorities and women.

The novel not only frames these questions but also provides an account of how storytelling, as an imaginative act, can answer them. Novels show how storytelling can provide a safety net for religious difference, incorporating stories of belief into a discussion that extends beyond the immediacy of marital conflict to larger community engagement. In this context, religious difference appears as one of the vicissitudes of everyday life, open to exploration as part of an evolving social plot about reciprocity and hospitality. Stories of the marginal and the vulnerable can be heard within the spaces the novel provides and granted authority by their interlocuters.

To suggest that narrative hermeneutics sustain modes of reciprocity is to enter into a well-established critical debate about the novel and tolerance.[44] The thesis that the novel, among literary forms, is best suited to fostering tolerance was promulgated by critics throughout the 1970s and 1980s. In 1984, Alain Morvan identified tolerance as the novel's central concern: "The path followed by the eighteenth-century English novel [is] both the logos and praxis of tolerance."[45] The formalist interest in Mikhail Bakhtin's theory of the novel as a species of "heteroglossia"—that is, of multiple social dialects—converged with the historicists' analyses of how the novel invites readers to identify with the "new and particular stories" of various social actors spread across the narrative landscape.[46] The novel gains its cultural authority, in these accounts, from its ability to draw the reader into a world of disparate voices and stories. This theory of the novel was sharply rebuked by the political criticism of the 1980s and 1990s, which countered with a reading of prose fiction as a tool of division and exploitation. According to this view, the novel's account of sympathetic identification masks its ideological investment, a thesis most notably advanced by John Bender's *Imagining the Penitentiary*, which allegorizes the novel as a carceral imaginary.[47] Read through this lens, the novel contributes to the cultural hegemony that maintains the exclusions and the asymmetries of state power. The novel's "tolerance" is merely a tool used to prop up these power relations, a top-down disciplinary regime.

The ethical turn in literary theory in the past twenty years has reframed this conversation, drawing on Emmanuel Levinas, Jacques Derrida, and others to advance an alternative understanding of how prose fiction addresses the problem of alterity.[48] Studies such as Rachel Hollander's *Narrative Hospitality in Late Victorian Fiction* read the novel as striving toward the ideal of recognition while foregrounding the limits of knowledge—a dynamic process of engagement.[49] Dorothy J. Hale, following a similar logic, shows how "the reader feels he or she comes to know more each time his or her knowledge is confounded." The reader can imagine herself "free" only to the extent that she recognizes herself as being "socially bound . . . in a constitutive relation with the other."[50] Approaching the novel through the lens of the new ethics helps us to move beyond accounts of the novel as either emancipatory or ideologically instrumental. Hale uses Henry James as an example of how "the politicized struggle between art and its ideological instrumentality" comes to constitute "novelistic aesthetics itself."[51]

I bring the insights of Hale and Hollander into my reading of the eighteenth-century novel, arguing that its representation of interfaith marriage refuses the intellectual orientation of eighteenth-century political philosophy and by doing so, creates the conditions for what Hale describes as "a felt encounter with alterity."[52] To theorize that encounter, I draw on Lars Tønder's *Tolerance: A Sensorial Orientation to Politics* (2013). Looking for a way to break the impasse in contemporary political discussions of toleration, where toleration represents either a liberal virtue (John Rawls) or an instrument of repression (Wendy Brown), Tønder advances a theory of "active tolerance," one that aims to confront, rather than avoid, the anxieties that attend disagreement and conflict.[53] Active tolerance sustains more equitable relations by attending to the body's "affective intensities" and how the experience of pain, in particular, enables "the desires, powers, and limits of becoming tolerant."[54] Pain becomes productive when "our desire to express it perpetuates the creation of new relations among self, other, and world."[55] Until we learn to understand the pain we feel in the face of difference as productive, rather than destructive, we will experience tolerance as a burden.[56]

Tønder's exploration of toleration's sensorium helps me describe how the interfaith marriage plot attends to the dark feelings that emerge when religious alterity is encountered at close quarters. The novel moves away from a world organized around the neatly separated positions, "between a 'tolerator' and something 'tolerated,'" that govern public discourse, toward what Tønder, drawing on Merleau-Ponty, describes as a "tolerance of the incomplete."[57] Unlike the public sphere, which channels toleration through the buffered self of white masculine Protestantism, the private sphere of the novel takes, as its starting point, the vulnerable bodies of women and religious minorities. In this register, Tønder's sensorial tolerance speaks to recent feminist accounts of vulnerability, which reflect on the possibilities of resistance it might afford.[58] In this study, the experience of vulnerability and failure signals not defeat but the possibility of starting again from a different vantage point.

And, indeed, the interfaith marriage plot breaks down, more often than not, in the novels I examine here. But its flaws represent "evocative symptoms of social transformation," to use Rachel Hollander's words, pointing toward an alternative world that could sustain these marriages.[59] There are not many eighteenth-century novels that represent the interfaith marriage plot in detail. The rarity of the plot speaks to the importance of uniformity in family religion both as a *reaction* to Whig policy that supported religious toleration and as a *confirmation* of the political theory that shaped that policy. That is, we see, on the one hand, a widespread fear, after the passing of the Toleration Act of 1689, that religious pluralism would dissolve communal bonds. Tracts promoting family religion as a safeguard against toleration were legion throughout the eighteenth century. At the same time, toleration theory, as defined by Locke, *also* rests on the security that civil speech in the public sphere can dispense with the strong feelings needed to secure faith by displacing those feelings to the private sphere—that is, to family religion, where conformity is the norm. Thus, whether the novel is coming at the problem of toleration from a conservative or liberal standpoint, it proves equally committed to religious sameness in marriage.

In this book, I focus on four novels to map an alternative history of the realist novel, one that focuses on Samuel Richardson's *Sir Charles Grandison* and its rewriting by three canonical women authors. Each novel was chosen for the complex rendering it offers of interfaith marriage and the sexual politics of toleration.[60] These authors were widely read, and their works generated lively debates among critics and the reading public. Analyzing how these particular texts engage the novel of sensibility and its gendering of tolerance, I revise the narrative of the novel's development that takes *Pamela* and its marriage plot as its starting point for discussions of sexual politics and social transformation in the eighteenth century. Each of the novels that I read complicates *Pamela*'s plot, as well as the trajectory that positions Jane Austen's perfection of that plot as the novel's point of arrival. Instead of charting the novel's progress toward nineteenth-century developments, including secularism, I watch it circle back, through Maria Edgeworth's *Harrington*, to the Jewish Naturalization Act and the Gordon Riots, to the persistence of questions that were first raised by Richardson in *Sir Charles Grandison*. How can tolerance negotiate with intolerance? What kinds of sociability foster religious pluralism? How can the weak affect of tolerance in the public sphere accommodate the powerful feelings of courtship and marriage? These questions continue to trouble us today.

Although the story of the novel it tells begins in 1753, this study starts by tracing the origins of that story to the 1640s, when questions of marriage and toleration emerged alongside one another, two threads woven together in the tapestry of the Civil War and Interregnum. Chapter 1 traces how claims to liberty of conscience underpinned Puritan attacks on Church of England hegemony in the years leading up to the Civil War and, in its aftermath, shaped a national conversation regarding England's future as a Protestant state. Claims for the radical individualism of conscience and its dream of spiritual perfection refused, most of the time, the idea of religious pluralism. Interregnum Presbyterians dreamed of a theocracy. The gap between religious toleration and liberty of conscience is made explicit in Milton's *Discipline and Doctrine of Divorce*, where interfaith marriage appears as a form of spiritual endangerment of the self. For Milton, religious difference in a marriage is *necessarily* experienced as a species of hatred by each spouse. The paradox here is that, on the one hand, Milton's argument for divorce promotes tolerance insofar as it acknowledges the believer's right to pursue her spiritual path without interference. On the other hand, it cannot abide the thought of living in close proximity to religious difference—in this sense, it is profoundly intolerant.[61] The questions raised by Milton's defense of divorce form part of a larger conversation about tolerance in the 1640s that repeatedly returns to the challenge of interfaith marriage: When does liberty of conscience take precedence over social norms? What kinds of affects are inspired by religious difference, and how can they be managed in a family? Is the domestic an extension of the public sphere or separate from it? Should the state interfere with private affairs?

I turn from the 1640s to John Locke, who answers the questions of the Civil War and Interregnum by imagining a state that protects the autonomy of individual conscience while creating safeguards against religious "zeal." In *A Letter Concerning Toleration*, Locke describes a public sphere in which reasonable men communicate their views freely and respect each other's differences. Religious conformity is advanced not as a theological tenet belonging to one denomination or another but as a moral contract among social equals. The problem with Locke's model of religious toleration, however, is that its commitment to civility cannot accommodate strong feeling; it fears, as Teresa Bejan has pointed out, "the difficulties of disagreement between partial and proud creatures in an inalterably expanded public sphere."[62] Strong feeling belongs in the family, where love fostered by mothers secures unity, a foundation upon which religious toleration can rest. The figure of a dissenting wife never appears in Locke's text.

By the middle of the eighteenth century, Whig politics were moving toward toleration policies that would support British commercial interests at home and abroad. But grassroots xenophobia (encouraged in part by the Whigs' own anti-Catholic polemic aimed at curbing sympathies for the exiled Stuarts) was moving popular sentiment in the opposite direction. It took very little for the Tories to rally anti-Semitic opposition to the Jewish Naturalization Act in 1753. Meanwhile, the growth of religious sentiment among evangelical Protestants put questions of individual conscience and women's rights of speech in the foreground. Rates of interfaith marriage, among various denominations of Christians and between Christians and Jews, continued to rise. The emergent novel revisits seventeenth-century controversies with the tools of realist narrative in hand. Samuel Richardson's *Sir Charles Grandison* (1753–54) represents a remarkable development in the early novel's history, and this study centers it in eighteenth-century literary studies. I read *Grandison* as an effort, on Richardson's part, to provide a counternarrative to the vision of antinomian individualism of *Clarissa*, which he continued to revise throughout the 1750s. *Grandison* counters the isolation and loneliness of that novel with a world teeming with characters whose conversations and modes of living dissolve the boundaries of self and space that Clarissa and Lovelace die to maintain. *Clarissa*, Toni Bowers observes, "declines to protect the hidden term—*rape*—behind its recuperative recastings, seduction and courtship."[63] How to raise a viable model of sociability and marriage—a social ethics of persuasion rather than compulsion—from the ashes of this vision of modernity? *Grandison* extends *Clarissa*'s reflections on sexual violence to the treatment of religious minorities, linking the conversation about misogyny and marriage to British responses to the Jewish Naturalization Act.

In chapter 2, I examine the questions *Grandison* asks about religious toleration. How can the novel foster an affective community capable of accommodating religious difference? How can women's rights as religious subjects, distinct from their duties as wives, find expression in marriage? Richardson introduces his readers to a Lockean gentleman who governs the public sphere through polite exchanges and demonstrations of Christian charity. His civility is expansive, generous toward religious minorities such as the English Methodists. Trouble arises, however, from two sources: the Portuguese Jew, Solomon Merceda, and the Italian Catholic, Clementina della Porretta. The Good Man's tolerance requires him to stand outside and above the arena of suffering and vulnerability inhabited by these marginalized subjects, but maintaining that distance compromises Richardson's efforts to situate religious toleration within the affective register of the novel of sensibility.

The next three chapters study how women novelists grappled with *Grandison*'s legacy, rewriting its narrative of toleration and women's liberty of conscience as a story about female authorship. Chapter 3 examines Frances Brooke's *History of Emily Montague* (1769), which takes the novel into Britain's newly acquired colony, where Brooke's husband, an Anglican clergyman, hoped toleration would prove a pathway to the cultural assimilation of French Canada. In her attempt to imagine how English culture might be transplanted in the colonies, Brooke represents, through an array of characters writing letters to each other, competing visions of what religious toleration and marriage mean in relation to each other. Brooke's long-standing preoccupation with the problem of "unequal" marriage—the marriage of individuals of different economic means—draws colonial questions into a feminist frame of reference. The dreams of Anglican hegemony sustained by *Sir Charles Grandison* are challenged, in this context, by French Catholic nuns.

They are further challenged by the presence of Indigenous women in the margins of Brooke's narrative. The Indigenous/French unions it recounts refuse Protestant norms entirely and reverse the logic of the captivity narrative that Nancy Armstrong and Leonard Tennenhouse read as constitutive of the modern novel tradition beginning with *Pamela*.[64] The mixed marriages between European men and Indigenous women find a correlative in a plot that exists only as a possibility, floating above the companionate marriage plot as it unfolds. The novel's Protestant hero contemplates buying property adjacent to that of a French Catholic widow, a French "native" of the Canadian colonies only recently acquired by Britain. The narrative of their relationship contains a love story that aligns women's sexual and religious autonomy with active tolerance. Even when this plot is abandoned, it overshadows the novel's happy ending. That is, Brooke's colonial imaginings shift our view of England and its domestic politics, challenging the alignment of the British woman author with the Protestant companionate marriage and exposing "the axis of colonialism, enslavement, and class exploitation that underwrites European wealth and by extension the prosperity of [the] fictional couple."[65]

Chapter 4 studies a neglected tradition: that of English Catholicism's toleration politics. Against the more familiar story of religious toleration and

Protestant Dissent in the 1790s, I trace a Catholic activism that focuses on the household as the space of community.[66] Feminist readers have analyzed the sexual politics governing the courtship plot that unfolds in the first two volumes of Elizabeth Inchbald's *A Simple Story* (1791) but rarely examine its religious aspect. I argue that one of the reasons the relationship between Miss Milner and her guardian goes so wrong is that it relies on a Protestant understanding of religious privacy—the central tenet of liberalism's understanding of toleration. The second half of Inchbald's novel, I argue, shows us how Catholic principles of hospitality inform an alternative interfaith marriage plot to that of the tragic story with which the novel begins. As in Brooke's novel, counterfactual love—imagined, in this instance, by an adolescent girl—allows new configurations of familial and conjugal affect to reform the religious and sexual politics of the companionate marriage plot.

My final chapter returns to Richardson's representation of the Anglo-Jew and the challenge he poses, in *Sir Charles Grandison*, to the British body politic. Maria Edgeworth's 1817 novel, *Harrington*, roots the literary history of English anti-Semitism in Shakespeare's *Merchant of Venice* and its dreams of conversion, writ large in the interfaith marriage plot of Jessica and Lorenzo. Edgeworth revisits this plot not only in the union she describes in the concluding pages of her novel but in two interfaith marriages she recounts earlier in the narrative. These marriages manifest the tolerance Richardson reaches toward in *Grandison*. Edgeworth embraces a tolerance forged in the crucible of persecution as the grounding of a sociable ethics capable of recognizing the rights of women and religious minorities. Interfaith marriage, within this frame of reference, refuses conversion in favor of hybridity. In the place of the aesthetic genius of Shakespeare, whose stature separates him from the crowd, Edgeworth imagines communal modes of art making as means of fostering community, practices that the woman author's "minor" status makes possible.

The interfaith marriage plot, I conclude, points a way forward that complicates the imperatives of the realist novel. In making this claim, I follow Laura Mandell, whose account of the novel's representation of "bad marriages" notes that "realism and revolution ... cannot co-exist generically—except to the extent that the classic realist novel's ending fails."[67] The interfaith marriage plot represents just such a failure in its refusal to naturalize the sex-gender and religious ideologies governing liberal modernity. Without claiming that Richardson, Brooke, Inchbald, and Edgeworth realize the interfaith marriage plot as a master narrative, I nonetheless argue that their novels contribute significantly to rethinking English Protestant triumphalism—and the sexual and religious economies that attend it—in the long eighteenth century.[68]

An extravaganza or young Solomon besieging Fitzhubbub shows the Prince of Wales, and future George IV, kneeling before Maria Fitzherbert, the Catholic he married, secretly, on December 15, 1785. The marriage was legitimate, insofar as it was performed by an Anglican minister and the marriage certificate, written by the prince himself, was signed by witnesses, but it was rendered null by terms of the Marriage Act of 1772, which required consent of the monarch and Privy Council for all royal marriages. Further, the provisions of the Act of Settlement (1701) excluded Protestants who married Catholics from the throne. Had the Prince of Wales fought to legitimate the marriage, he would have done so at the expense of his future title. The print portrays Fitzherbert with a dark complexion, a reference to the print's title. "I am black, but comely," reads the fifth verse of the first canticle of the Song of Solomon.[69] The satire draws on this verse to reinforce long-standing associations of religious alterity with racial difference. Maria Fitzherbert was a "neighbour" from Shropshire, but her presence in the prince's bed signaled

Anon., *An extravaganza or young Solomon besieging Fitzhubbub* (1786)

a threat to the "purity" of the monarchical line, marked here by the contrasting whiteness of the prince's skin to that of the darker countenance of his lover, who holds in her hand a document outlining "Articles of Capitulation," articles that include a "mock marriage." The Prince of Wales went on to marry his German cousin Caroline of Brunswick in 1795, in return for having his debts paid. But the Vatican maintained the legitimacy of Fitzherbert's marriage throughout her life.[70]

This book argues that prose fiction has the potential to reveal the limits of political philosophy and state practice and to provide a way of reconceptualizing what an alternative theory of religious toleration, one that accounts for sexual difference, might look like.[71] It also hopes to show feminism what the history of religious toleration can teach those attempting to build bridges in the global women's movement. After the Women's March of January 2017, controversy broke out when one of the leaders of the march in the United States, Vanessa Wruble, left the organization. The journalists covering her departure portrayed complex disputes and painful conversations among the leadership.[72] Wruble feared Tamika Mallory's ties to Louis Farrakhan and the anti-Semitism of his 1991 publication, *The Secret Relationship between Blacks and Jews*. Mallory defended the Nation of Islam as her community: "Wherever my people are, that's where I must also be." Carmen Perez published a list of "unity principles" that listed BIPOC, disabled, Muslim, queer, and trans—but not Jewish—women as minority groups that the march supported. The mainstream press found little in these exchanges to suggest that anyone was able to imagine how toleration politics could become part of the march's feminist agenda. The reasons for this failure are much larger than the women who found themselves embroiled in conflict, and they speak to the divisiveness of our current moment. As Teresa Bejan has recently pointed out, we have not yet found a way to tolerate the painful feelings that accompany talking about "the things that divide us most deeply."[73] Couples who entered into interfaith marriages in the eighteenth century were brave enough to undertake this difficult work. The novel's attention to the challenges they faced, I believe, allows us to imagine a deeper species of tolerance than Western liberalism has, as yet, been able to sustain.

CHAPTER 1

Religious Toleration and Interfaith Marriage, 1640–1720

> How far we ought to part with our own liberty to gratify another's scruple is a question full of niceness and difficulty.
> —*John Locke, "First Tract on Government" (1660)*

The question of intimate relations, this chapter shows, was embedded in toleration debates from the moment of their first articulation in early modern England.¹ Prompted by rising tension over Jewish naturalization, Catholic emancipation, and Methodist revivalism from the 1750s onward, eighteenth-century novelists revisited these debates as they tested emergent models of toleration, developed in the heat of seventeenth-century religious conflicts, against deep-seated xenophobia. Eighteenth-century novels ask, How do the different contexts of private and public spheres shape toleration discourse in theory and practice? Can the equality of women—and, by extension, racialized minorities—be realized in a liberal state? How does marriage regulation contribute to the shaping of national identity? As it contemplates these questions, the novel returns us to complex accounts of religious sociability generated by seventeenth-century thinkers and activists.

This chapter identifies the central role played by interfaith marriage in seventeenth-century toleration debates to show why these ostensibly minor plots deserve more attention, in our study of the eighteenth-century novel, than they typically receive. In both centuries, interfaith marriage challenged attempts to impose religious uniformity in the family and to limit toleration in the public sphere. John Milton's divorce tracts, I argue, serve as a fulcrum in early debates over toleration, liberty of conscience, and the companionate marriage. By establishing the rights of conscience as grounds for separation, they identify women's spiritual agency as an integral feature of marriage. They also establish the principle of religious sameness as a key feature of the companionate marriage. By linking religious conformity to love and attachment, they grant it a new emotional force. Forty years after the publication of Milton's tracts, John Locke sets the individual's religious subjectivity *apart* from the social body, whose coherence, he argues, can be maintained by civility and emotional regulation in the public sphere. But strong religious faith remains a key to preventing atheism from arising in a state governed by politeness. That strong faith belongs in the family, Locke suggests, where love secures religious conformity among family members. Like Milton, Locke assumes that conjugal conformity will organize itself around a husband's, rather than a wife's, religious identity. The contradiction in Locke's thinking between an assertion of the inalienable rights of conscience and the naturalization of male authority lies close to the surface.

Throughout the seventeenth century, a range of thinkers on the subjects of toleration and marriage exposed this contradiction. Independent polemicists and radical activists conceptualized theories of the family and nation that allowed for the possibility of both women's equality and religious pluralism. I conclude this chapter with two case studies concerning the interfaith marriages of Samuel and Susanna Wesley, and the Duke and Duchess of Norfolk. In each case, an understanding of women's claims to liberty of conscience contributes to a sense of what a strong religious pluralism, rather than a weak tolerance, requires. Finally, I turn my attention to how storytelling serves as the conduit by which this vision of sociability might be realized, setting the stage for the eighteenth-century novel's intervention in the debates framed by seventeenth-century polemicists.

Civil Wars, Public and Private

For those contemplating interfaith marriage in the early decades of the seventeenth century, the English had one word: "don't." In 1634, William Gouge, a proponent of Protestant companionate marriage, wrote strongly against interfaith unions: "Contrary are marriages with persons of different dispositions, and divers professions in religion: especially when they are made with infidels or idolaters. This is one of those unequall yoakes, wherewith the Apostle forebiddeth Christians to be yoaked."[2] While acknowledging the authority of 1 Corinthians 7:12 ("If any brother hath a wife that believeth not, and she be pleased to dwell with him, let him not put her away"), Gouge explains it away as an expedient for making the best of a bad situation in the days of early Christianity. The 2 Corinthians 6:14 prohibition—"Be ye not unequally yoked together with unbelievers"—takes the upper hand for Gouge, and it continued to do so in the decades that followed, its urgency becoming more marked with the rise of Protestant sectarianism.

Fears about interfaith marriage, by the middle of the seventeenth century, encompassed politics both high and low. Charges that Charles I was being corrupted by his Catholic queen proved a mainstay in anti-Royalist polemic in the years leading up the outbreak of civil war. In 1643, Puritan William Prynne wrote, "The Kings match with the Queen was both in designe and event, the greatest means to advance Popery in England, to suspend the Lawes and proceeding against Popish Priests and Monkes; and to reduce both the King and the Prince to the entertaining and professing of the Roman Catholick Faith."[3] The queen's Catholicism compromises both the rule of law and the king's integrity, Prynne argues, allowing the unjust usurpation of authority by a consort, thereby compromising the nation's religious identity. "Popish Priests and Monkes" can advance the interests of the Vatican in the absence of a strong judiciary supported by the monarch. In Milton's account of the marriage of Charles I, we see an argument common to the period: interfaith marriage provides an occasion for spiritual corruption that flows only in one direction—from wives to husbands. Nine months after Charles I's execution in 1649, Milton argued that the queen's Catholicism gained the upper hand: "It is op'nly known that her Religion wrought more upon him, then his Religion upon her, and his op'n favouring of Papists, and his hatred of them call'd Puritans, . . . made most men suspect she had quite perverted him."[4] The corruption of the marriage had spread, Milton claims, from the king's bedroom into the body politic, where the persecution of Puritans set the scene for the conflict that unfolded in the 1640s.

Closer to the ground, antipathy to interfaith marriage became particularly marked as new Protestant sects emerged and attempted to render themselves socially recognizable both to their own communities and to the world around them.[5] Different congregations exhorted their members to distinguish themselves from their Protestant neighbors by marrying in, aligning the marriage bond with the larger project of community growth as a sign of each sect's spiritual success. In 1655, Baptists debated the practice of interfaith marriage: "After prayer and supplication to the Most High, this question was propounded, viz.; Whether or no it is lawful for any member of the congregation, to marry any without the congregation? Upon this question there was very much debate; but at length it was resolved, that it is not lawful for any member of the congregation to be married unto one without the congregation."[6] That same year, Jane Johnson was "separated from the congregation" after marrying a man outside the community. In this instance, the integrity of Johnson's belief, as well as that of the man she chose to marry, was called into question: "She knew that he was so far from embracing the truth, that he was as great an enemy as could be."[7] Jane Johnson cannot herself be a sincere believer if she is so ready to bring the enemy into the congregational fold. A similar argument informed the excommunication of Congregationalist Anne Pharepoint in 1651: "There is now none but the church and the world; if your husband were not of the church, he must be of the world, and so a stranger; and if a stranger, then he will turn your heart from the Lord."[8] Here the ministers of Pharepoint's congregation, Edmond Maile and Henry Browne, draw on Deuteronomy 7, which describes the Israelites taking possession of their new land and casting out the tribes who live there: "neither shalt thou make marriages with them . . . For they will turn away thy son from following me," God tells his chosen people (Deut. 7:3–4). In England, the Baptists imagined themselves as the new elect and created a spiritual geography that separated the worldly from the true believers, shunning the "strangers" in their midst.

The cases of Jane Johnson and Anne Pharepoint show us that women's religious independence was particularly concerning for Protestant church elders. Their discourses argue that the corruption of interfaith marriage involves more than unholy pairings; its acknowledgment of a woman's religious rights compromises a husband's conjugal authority.[9] Wifely obedience was a mainstay of Protestant family discourses, and only the most extenuating circumstances could overrule this imperative. In a 1645 tract, Presbyterian John Brinsley reflects on this point at length, defining the limits of religious freedom within a marriage and the problems that arise when a wife contemplates moving to a new Protestant church. I quote Brinsley's text at length because it makes several important arguments:

> Conscience must be directed and regulated by the word, otherwise it is not conscience but will, (which too often is mistaken for conscience) or at the best an erronious conscience, which must rather be rectified th[a]n satisfied. . . . I might here instance in some particular cases, such as the scruples of the times bring to hand. I shall only single out one, and that I will but touch upon: viz. The womans forsaking of that Church whereof her husband is a member, and joyning her self by Convenant to some other, and that without his consent, if not against his will.
>
> In this case it must be acknowledged, that could it be made good by clear evidence, that that Church from which this departure is made, were no true

> Church, but Anti-Christian, now there might be some plea for this their Separation: But this being granted, that that Church is a true Church, such a Church as wherein salvation may be had in an ordinary way (though possibly not so perfect as some other may be conceived to be) now in this case for the wife to desert that Church, and to joyne her self to another, so as they who lie in the same bed, and in the eye both of Gods Law and mans are both one, should yet be of two Churches, it is such a solecisme, such an absurdity in Christianity, as I think the world never saw practised, much less heard pleaded for, until this last age. So it is, though it should be with the husbands consent. Much more if without it; much more if against it.[10]

Brinsley begins by reflecting on errors regarding conscience. When conscience finds itself inclined toward disobedience, it should be examined for signs of "will," an unlawful exercise of self-determination. Education by the "word" should correct both the inclinations of the will and the lesser mistake of "erroneous conscience." (We will return to this understanding of conscience below.) Reflecting on "the scruples of the time," Brinsley addresses the particular case of a wife leaving her husband's church for another. When in doubt, Brinsley argues, women should trust their husband's judgment rather than their own. Their conversion to another doctrine is only justified if the home church can be proven to be "Anti-Christian." One can assume, given Brinsley's Calvinism, that a Roman Catholic church would fall into this category. In all other cases, a woman should trust that her salvation can be achieved in an "ordinary way." She can put aside her desire for a "more perfect" spiritual discipline without fear of damnation. Marital obligation, in other words, takes precedence over any spiritual preferences, beyond the essential Christian/anti-Christian divide. Otherwise, a wife risks sundering the "one flesh" she and her husband became when they married. It is impossible for the marital body to inhabit two churches simultaneously, Brinsley asserts, even if a husband consents to his wife's move. God's law—that conjugal relations constitute, in and of themselves, conformity—requires women to give up their dreams of spiritual perfection in favor of domestic and church unity.

We see, here, how marriage vows weigh almost equally in the balance with the claims of conscience. No one went so far as to claim that a husband's authority takes precedence over Christ's. A generation earlier, Anglican Richard Greenham had made it plain to wives that husbands were not allowed to incite un-Christian thoughts or actions: "Neither doe I thus charge you with any obedience but in the Lord: for if he [the husband] should require any such thing of you, as should cause you to depart from Christ, I would have you in any case remember that you are principally espoused unto Christ."[11] But fifty years later, Protestants at the crossroads of denominational schism and divided political loyalties asked, What constitutes a "departure" from Christ? As we have seen, John Brinsley considered women subject to their marital duties right up to the border of Roman Catholicism. But, in arguing that Jane Johnson and Anne Pharepoint should not marry out of their Baptist and Congregationalist communities, other church elders brought the "anti-Christian" much closer to home. Who is to judge?

Milton's *Doctrine and Discipline of Divorce*, published over the course of 1643–44, makes a sharp turn in direction by setting the radical independence of conscience against the marriage vow. Individuals are "principally espoused unto Christ" and only secondarily to an earthly partner. In the absence of religious agreement between spouses, he maintains that a timely separation protects the religious integrity of each spouse.[12] Chapter 8 of *Doctrine and Discipline* is devoted to the question of religious incompatibility, which constitutes, for Milton, "the whole question of divorce."[13] Against Brinsley, Milton claims that religious difference within marriage constitutes a form of spiritual endangerment: "There is a spiritual contagion in Idolatry as much to be shunn'd; and though seducement were not to be fear'd, yet where there is no hope of converting, there always ought to be a certain religious aversion and abhorring, which can no way sort with marriage" (2:262).[14] The spouses each fear "contagion" by the other in the cases where the faiths are not aligned, and even confidence in their own faith does not help. Living with religious disagreement, in the absence of any hope for conversion, breeds hostility, and this affect, in turn, corrupts the marital bond.

In advocating for divorce, Milton claims that the righteousness of men and women represents the highest law, over which the magistrate and ecclesiastical courts have no authority. Designating marriage an "inferior calling" to Christian duty, Milton warns his readers against the "dangerous subjection to that Ordinance" (2:268), which has the potential to transgress the moral law of God in those instances where religious integrity may be compromised. The scandal of "misbelief," Milton argues, overrides "the due progresse of reason, and the ever-equall proportion which justice proceeds by it." Nothing less than "a total and final separation" can stop the spiritual defilement that results from interfaith marriage (2:263). God mandates divorce so that the religious duty he is owed might be properly exercised by his subjects.

We have already seen the arguments against interfaith marriage that Milton rehearses here. What is different is that those before him considered their arguments preventative—that is, they issued warnings against engagement, rather than imagining separation in the event of religious conflict *after* the exchange of vows. Divorce meant severing the "one flesh" of husband and wife constituted by those vows. To justify such a radical act, Milton aligns the individual conscience with a "pure" scriptural authority derived from God and his Son, one that grants men and women the authority to dissolve a marriage that does not satisfy their religious scruples.[15] Like Gouge before him, Milton argues away Paul's injunction regarding the permissibility of unbelievers and believers remaining together in the verses of 1 Corinthians by claiming that the apostle was speaking only to the practical concerns of his historical moment. He goes on to argue that Christ's pronouncements on the subject, which *do* suggest setting aside a spouse (Matt. 19:29, Luke 14:26), should always take precedence over Paul's strictures: "The counsell we have from S. Paul to hope, cannot countermand the moral and Evangelick charge we have from God to fear seducement, to separate from the misbeleever, the unclean, the obdurat" (2:267). Milton considers Paul's hope of conversion among the unbelievers— "For what knowest, O wife, whether thou shalt save thy husband?"—as a last ditch effort to make the best of a bad situation. Only Christ's words, with their intimations of sin and punishment, reflect God's mandate.

Milton plays close attention to the demands of marriage, focusing particularly on its affective demands and how they shape the experience of living with religious difference. The intimacy of marriage requires that we live with our partners "perpetually at our elbow" (2:263). Milton notes the difference between a marriage and other family relations, where religious toleration might be extended, for example, to an unbelieving father or sibling:

> It will easily be true that a father or brother may be hated zealously, and lov'd civilly or naturally; for those duties may be perform'd at a distance . . . : but how the peace and perpetuall cohabitation of marriage can be kept, or how that benevolent and intimate communion of body can be held with one that must be hated with a most operative hatred, must be forsak'n and yet continually dwelt with and accompanied, he who can distinguish, hath the gift of an affection very oddly divided and contriv'd. (2:264)

Conviction might require us to hate the unbeliever "zealously"—that is, as a religious subject. But we may continue to love that unbeliever "civilly" or "naturally." In other words, given enough space, civil relations between different kinds of believers might be maintained. But these relationships do not include sexual intimacy. An engagement with another's body, in particular, necessitates a more complete "communion" of souls, Milton argues. The "distance" between selves and the compartmentalization of different affects required by religious toleration proves inimical to the success of marriage.[16]

Milton set the course for the companionate marriage over the course of the long eighteenth century by prioritizing the importance of fellow feeling between spouses. By insisting that this feeling cannot survive the introduction of religious difference, he also established a clear distinction between liberty of conscience and toleration. "For Milton," Lana Cable observes, "the objective in the practice of toleration is civil concord. By contrast, freedom of conscience is necessitated by the unchanging certitude that is presumed to characterize the realm of the divine."[17] Each individual must aim for the spiritual perfection that realizes the alignment of conscience and godliness in his personal life. But, as a subject in the public sphere, he can bracket that perfectionism to advance the goals of sociability and political compromise.

Today we tend to conflate the discourses of conscience and toleration. It is important, for the arguments of this book, to maintain the distinction. After the Reformation, "liberty of conscience" became a hallmark of English Puritan discourse, signaling freedom from priestly interference in the affairs of the believing heart. William Ames, a forerunner of Nonconformity, articulated in 1639 the discourse's central paradigm: "The interpretation of the Scriptures, or a judgement to discerne Gods will for a mans selfe, in his owne Conscience, belongs to every man."[18] This idea of conscience as "property" encompasses two meanings. In the first place, it is a faculty innate in every human: "The Conscience of her selfe, hath in every man, a naturall light, though it bee but dim and clouded, this was never quite extinguished, by the fall," writes the author of *An Expedient to Preserve Peace and Amity Among Dissenting Brethren* in 1647.[19] In the second place, property appears as the political right of English subjects. John Goodwin, in 1647, writes that "every man esteemeth it as properly his own, as any Immunity contained in Magna Charta, to use his Conscience without controule."[20] In both instances, conscience proves inalienable. The question, for seventeenth-century theologians and political theorists, was the extent to which conscience was *malleable* in relation to church or familial allegiance.

The degree to which an individual's conscience was unchangeable became important in debates about the authority of the Church of England before and after the interregnum. For some, conscience could benefit from enforced exposure to Anglican doctrine (in the interest of religious conformity). Alternately, it could be readily compartmentalized so as to resist the effects of that exposure. People would not be harmed by membership in the Church of England, regardless of what their conscience told them was the correct way to worship. This was John Locke's early view and Thomas Hobbes's. For others, conscience was too central a feature of personal identity to remain unviolated in the face of these threats. It had to find expression outside the Church of England, whose teachings failed to square with alternative religious sensibilities. For these thinkers, the "liberty of judgement" (that is, conscience) could not be separated from the "liberty of the will."[21]

Those advocating for liberty of conscience under Charles I did not promote religious toleration.[22] As Gordon J. Schochet points out, "Of religious liberty per se—that is, of the right of all people to practice their religion without interference from the civil authorities and without any consequent loss of social or political status—we read very little."[23] The 1645 *Letter of the Presbyterian Ministers in the City of London . . . Against Toleration* describes it as "utterly repugnant and inconsistent" with the solemn league and covenant that the ministers had fought so hard to achieve. "That blessed fruit of a pure and perfect Reformation," its authors wrote, "is in danger of being strangled in the Birth, by a lawless Toleration, that strives to be brought forth before it."[24] During the interregnum, only a small minority of radical thinkers associated liberty of conscience with the freedom to build diverse religious communities.

Questions of liberty of conscience and religious toleration became intertwined, however, in debates about interfaith marriage. We see this in the hostile reception of Milton's treatises on divorce. Critics repeatedly conflate his arguments for the right of spouses to pursue their religious freedom with a political mandate to establish a state practice of religious toleration. Daniel Featley, for example, lists the divorce tracts alongside the writings of both radical sectarians and tolerationist Roger Williams, author of *The Bloudy Tenent* (1644), in his complaint about the publishers of Milton's works in 1645: "They print not only Anabaptisme, from whence they take their name; but many other most damnable doctrines, tending to carnall liberty, Familisme, and a medly and hodge-podge of all Religions. Witnesse the Book printed 1644. Called *The Bloodie Tenet* [sic]; . . . Witnesse a Tractate of Divorce, in which the bonds of marriage are let loose to inordinate lust, and putting away wives for many other causes besides that which our Saviour only approveth, namely, in case of Adultery."[25] Featley conflates Williams's willingness to release individuals from the bonds of religious conformity with Milton's defense of an individual's right to break the marriage vow. The unorthodox views of both authors contribute to the "hodge-podge of all Religions" now circulating in the public sphere. By publishing these texts, the press has facilitated the replacement of the will of "our Savior" with the unregulated appetites of individuals masquerading as religious discourse. The agendas of Williams and Milton alike are driven by selfish and irrational desires, here identified as "inordinate lust." Both release individuals from their duty to follow established norms and religious prescriptions.

Even the most sustained commentary on Milton's essay, *An Answer to a Book, intituled, The Doctrine and Discipline of Divorce restored to the good of both Sexes from the bondage of the Canon Law*, dismisses most of its arguments out of hand, suggesting along the way that Milton's examples of unhappy unions point to individuals who chose badly in the first place, an intimation that must have rankled Milton in light of his precipitous marriage to, and subsequent separation from, Mary Powell. Like Featley, the author focuses on how Milton's text might be used to justify irregular appetites, as in the case of husbands looking for excuses to leave their wives for other women: "Who sees not, how many thousands of lustfull and libidinous men would be parting from their Wives every week and marrying others: . . . what reproach would the woman be left to, as being one left who was not fit for any ones company?"[26] For both authors, the individual's claims to liberty of conscience too easily serve as a cover for other individual appetites to justify dismantling social norms.

An Answer recognizes how a woman's claims to liberty of conscience might serve as grounds for larger claims, such as the right to speak about religious matters in the public sphere. Milton's *Doctrine* appears as a species of antinomianism, similar to that associated with the women preachers appearing in the streets of London: "This is a wilde, mad, and frantick divinitie, just like to the opinions of the Maids of Algate: Oh say they, we live in Christ, and Christ doth all for us; we are Christed with Christ and Godded with God, and at the same time we sin here, we joyned to Christ do justice in him, for our life is hid with God in Christ."[27] In *Gangraena* (1646), Thomas Edwards makes the same connection between Milton's text and the preaching of Mrs. Attaway, a Baptist whose preaching over the course of 1645–46 drew the notice of Edwards and others. "She spake to [two Gentlemen]," Edwards recounts, "of Master *Miltons* Doctrine of Divorce" and of her "unsanctified husband" (whom she appears to have left for William Jenney, a fellow preacher, sometime after this conversation took place).[28] For Edwards, Milton's text grants women illegitimate authority under the guise of religious principle, which they use to contravene social law.

We see, in each of these accounts, how Milton's reflections on the liberty of conscience—a principle separate, in his mind, from that of toleration—become connected, in the minds of Milton's detractors, to the idea of religious pluralism. His opponents recognize that divorce justified on the grounds of conscience generates an authority for women that counters the disciplinary regimes of custom and the law. The same logic applies to religious communities that want to separate from the hegemony of state religion. Milton's reading of conscience leads directly into conversations that extend his model outward into social groups and communal imaginings. Thus, we should not be surprised that marriage and family religion so often shape debates about religious toleration in this moment. In 1645, Presbyterian John Bernard asked rhetorically:

> *Quest.* May diversities of Religions be tolerated amongst Christians, or were they ever tolerated in the Old or New Testament?
> *Answ.* The practise of the holy men of God sheweth they may not, and their practise is our imitation; ... [I]t is cleare that *Abraham, Isaac, Jacob,* and *Joshua* suffered no Idolatry nor Sects in their families, for this had been to tolerate all Religions, or to worship the true God in a false manner.... Now these that labour for a toleration of all Religions must needs be Luke-warme, such as God will spue out of his mouth.[29]

In advancing the case for Presbyterian citizenship in England, Bernard upholds paternal authority against religious pluralism. Strong patriarchs ensure religious conformity. He, like Milton, identifies strong feeling as the key to proving one's religious integrity; those who are able to tolerate religious difference appear suspiciously "Luke-warme" in their belief.

Lazarus Seaman similarly turns to biblical precedent to argue against religious toleration. Reflecting on King Solomon's legacy, he observes, "*Consider also his failings, and beware of them.* 1. He had many wives, even *seven hundred Wives, Princesses, and three hundred Concubines (i).* Let not us have as many Religions. There's some anology [sic] between the one and the other. 2. There was in his daies first a connivance at Idolatry, then open toleration, and withall Apostacy."[30] Seaman draws us back to mixed marriage as the source of national corruption that we saw in Milton's description of the marriage between Charles I and Henrietta Maria. Alien wives introduce alien beliefs to the nation, the nation indulges their practice, and apostasy follows. Interfaith marriage leads to toleration, which in turn leads to national disintegration.

Thomas Thorowgood takes the family as his starting point. Toleration in the public sphere must necessarily enter, like a worm into an apple, the heart of the nation—its homes: "Such allowance [i.e. toleration] would prove destructive to holiness, both personall and domesticall.... Suppose the husband of one opinion, the wife of another, the children, it may be, of one or two other, and the servants of as many more; what shall the Master of the house doe here? how performe the family duties? diversitie of opinions, like so many *hatchets interrupting their prayers*, 1 Pet. 3.7. *chopping all devotion and piety in pieces*."[31] Religious pluralism, granted legitimacy by the state, will sow civil discord within the family, undermining paternal and conjugal authority. "Devotion and piety" are housed by the corporate body of the family, which has the master as its head. The integrity of that body is threatened by "diversitie of opinions." The unified church of the home mirrors the unified church of the state, which keeps the nation on its path to salvation.

The few thinkers who wrote in defense of toleration in the 1640s maintained that the body politic could house many faiths without losing its integrity or security. Their arguments pursued the logic that led to the Puritan rebellion against the king and his church: to give a magistrate jurisdiction over religious matters is to set him in Christ's place, a practice of the corrupt regimes "we have puld downe." Only Christ knows the final truth in matters of religious dispute: "Christ is the Judge of Controversies, and the interpreter of holy Scripture."[32] Toleration is the necessary conclusion of the revolution that has enabled spiritual growth in the nation. Independent John Goodwin advocates for the full realization of Protestant liberty initiated by the overthrow of Anglican hegemony. "Men now, are grown more various in their opinions than ever before, and will be as easily perswaded to forsake their meat, as to relinquish their Tenets; ... therefore is not only a reason, but also a necessity of Toleration."[33] Without toleration, civil war will prove interminable, Goodwin suggests. These two lines of reasoning—the one theological, the other practical—are brought together by Henry Burton, who indicts the Presbyterian push for conformity: "To set up in the Church an Oracle of Infallibility, and such a supremacie, as no true-bred English Christian can interpret for other than antichristian tyrannie? And all under the name of a Christian Presbyterian Church-government? ... Such as conform to a State religion, or a State church-government, make that the supreme law and lord over their conscience, and so exclude Christs supremacie."[34] Here, the Presbyterians seem to be falling into tyrannical modes of government, in direct contravention of the norms of "English Christian liberty." They exhibit signs of theological hubris, likewise, imagining themselves, rather than Christ, as the "law and lord" of conscience. Only toleration can curb these twin evils. Any other policy represents a popish imposition of worldly authority in the place of English Protestant spiritual independence.

Those who advocated for religious pluralism moved back and forth between the family and the state in their arguments. In 1645, Presbyterian ministers charged that religious toleration would disrupt "the whole course of religion in private Families" and would, further, impede "Reciprocal Duties between persons of nearest and dearest Relations."[35] In replying to these charges, Independent William Walwyn addresses the claim that religious difference necessarily inspires hatred. The supposition, Walwyn argues, "that difference in judgement must needs occasion coldnesse of affection . . . proceeds from the different countenance and protection, which States have hitherto afforded to men of different judgements."[36] It is a persecuting spirit fostered by state intolerance, rather than the difference in judgment, that leads to the "coldnesse of affection." The inability to separate love and judgment points to a lack of charity. A true Christian refuses the mask of intolerance that the persecuting state would have him put on and instead draws on a principle of universal love to sustain the divided family. Here Walwyn counters Milton's claims regarding the "hatred" inspired by religious difference between spouses. Conjugal love is borne out of a Christian love that recognizes only God as the final arbiter of religious truth, rather than relying on political categories imposed by the state.

Roger Williams uses interfaith marriage as a metaphor for the virtues of religious pluralism on a national scale, stressing the "civill covenant" that allows individuals of differing beliefs to live together peaceably. He begins with the Pauline doctrine that Milton attempts to discredit in the *Doctrine*:

> Now in *families*, suppose a beleeving Christian Husband hath an unbeleeving Antichristian wife, what other charge in this respect is given to an *husband*, I. Cor. 7. but to dwell with her as an husband if she be pleased to dwell with him: . . . Consequently the *Father or Husband* of the State differing from the *Commonweale* in *Religion*, ought not to force the *Commonweale*, nor to be forced by it: yet is he to continue a *civill husbands* care, if the *Commonweale* will live with him, and abide in *civill covenant*.[37]

Civility precludes the use of force and here appears as the proper affect of both an interfaith marriage and a religiously plural state. A husband's "care" characterizes the state's proper relation to its religious dissenters, who can choose whether to stay or go. For Williams, Christian duty requires a willingness to live with difference, and its integrity is threatened by demands for conformity. Like Walwyn, Williams imagines the national community as a corporate body that flourishes, rather than decays, when individuals feel free to answer the dictates of their conscience. The presence of religious difference does nothing to diminish those ties, nor are the affects that attend it less heartfelt than those of allegiance to a state church.

We have seen that the 1640s bring into sharp focus competing imperatives: to establish the political and cultural hegemony of a new Protestant dispensation without falling into the hierarchical modes of Laudian Anglicanism, to shore up the Protestant family while acknowledging the integrity of its members' pursuit of spiritual perfection, to assert the integrity of conscience without conceding the necessity of religious pluralism. Each of these dramas played out in private and public arenas and blurred the boundaries between them. The Puritan emphasis on scriptural authority—and the individual's right to interpret it—muddied waters that were already murky in the face of competing biblical injunctions on interfaith marriage and the tolerance of religious difference. Milton and his wife separated and then reconciled: their conflict was both political—Puritan/Royalist—and personal.

John Locke and Family Religion, 1690–1720

We now turn to the 1690s, to a moment when (limited) religious toleration became law. Interfaith marriage, however, remained culturally taboo. What follows suggests how Locke's toleration theory reinforces this prohibition by underlining Milton's insistence that the private family's religious uniformity and strong affective bonds make possible the public sphere's tolerance, organized around the male, Protestant subject. The sense of urgency around family religion in cultural discourses of the period reinforced this division, rendering interfaith unions a more, rather than less, sanctioned practice—even as numbers of these marriages continued to increase.

My reading of the Locke follows two lines of investigation.[38] The first considers Locke's understanding of religious experience and the impropriety of trying to regulate the beliefs of another person, the second, Locke's account of marriage in the *Second Treatise on Government*. In placing these subjects alongside one another, we see how the idea of religious autonomy advanced by the *Letter* undermines the masculinist imperatives that inform the *Second Treatise*. The social plan Locke engineers for the control of religious difference in the public sphere cannot be used to regulate the family. Taboos against interfaith marriage expose the paradox that religious toleration in the public sphere, after Locke, requires more, rather than less, conformity in the private.

"Toleration, like all Lockean political principle, is anchored in resignation to a fact: the ubiquitous subjectivity of human wills," George Windstrup observes.[39] "Resignation" aptly sums up the attitude Locke expressed after thirty years of reflection on the subject.[40] But once having reached the conclusion that "every one is orthodox to himself," Locke never retreated from this assessment.[41] In the *Letter*, Locke's commitment to religious freedom turns on the particular quality of religious conviction each of us manifests—and on the status of that conviction as a property of character that cannot be alienated. Echoing earlier Protestant writing, Locke claims that "the care of each man's soul, and of the things of heaven, which neither does belong to the commonwealth, nor can be subjected to it, is left entirely to every man's self" (*LCT* 243).[42] The idea that conviction is "left" to the self suggests a kind of husbandry. Each of us must cultivate our own spiritual garden. Even more importantly, our religious conviction is an involuntary *aspect* of the self that distinguishes one individual from another: "No man can, if he would, conform his faith to the dictates of another" (219). Each man's faith, Locke reasons, is inseparable from his sense of himself. "An under-appreciated feature of the *Letter*," Richard Vernon notes, "is its adoption of a sort of aesthetics of belief that connects forms of worship with deep tastes or temperament."[43] To try to exercise religious authority over the belief of another is to violate her personhood.

Conscience is the sign of an individual's mature agency, his viability as a social subject: "No man can so far abandon the care of his own salvation as blindly to leave it to the choice of any other" (*LCT* 219). True belief can be established only "by meditation, study, search, and [an individual's] own endeavors" (229). And salvation follows adherence to the path one has chosen: "Although the magistrate's opinion in religion be sound, and the way that he appoints be truly evangelical, yet if I be not thoroughly persuaded thereof in my own mind, there will be no safety for me in following it" (232). The individual must chart her own course rather than conform to externally imposed values or fall short of the mark of proper conviction. Salvation stands not on theological principle but on sincerity: "True and saving religion consists in the inward persuasion of the mind, without which nothing can be acceptable to

God" (219). Sanford Kessler highlights the significance for modern religious subjectivity of this shift from reason to feeling in Locke's *Letter*. By separating conscience from rationality, Kessler observes, Locke underscores "the individual's subjective state of mind" as the key determinant of religious rectitude.[44] Individual affect, rather than divine regulation, guarantees religious conviction, securing the integrity of the belief in a sincere heart.

I use the gendered pronouns "he," "she," "his," and "hers" interchangeably in my reading of Locke's account of religious subjectivity, because the theory of mind that subtends this account is not, I believe, gendered. The move from interiority to the social practice of toleration is where religious identity takes on an embodied form. Tolerant gentlemen form community in the public sphere by upholding the rules "of virtue and piety" (*LCT* 215). These rules focus our attention on moral conduct, rather than religious contests. So, for instance, theological rigor in the pulpit is not the purpose of church service, and the clergyman who preaches doctrine without attending to the correction of vice "plainly demonstrates by his actions, that it is another kingdom he aims at, and not the advancement of the kingdom of God" (217). Clerical self-interest reveals itself through theological ardency. True Christianity is reflected in the practices of polite sociability.[45]

Locke's desire to ground Christian sociability in moral conduct rather than specific religious tenets means that "toleration [i]s closely tied to pastoral issues for the evangelising Christian."[46] In a community where sincerity marks the integrity of belief, outward signs of conviction take the form of right conduct and community governance. The common sense fostered by these codes limits the externalization of liberty of conscience as any kind of personalized action plan, in particular refusing it as the grounds for exceptionalism—whether individual or that of the Protestant and Roman Catholic Churches.[47] This exceptionalism, or "false" liberty of conscience, Locke labels "zeal." It is recognizable by the trajectory it pursues—moving from appeals to toleration to quests for power. Toleration is, for the zealot, a haven that protects his faith until such a time as it can be imposed on the body politic (*LCT* 226). As in the case of the clergyman exhorting theological purity from the pulpit, the desire for power will always reveal itself in the intemperateness of the zealots, which "betray[s] their ambition, and show[s] that what they desire is temporal dominion" (228). It is the opposite of the quiet Christian charity that reveals itself in the practice of neighborly respectfulness and church attendance.

What happens when we move Locke's model of religious toleration into the household?[48] In his *Second Treatise*, Locke argues that "conjugal society is made by a voluntary compact between man and woman." "The power of the husband [is] so far from that of an absolute monarch," he writes, "that the wife has in many cases a liberty to separate from him."[49] In the instance of marital disputes, Locke gives husbands the upper hand—"it therefore being necessary that the last determination, *i.e.* the rule, should be placed somewhere"—but places strict limits on their exercise of authority: "This reaching but to the things of their common interest and property, leaves the wife in the full and free possession of what by contract is *her peculiar right*, and gives the husband no more power over her life than she has over his" (*ST* 135, emphasis added). More than any other aspect of humanity, liberty of conscience, according to Locke's own model of religious belief, constitutes "a peculiar right." The rules enforced by "nature" cannot regulate religious autonomy, and the imposition of a husband's belief on his wife could only ever represent forcible conversion. Locke does not answer the question of religious difference within a marriage in either the *Letter* or *Second Treatise* but not, I believe, because he was not thinking about dissent within the family. When he turns to the subject of religious persuasion in the family, in *Some Thoughts Concerning Education* (1693), he "prudently," Elizabeth Pritchard observes, "returns to the stage of childhood rather than marriage."[50] Locke's silence on the subject of religious difference between spouses, I believe, acknowledges that women are "mature" and therefore cannot be subjected to the educational practices that ensure right belief in children.

Locke's silence, in this instance, manifests the self-restraint he recommends for the maintenance of religious toleration in the public sphere. The civility of tolerant gentlemen promotes a strong charitable ethic, on display in the forbearance shown in this instance. Civility shaves off the rough edges of belief—that is, the spiritual zeal that might encourage one person to impose his belief on another. But this self-restraint does not work, affectively, in the arena of family affairs. The affective enthusiasm that Locke deplores as an exercise of zeal in the public sphere means something different in a family. That is, the impulses that Locke hopes to control in the *Letter*—the desire to imprint one's own religious conviction on the mind of another, to impose theological imperatives on a corporate body, to express enthusiasm as a social feeling—are forces that, within a marriage, are likely to be understood as instances of love and attachment. In 1702, nonjuror Charles Leslie argues just this—that religious difference in a marriage must be overcome because love for a spouse *requires* it: "Can I Covenant (or ought I to keep it) to suffer my Wife to go on in what I am persuade is a great Sin, to continue all her Life in idolatrous Worship, or in open and notorious Schism, without so much as once interposing even my Advice, or attempting to satisfie her Scruples, or convince her Reason? Will not the Blood of her Soul be requir'd at my Hand?"[51] Where Locke attaches religious zeal to hypocrisy—a desire for power over another, rather than for a reconciliation of beliefs—here the presence of zeal speaks to a caring sensibility. To seek conversion of a wife is to honor her. John Shower similarly argues that the quality of love is compromised once religious difference appears in a marriage: "But if they find themselves mistaken in their Choice in that respect, they must use the greater Care to perswade them to be such, as they supposed them to have been: Remembring however, that if they cannot as yet love them, *as real Saints*, they must love them, *as Husbands and Wives*."[52] True love—the love of a fellow Christian—cannot withstand religious dissent, and in its absence an affectively thin sense of conjugal duty must take over to fulfill social obligations.

It should not surprise us, then, that following the lead of *Some Thoughts Concerning Education* (1693), Locke's contemporaries were preoccupied with family religion, the practices of religious education and worship that Protestant households were expected to maintain.[53] J. Paul Hunter has observed that, in the years of William and Mary, "worry about the decay of family religion became heated."[54] The Act of Toleration did not grant Dissenters the right to public office or university education, rendering the family an important site of community building.[55] Further, the passage of the act deepened the rift between nonjurors and High Church Anglicans, who evoked the destruction of the nation's "family" ties in their lament for the loss of Stuart and church authority. The family/nation analogy remained a governing trope throughout the period and worked in both directions: the decay of the nation was reflected in the breakdown of family relations, and instability within families contributed to national degradation. The archbishop of Canterbury, John Tillotson, starts with the nation, focusing on the trickle-down effects of Dissent's commitment to the liberty of conscience: "This great Neglect and Decay of Religious Order in Families is chiefly owing to our Dissentions and Differences in Religion, upon occasion whereof many under the pretence of Conscience have broke loose into a boundless Liberty."[56] In the absence of a comprehensive Church of England, individual families cannot expect religious uniformity within the home: "Till the Publick and unanimous Worship of God do in some measure recover its Reputation, the good Order and Government of Families as to the great ends of Religion is never likely to obtain and to have any considerable effect."[57] The question of "reputation" speaks to the necessity of a stable discursive realm in which the Church of England can circulate as the sign of national religious identity. Without this placeholder, families and individuals have no tool with which to shape their religious identity. More optimistically, fellow Anglican William Payne considers family religion the place to start in reuniting the Church of England. Family discipline can produce social discipline: "Could we then be so happy as to perswade Men but to the constant use of this [family worship], it would quickly bring them to Publick Worship, and make an hundred times fewer Dissenters, and a thousand times more Religious and Good Men in a very little while." Payne, significantly, suggests that the use of patriarchal authority to enforce religious conformity in the home "will never I suppose be thought any breach of Toleration or of the fullest Liberty of Conscience."[58] Of course, as we will see, it *was* thought such a breach by women who found their religious freedom curtailed by their husbands.

Dissenters equally looked to family religion to shore up their values. Michelle Wolfe and Andrew Cambers note that "proscribed from public worship, participation in nonconformity was legally limited to two venues: domestic piety and shared text."[59] Presbyterian John Shower argues that Dissent's Protestant integrity, grounded in allegiance to scriptural authority, starts from the family and moves outward: "What Hope of *a National Reformation*," writes Shower, "if it begin not in *Families*? If they, who have the Care and Government of these lesser Societies, will not faithfully do their part; neither Magistrates, or Ministers can expect success in doing Theirs."[60] Shower narrates a history of religious identity, organized around the family as the foundational unit: "Family-Worship was the first kind of Social Worship: Religion was at first confin'd to single Persons; upon the Increase of Mankind it begun in Families. Every Ruler of a Family was then a Priest to his own House, or offered his own Sacrifice, and governed his Family, not only as such, but as a Religious Society."[61] Here, each family serves as a microcosm of an independent Protestant congregation. The argument here does not move outward toward a Filmerian vision of government but rather centers itself on the integrity of those family values capable of sustaining religious community.

For Samuel Slater, family religion serves the same role that Locke ascribes to public worship, drawing the individual into a larger community, where faith can be translated into "useful" virtues. Individual prayer and family worship work in tandem to form the religious subject: "It is not enough for them to worship God in their Families, but they ought to do it in their Chambers too; nor is it enough for them to worship God in their Chambers, but they ought to do it in their Families too.... Secret duties are plainer Evidences of Sincerity, Family and publick duties are of larger influence and usefulness."[62] In a household where family religion is not practiced, Slater notes, the believing individual is set adrift and has no recourse but to God: "You that are fixed, as a Wife, Child, an Apprentice, count the want of Family-duty as your Affliction, and groan under it as such, and in your private addresses beg down, if possible, Mercy and Grace upon them. Pray heartily for them who will neither pray for you nor for themselves, the godly Wife for the ungodly Husband, the gracious Child for the profane Parent, and the Religious Servant for the Wicked Master or Mistress."[63] Significantly, Slater speaks only to the powerless members of the family. He assumes a husband/father/master can impose family prayer on a wife/child/servant: "The Family is a *Body*, bigger or less, and the Master is the *Head* of it, and he should rule, order and influence all the *Members* thereof."[64]

Needless to say, interfaith marriage proved a particular threat to the practice of family religion. Slater and his contemporaries turn repeatedly to interfaith marriage as the occasion for the institution's degradation. Dissenter Matthew Henry writes, "If a Church in the House be so necessary, so comfortable, then *be not unequally yoked with Unbelievers*, who will have no Kindness for the Church in the House, nor assist in the Support of it, but instead of *building this House, pluck it down with their Hands, Prov. 14.1*."[65] "It too often comes to pass," James Kirkwood observes, "that they who are unequally yoked, either with Persons of a false Religion, or of a Wicked Life, do by degrees degenerate from their strict and Virtuous Education."[66] The habits of everyday life that underwrite family unity, in other words, cannot be maintained in interfaith households.

The editors of the *Athenian Mercury* tackled the subject in response to a question regarding the viability of a Catholic-Protestant union in 1692:

> Its very unlikely she shou'd have any great share in his *Heart*, if he's but true to his own *Principles*, for we can't see how is't possible for him heartily to love one he believes is certainly damn'd as that the Pope is St. *Peters* Successor, and has the Keys of Paradice in his Girdle.... Add to all this, what's more than all, the perpetual hazard she'll be in of changing her Religion, and losing her *Soul* by their plausible Insinuations, and we're then sure we shall have said enough to hinder any wise Woman from making the Experiment.[67]

The question of sincerity structures this debate. The Catholic husband cannot help but interfere with his Protestant wife's spiritual life if "he's but true to his own Principles." Indeed, the quality of his love *depends* on his bringing her to his faith if he wants to ensure her eternal salvation, according to Catholic doctrine, the editors argue. The woman involved with a Catholic man, however firm her faith, faces at the very least the unhappiness of continually guarding herself against religious violation. In another instance, a woman finds herself duped into an engagement to a Catholic and asks whether she is required to honor it. The editors of the *Athenian Mercury* write:

> In our Opinions th[e] Contract is void, which cannot be kept without Sin. If the Contract is not ratifi'd to all intents and purposes in the Eye of Law; we believe the Laws of God requires it not, but rather forbids it, *Be ye not unequally yoked together with unbelievers*: . . . And thô we have given our Opinion, we desire you not to rely on it, unless confirm'd by the Approbation of some of *our Bishops*, for 'tis a matter of great Moment, that pretends to the decision of an Interest in both Worlds.[68]

The editors argue that religious law requires that the Protestant break with her Catholic partner, whom she cannot marry "without sin." But they also recognize that breaking a civil contract, even in the case of marriage fraudulently engaged and not yet ratified by law, requires a strong defense, and they look to the bishops for guidance.

In 1702, nonjuror Charles Leslie identifies interfaith marriage as "the particular Sin, for which it is said, God sent the Flood to destroy the whole Earth, except eight persons."[69] Quaker Moses West, whose treatise against interfaith marriage was reprinted eight times over the course of the eighteenth century, makes the same connection five years later: "It [interfaith marriage] appears to have been a great step, that lead to the Destruction of the old World, the Door that gave the Inlet to those Corruptions and Violence, which filled the Earth and provoked the Lord."[70] He goes on:

> If two Persons of *differing* Judgments about Matters of Faith and Religious Exercises (as going to Meetings, Preaching, Praying, Thanksgiving, &c.) should incline to marry each other, presuming in their fond *Affections*, that, notwithstanding that *Disagreement*, they may live comfortably together, they will find *too late* that they were greatly mistaken. . . . [I]f their Love to God and Religion, be not quite *consumed* by those *passionate Flames*, which engaged them into that *unwarrantable* Undertaking; they will feel, *after Marriage*, their Spirits more plainly and warmly *conflicting* with another, and striving to bring into a *Conformity* unto that Way of Worship, which he or she is in. And then, whichsoever of

them prevails, the other must lose *Peace* of *Conscience* (the *greatest* of all Losses) unless such *Compliance* spring from a true and unfeigned Conviction, that the Worship so conformed to, is the *right*: Which is more than may reasonably be expected by any, who are guilty of *tempting* the Lord with such *Mixt-marriages*.[71]

Here, two threats appear. The first—the one that allows the couple to consider marriage in the first place—is the subordination of religious principle to love: that is, a secular approach to marriage. The second is the reawakening of religious principle after the honeymoon is over. Each conscience retreats into the integrity of the theological tenets that consign the other to hell for unbelief. The passion of romantic love gives way to the warmth of religious "Spirits," and discord is inevitable. Even if one partner is persuaded to convert by the other, a shadow of doubt will hang over the marriage. This portrait of spouses engaged in their own private religious war suggests that toleration as a species of mutual regard or recognition is not only unattainable but undesirable—those who embark on the experiment are "tempting" the Lord to visit his displeasure upon them.

We hear, in these polemics, the urgency of maintaining religious conformity in the face of state-sanctioned toleration. The vast majority of eighteenth-century novels uphold the prohibition against interfaith marriage. But for the novelists I study in the chapters that follow, interfaith marriage serves as an occasion to explore the limits of Protestant triumphalism and the racial and sexual logics of an emergent liberalism. The limited toleration afforded to Protestant Dissent by the 1689 act, and its exclusion of Catholics, raised questions for the novelists attempting to imagine affective communities and an ethics of sociability capable of mitigating conflict. The persistence of anti-Catholic and anti-Semitic xenophobia revealed the limits of statecraft's ability to foster social bonds. For women novelists, the question of women's religious subjectivity and freedom of speech informed how they imagined the woman author and the writing of women's lives. The form of the realist novel proved sufficiently expansive for the abbreviated plots recounted by polemicists to grow into a developed storyline.

Before turning to Samuel Richardson, however, I want to examine two historical marriages to reveal how ideas about family religion and conjugal love were tested by instances of marital conflict. The stories of the Duke and Duchess of Norfolk and of Samuel and Susanna Wesley reveal the fault lines in the discourses that structured seventeenth- and early eighteenth-century understandings of toleration and marriage. They remind us of the Protestant radicalism of the mid-seventeenth century that shaped cultural understandings of both toleration and divorce, as well as the disciplinary regimes that maintained the spousal authority of husbands in the Protestant household, before and after the Restoration. The transformation of religious toleration into statecraft by the regime of William III revitalized the agendas of moral reform and family religion, both of which attempted to ameliorate the tensions created by deep cultural and religious schisms. Throughout the seventeenth and early eighteenth century, women made claims for their liberty of conscience, a discourse that challenged the prerogatives of family religion.

At the heart of each story are the rights that attend a woman's religious identity. In 1692, Protestant Henry Howard, Duke of Norfolk, asked Parliament to grant him a divorce from his Catholic wife Mary, ostensibly on the grounds of adultery.[72] But at least one source defined the case in religious terms, accusing the duke of inciting anti-Catholic sentiment to advance his case by mobilizing parliamentary interests in noble estates descending to Protestant heirs. Robert Welbourne, a witness who testified before the lords, claimed that the duke told him to threaten his wife with divorce on religious grounds when he had wanted her to cede properties to him several years earlier: "[Duke:] I do not say it to threaten her: But I am told, that for the Reason of there being either One and Twenty, or Two and Twenty *Catholick* Heirs of my Family before One *Protestant* One; if I would bring in a Bill of Divorce, I should obtain it on that account." As Welbourne pointed out, the Duke's remarks about his Catholic heirs "seem'd to turn the Case of Adultery into a Case of Religion."[73]

Opponents of the Duke of Norfolk's petition for divorce argued that a larger national principle was served in preserving, rather than dissolving, the marriage. Nonjuror Roger North was particularly eloquent on the subject, claiming that a Hobbesian nihilism would be advanced by a divorce: "The policy will not rest between papist and protestant, but will descend down thro all the subdivided sects, of Presbyterian, Independent, Quaker and so that party that is uppermost must oppress all the rest and the nation become a desart of wolves."[74] North goes on to suggest that a divorce would effectively create a new legal precedent for the disinheriting of "absent & defenseless" heirs, as well as laying the groundwork for civil unrest created by self-interested parties: "It will make such a disturbance & turmoil among the subjects of England, supposing an Equity . . . that all men's bills are received; that none will be contented with what is their own by law."[75] The duchess, most immediately, is harmed by the duke's appeal, North argues. Having been born a Catholic with few legal rights, "surely there is little reason or justice in taking from her, & forcing a new penalty upon her."[76] The duchess herself advanced this same line of argument in her appeal to the House of Lords: "Your Lordships are now creating new ways of Proceeding against me, and a new Law to Punish me."[77]

Two models of government, as well as two models of toleration, are in play here: James II's monarchism versus William's parliamentarianism, and James's Declaration for Liberty of Conscience (1687, 1688) versus the Act of Toleration.[78] Where James's declaration granted religious freedom to all of his subjects, including Catholics, as an instance of monarchical indulgence, William and Mary advanced a restricted toleration organized around a collective Protestant "consent" to the new regime. For William's opponents, the new disposition signaled a descent into individualism and self-interest, breaking the oaths that tie a nation to its king and to a larger collective good. To support the interfaith marriage of the Duke and Duchess of Norfolk, by this account, is to move beyond the nominalism of "Protestant" or "Catholic" to a deeper account of the family members' integrity. John Evelyn described the duke's nephews, heirs to the estate, as "Papists indeede, but very hopefull & vertuous Gent: as was their father: The now Duke & Unkle, a dissolute protestant."[79] The social compact has been broken by the husband whose self-interested Protestantism masks the absence of an ethical character.

In the case of the Duke and Duchess of Norfolk, the religious rights of the duchess were overridden by the interests of the state—and its interests in the Protestant transmission of property—when Parliament granted the divorce. But defenses of the duchess show us how those rights were recognized as well as how interfaith marriage set the stage for competing narratives about how religious identity contributed to the maintenance of social bonds. The duke's victory, for many, represented a violation of the trust in his private character upon which the nation's reputation rested. While this marriage was not typical, insofar as the nobility of the family meant that the state had a vested interest in the outcome of this case, I suggest that the terms governing this dispute did not differ substantially from those surrounding the second marital conflict over religious difference we now turn to, involving Susanna and Samuel Wesley.

Susanna Wesley is best known as the mother of Charles and John Wesley, founders of the Methodist movement. It is not difficult to trace the roots of Methodism to the family household in which Charles and John were raised, where Susanna served as a religious educator of both her children and her parish community and developed a rigorous program of spiritual discipline that her sons would later formalize. Raised a Dissenter, Susanna Wesley converted to Anglicanism at an early age, "not being full 13." She married Samuel Wesley, an Anglican clergyman, at nineteen, in 1688.[80] Sometime in the early years of her marriage, Susanna Wesley developed the nonjuring sympathies that sparked a standoff with her husband in 1702, when she decided that she could no longer, in good conscience, participate in prayers for the king. She describes her husband's response in a letter to Lady Yarborough:

> Tis but a little while since he one Evening observ'd in our Family prayers I did not say Amen to his prayer for W[illiam] as I usually do to all others; upon which he retir'd to his study, & calling me to him ask'd me the reason of my not saying Amen to the Prayer. I was a little surpris'd at the question & don't well know what I answer'd. [B]ut too well I remember what follow'd: He immediately kneel'd down & imprecated the divine Vengeance upon himself & all his posterity if ever he touch'd me more, or came into a bed with me before I had beg'd God's pardon & his, for not saying Amen to the prayer for this King.[81]

Samuel Wesley's response identifies Susanna's disobedience to the king as a violation of both conjugal and divine law. As punishment, he renounces the marriage bed. We see, in a poem written a few years earlier, how Samuel Wesley's understanding of the Protestant household might have shaped his response to his wife's disobedience. In *The Life of Christ* (1697), Samuel writes a portrait of the Virgin Mary as a model for the ideal wife. Joseph describes Mary thus:

> She grac'd my humble *Roof*, and blest my *Life*,
> Blest me by a far *greater Name* than *Wife*:*   [. . . That of *Friend*]
> Yet still I bore an *undisputed Sway*,
> Nor was't her *task*, but *pleasure* to *obey*:
> Scarce *thought*, much less cou'd act, what I *deny'd*;
> In our *low house* there was no room for *Pride*.
> Nor need I e'er *direct* what still was *right*,
> Still study'd my Convenience and Delight.[82]

The problem with Susanna was that she did not study her husband's "convenience and delight" but rather her own conscience in considering the laws she needed to obey. It's clear that Susanna considered the religious difference created by her nonjuror obligations a private matter that posed no threat to her marriage vows. In her letter to Lady Yarborough, she argues that Samuel transgresses the boundary of her religious autonomy, while she respects his: "I've unsuccessfully represented to him the unlawfulness & unreasonableness of his Oath; . . . that since I'm willing to let him quietly enjoy his opinions, he ought not so deprive me of my little liberty of conscience" (238).

Presumably Samuel did not register that his wife was exercising forbearance by allowing him to "quietly enjoy his opinions" but rather assumed that his views were hers as well. Confronted with evidence of her independent mind, Samuel chose to separate from his wife rather than make room for it in the marriage. Susanna sought counsel from George Hickes, who supported her claims and provided her with arguments to use in the event Samuel Wesley brought his bishops into the conversation: "I am persuaded if it were so represented to the two persons to whom you say Mr. Wesley will refer it, that they would pity you & blame his conduct & tell him, that his Oath lays no obligation upon him, but that of repentance for the rashness & iniquity of it, the matter there being wholly contrary to the prior obligation of his marriage-promise, & the relative duties of an husband resulting from thence." According to Hickes, the marriage oath binds Samuel Wesley to his wife, who is free to pursue her religious independence within the marriage. Hickes does not stop at her dissent, however, but brings in the hypothetical case of an interfaith union: "You may tell them that you humbly conceive that if you had renounc'd your Religion by turning Papist, Anabaptist, or Quaker, as some Clergymen's Wives & children have done, he neither ought to have made such an oath, or if he had, to have kept it." Echoing the radical tolerationists of the mid-seventeenth century, he argues that it is up to God, not husbands, to show individuals the errors of their ways: "God, if you be in the wrong, [will] convince you of it by the illumination of his holy Spirit, who shews to them that be in error the light of his truth that they may return into the way of righteousness" (239). Marriage is capable of supporting religious difference because God is the arbiter of religious truth and the guide to spiritual awakening. Hickes concludes with words of comfort for Susanna: "Wherefore good Madam, stick to God & your conscience, which are your best friends, whatever you may suffer for adhering to them" (240).

Samuel Wesley was forced to return to the family when their home burned down several months after he left his wife, and perhaps this particular fight was resolved by the death of King William the same year.[83] But religious conflict continued to strain the Wesley marriage. Susanna notes, in a letter to her son, that dispute defines her relationship with Samuel: "'Tis an unhappiness almost peculiar to our family that your father and I seldom think alike" (106).

Early in 1712, Samuel was in London when he received a complaint from his deacon that attendance at Susanna's family prayers on Sunday evening was affecting Sunday morning church attendance. We don't have Samuel's letter, but Susanna's response recounts its criticisms: "The main of your objections against our Sunday evening meetings are, first, that it will look particular; secondly, my sex; and lastly, your being at present in a public station in character" (79). Having answered each concern individually, Susanna concludes, "If you do after all think fit to dissolve this assembly, do not tell me any more that you desire me to do it, for that will not satisfy my conscience; but send me your positive command in such full and express terms as may absolve me from all guilt and punishment for neglecting this opportunity of doing good to souls, when you and I shall appear before the great and awful tribunal of our Lord Jesus Christ" (82–83). By this directive, Samuel will assume the guilt that Susanna would otherwise feel in refraining from doing good, and in return for exercising his worldly prerogative—that is, his authority as a husband—he will find himself accountable to a higher law. Susanna acknowledges masculine authority as a custom to be observed, but she refuses to grant it credence as an extension of divine law. Here, Susanna's conscience can suspend its conviction in deference to a marital obligation, but it is a suspension only—not a concession to her husband's understanding of the evening prayer meetings.[84]

A transcript of Susanna Wesley's "A Religious Conference" housed in the John Rylands Library has a manuscript note written by Thomas Marriot on its final page, dated December 20, 1847: "This MS shows she was nice under the teaching of *Bp* [Bishop] *Bull* & was somewhat lectured with Socinianism to which her Husband Sam Wesley was *so strongly opposed*."[85] Marriot's note on the religious differences between Susanna and Samuel Wesley reminds us of the radical shifts that occurred in Protestant theology and English religious culture more generally in the early eighteenth century. That the Wesleys' sons, Charles and John, became the founders of a new denomination reflects this broad transformation, as well as the schisms that attended it. The effect of these schisms on marriages reveals how easily one could find oneself "unequally yoked." How to navigate this terrain at the dawn of a new political and religious dispensation?

Samuel and Susanna Wesley provide one instance of how storytelling could ameliorate the challenge of interfaith marriage in early eighteenth-century England. In a letter to George Hickes, Susanna Wesley writes of her husband's departure from the family home:

He staid 2 days & then left me early one morning with the resolution never to see me more, but that infinite Power that disposes & overrules the minds of men as he pleases, & can speak to their wild unreasonable passions as he does to the waves of the sea, hitherto thou shall go & no farther, so order'd it, that in his way he met a Clergyman to whom he communicated his intentions, and the reason that induc'd him to leave his Family: He extremely pitied him & condemn'd me, but however he prevail'd with him to return. (240–41)

Susanna establishes, through the parallel construction of her sentence, a connection between God's ability to limit our passions—"hitherto thou shall go & no farther"—and the clergyman's ability to engage Samuel in a conversation that both draws out the story and leads to the right moral decision.[86] The clergyman's sympathy for Samuel does not prevent him from upholding the law of the marriage vow, softened into a human form through the intimacy of conversational exchange. Samuel trusts the clergyman in ways that, the record shows, he did not trust higher church dignitaries.[87] Religious sociability depends on these structures of exchange capable of maintaining—in their distance from the public sphere—the sincerity of those who engage in them. It is not religious principle as law, then, that maintains the integrity of belief but its articulation in the everyday negotiations of moral and affective relations through social and narrative exchange.

In the years that followed the Wesleys' marital conflicts (resolved only by Samuel's death in 1735), a new dispensation arose in the preaching of their sons, John and Charles. Although Methodism did not separate from the Church of England until the end of the century, its evangelical beginnings drew attention to a new religiosity, one that provided women with an opportunity, in the early years, for preaching and writing, bringing questions of their religious rights into sharp focus while theorizing, at the same time, a feminized religious subject. Misty Anderson places a "penetrable, vulnerable self" at the center of eighteenth-century evangelicalism.[88] An increasingly influential print culture kept Methodism in the public eye, as Brett McInelly has argued, and set the stage for the convergence of religious and literary interests in the early realist novel.

After 1700, Protestant toleration advocates made steady gains on the political front: "Although the [Protestant Dissenting] Deputies failed to get [the Test and Corporation Acts] repealed, they did remarkable service in dealing with local grievances."[89] But these gains for toleration were countered by divisions within Protestantism, brought about by the evangelical turn and by the spike in anti-Catholic sentiment in the aftermath of the Jacobite Rebellions of 1715 and 1745. R. K. Webb observes, further, that "a horrendous series of medieval anti-Jewish statutes remained unrepealed."[90] By the 1750s, the government's commitment to toleration as a means of fostering commercial interests had to confront the persistence of religious xenophobia, a product of earlier state commitments to marginalizing minorities and shoring up Protestant hegemony. The structural flaws in the architecture of limited toleration imagined by the 1688–89 revolution began to reveal themselves.

CHAPTER 2

Sir Charles Grandison's Religious Disturbances

> The persuasions of religion are not to be compell'd: but the disturbances by religion are to be restrained by the laws.
> —*Jeremy Taylor,* Ductor Dubitantium, or The Rule of Conscience *(1660)*

The evangelical movement launched by John and Charles Wesley makes a cameo appearance in Samuel Richardson's *Sir Charles Grandison* (1753–54), when a minor character, Mrs. O'Hara, recovers from alcoholism by converting to Methodism.[1] This conversion serves as the starting point for Charlotte Lennox's satire of Richardson in her 1758 novel, *Henrietta*. Miss Woodby, a friend of the novel's heroine, remarks,[2] "A writer ... who is greatly admired by our sex, ... has introduced these modern saints reclaiming a woman who had led a very vicious life. ... [A]nd he has not thrown away his compliment: I dare say this numerous sect has bought up an impression of his book; and is not the third edition upon the title-page a very good return to it?"[3] Lennox implies that Richardson has flattered the Methodists to increase sales of his novel, reducing the conversion story to a marketing strategy. The critique does not stop there. Religious toleration, more generally, turns out to be a species of authorial self-promotion. "Oh! my dear," Miss Woodby goes on, "there is no vanity like the vanity of some authors: it is not to be doubted but if there were musselmen [Muslims] enough in the kingdom to add a unit more to the account of those editions, but we should find him introducing the alcoran, making proselytes from luxury."[4] By this account, any author who expresses interest in, or sympathy toward, minority faiths is simply expanding his market share. The move from Methodists to "musselmen" suggests, further, that toleration, once indulged, has no limit—that, indeed, the absence of discrimination might well signal a dangerous lack of Christian interiority. Richardson "pays court to all religions, carrying himself so evenly amidst them, that it is hard to distinguish to which he most inclines," Miss Woodby notes.[5] Richardson's tolerance looks suspiciously like religious apathy.

Charlotte Lennox was not alone in attacking the tolerationist tendencies of Richardson's third novel. One reader accused him of facilitating a Catholic invasion of the body politic through his sympathetic portrait of Clementina della Porretta, Sir Charles Grandison's first love interest: "What a Glorious opportunity lost in a work so Generally read the time so critical, the hope of the nation in the hands of papists . . . papists in offices about the court conceal'd papists in the great Council of the Nation; priests creeping universally into houses leading Silly women captive many so led sending their Children to nunneries for Education (as tis called) where from the subscriptions of the deluded in England, they learn many triffles [sic]."[6] Regardless of the fact that it never reaches the altar, here the Grandison-Porretta union allegorizes a captivity narrative. England becomes subject to the Vatican when Catholics find their way into court circles and British homes, where "silly women" are told by meddling priests how to educate their children. The novel represents an important agent for the transmission of cultural values. The reader bemoans the "glorious opportunity" lost for advocacy of the Protestant cause against Catholic encroachments. The mere inclusion of the interfaith marriage plot in *Grandison*, regardless of its failure, creates a tear in the cultural fabric through which dangerous ideas might make their way into the minds of readers.

Given that Richardson could have anticipated the rebuke, it is worth asking, Why did he venture into these dangerous waters at all? We know that, despite his support for the Jewish Naturalization Act of 1753, when popular outcry rose up against it, Richardson advocated privately for the law's repeal, worrying that controversy would harm the Jewish community.[7] Richardson did not consider religious toleration a policy worth the public fight, in this instance. But this chapter argues that the social ethics he promotes in *Sir Charles Grandison* identify toleration as a key aspect of what Tita Chico describes as the novel's "affective communities."[8] That is, Richardson recognizes that the failure to accommodate religious difference signals a larger problem of communal engagement. Critics have analyzed *Grandison*'s account of toleration in their studies of the novel's representation of Italian Catholicism, and what follows builds on their insights.[9] But where critics have tended to map the novel's politics onto the either/or logic of contemporary political theory— tolerance represents a tool of repression *or* a liberal virtue—I hope to map the novel's understanding of tolerance in a way that helps to move us beyond this binary. Even as *Grandison* endorses Locke's model of paternalist governance, it also recognizes how that endorsement impedes a more ambitious literary and philosophical project, one that engages directly with the darkness of *Clarissa*'s world, where compulsion, rather than persuasion, proves the norm.[10] The interfaith marriage plot, I argue, allows Richardson to circle back to the questions of sincerity, conscience, and community central to *Clarissa*, and to answer them in different ways.

I begin this chapter by placing Solomon Merceda, the novel's Jewish rake, against the backdrop of Anglo-Jewish libertinism and interfaith marriage in eighteenth-century England. This figure, I suggest, foregrounds the problem of conversion that attended disputes over interfaith marriage. As we saw in chapter 1, Pauline doctrine encouraged Christians in interfaith marriages to hope for the conversion of their partners. But several questions arise from this tenet: If a spouse proves willing to convert, can his sincerity be trusted? If he does not convert, can he be trusted not to impose his beliefs on his spouse? Solomon Merceda is not, himself, the subject of an interfaith marriage plot. He represents, however, a masculine subject whose status in English culture was defined by that plot. He foregrounds, further, how race was embedded in ideas of toleration and civility and how whiteness adhered to the gentlemen charged with upholding them in the public sphere. Questions about conversion thus cast light on Sir Charles, both in relation to his efforts to assimilate those he meets into his social program and to his proposed marriage to Clementina della Porretta. How does the defeat of Merceda that *Grandison* stages compromise, rather than enable, Richardson's social vision?

I then turn to the question of women's spiritual authority as it is framed by the characterization of Clementina della Porretta. Like Clarissa before her, Clementina puts her conscience first. Richardson's respect for the claims of conscience competes with his respect for patriarchal authority in the family, and we see in the contest between Clementina and Charles how religious principle interrupts emergent norms of both toleration and sexual discourses in England. Of particular interest to me is how Clementina's linguistic mastery reinforces her religious autonomy—a configuration that reappears in the novels of women authors responding to *Grandison*. That is, Clementina prefigures how women authors aligned religious freedom with their claims to independence as writers.

Both Solomon Merceda and Clementina della Porretta represent cracks in the edifice of the community that supports the marriage of Harriet Byron and Charles Grandison. Merceda and Clementina maintain plots of refusal—to believe, to love, as Grandison does—but their stories signal the arrival of religious pluralism as a discursive, as well as a political, practice. How might we engage their stories to provide an alternative trajectory, one that draws religious minorities into a larger social narrative?

The second half of this chapter shows how these characters shadow the Protestant marriage plot as it unfolds. The triumph of Protestant companionate marriage over the vicissitudes of religious difference is compromised by our awareness of the restrictions on freedom this marriage requires. First and foremost, it foregrounds the sublimation of strong feeling into maternal duty for Harriet Byron and into arranged marriage for Clementina. Second, it exposes the dependence of Sir Charles's tolerance on that sublimation. The civility he maintains seals off his interiority from the incursions of feeling and, in doing so, prevents Sir Charles from fully entering into the social world over which he rules. *Sir Charles Grandison*, I argue, recognizes the limits of an emergent liberalism—as well as its gendered and racial character—at precisely the moment it tries to translate its principles into narrative. It is the *failed* plots of conversion and marriage, I contend, that reveal the conditions that would sustain, most fully, the ethics of sociability and tolerance Richardson hoped to advance.

Converso Libertinism

The index of volume seven of *Sir Charles Grandison* includes an abbreviated account of Solomon Merceda's final days: "Desperately wounded. . . . Vows penitence. . . . Dies miserably. . . . His exit full of horror and despair."[11] This rake's progress follows the telos of all libertine narratives—at least as they are told by moralists—but, more particularly, it reminds Richardson's readers of *Clarissa*'s final pages. We know that Richardson was offended by readers' willingness to forgive Lovelace for the rape of Clarissa and darkened his character in subsequent editions of the novel. Although Richardson claims, in his preface, that Lovelace is a Christian, Clarissa's downfall can be attributed, in part, to her failure to imagine that anyone could hold belief in as little regard as Lovelace holds his. Indeed, her confidence that a common standard of Christian morality operates in the world is one of the imperatives that Lovelace uses against Clarissa. The novel's tragedy stems from the confrontation of sincere belief and a belief whose evisceration reflects a wider cultural corruption. In the character of Solomon Merceda, I believe, Richardson brings this question of sincerity, left unanswered by *Clarissa*, into focus.

The character of Solomon Merceda emerges from a tradition that was well established by the 1750s: that of the Anglo-Jewish rake, whose libertinism provoked cultural anxieties only matched by the rise in interfaith marriages between Jews and Christians. The historical facts of Anglo-Jewish engagements with London's sexual underworld, actively satirized in images like Hogarth's plate 2 of *The Harlot's Progress*, identify an increasingly close alliance between Sephardim and Christian cultures in eighteenth-century England. In Hogarth's print, the Jewish protector, defined by his dark eyebrows and caricatured nose, is duped by his mistress, who distracts him while her lover slips away.[12] In these circles, celebrity status was achieved by a few notable Jewish men.[13] Hogarth represents this achievement as a species of fraud, and he marks the Jew as "damned not only for his inescapable otherness, but also for his transgressive desire to merge his identity with that of the self."[14]

Take, for example, the case of Jacob de Castro Sarmento (1692–1762), a contemporary of Richardson's.[15] Sarmento's parents were hounded by the Inquisition, and Sarmento and his wife escaped the Continent in 1721. He achieved prominence early as the author of tracts on smallpox vaccination and the benefits of drinking mineral waters, and was inducted into the Royal Society in

William Hogarth, *The Harlot's Progress*, plate 2 (1732)

1729.[16] His Christian mistress, Elizabeth, gave birth to a son in 1748. He married her in 1756, after his Jewish wife died, and the couple had a second son in 1758.[17] Interfaith marriage, on this and other occasions, became part of the cultural conversation about the place of the Sephardim elite in the English social landscape. Sarmento appears in a satirical print published in 1749 titled *The Jerusalem Infirmary, Alias, a Journey to the Valley of Jehosaphat*, circulated after a Jewish apothecary, Mordechai de la Penha, was suspended in the wake of charges of assault against an English woman. The print represents the meeting where the suspension occurred, but the debate it stages attends to a different matter: that of excluding lower-class Ashkenazi Jews from the hospital. The status of the four Sephardim gentlemen standing on the left is marked by the white angel hovering over them. The blackness of the devil racializes the non-elite Jews seated at the table below him. The closer to the status of Protestant gentleman a Sephardim gets, the more likely he is to pass as "white." In a farce of the same name, *The Jerusalem Infirmary*, Sarmento appears as "Hypocrates," father of "Babe H*rry" (the child Sarmento had with Elizabeth). "The best thing he ever did in his Life," the servant character observes, "Is to have his Babe baptized in his name."[18] Here, interfaith marriage allows the body politic to transform both cultural difference and sexual mis-

Anon., *The Jerusalem Infirmary* (c. 1750)

conduct into comedy via conversion and the reproduction of British Protestant subjects. Anglican baptism appears to work in both a theological and ethnic register simultaneously, cleansing father and son simultaneously of their respective "sins."[19]

Andrew Crome notes that, by middle of the eighteenth century, "wealthy Sephardim were indistinguishable from other members of the English upper classes: they wore fashionable clothes, owned country mansions and married into the higher echelons of English society."[20] Although the story of acculturation is not necessarily one of assimilation, as Tijl Vannesta has pointed out, assimilation did become a reality when Sephardim married out.[21] The result of these marriages was, according to Todd Endelman, more often than not conversion to Christianity: "Mixed marriages contracted by respectable Jews almost always ended with the apostasy of the Jewish partner or with the eventual baptism of his or her children."[22] In his renunciation of Judaism in 1758, Sarmento commended secular sociability to his Jewish community as an alternative to religious affiliation: "I now therefore take my leave of you, hereby renouncing expressly that communion in which I have been considered with yourselves. I do not however renounce the intercourse I have with you in the general society of men of honour and probity."[23] Within this frame of reference, toleration is made possible by a replacement of religious conviction with moral benevolence of the kind encouraged by Locke's *Letter* and by *Grandison*.

The conversion undertaken by Jacob Sarmento on his way to achieving this sociability seems to involve the bracketing not only of Jewish belief but of all belief. How sincere, then, was his conversion to Christianity?[24] This question had dogged the Jewish community since the early days of the Spanish and Portuguese Inquisitions. Portuguese Jews, having been promised safe passage from the Iberian Peninsula by John II after their expulsion from Spain in 1492, faced forced conversion instead under Manuel I in 1497. "For the next several hundred years," Jane S. Gerber notes, "the fading remnants of Judaism were secretly cultivated in Portugal."[25] Those who managed to escape Portugal faced the challenge of reconstituting a Jewish identity in the absence of an established community. Portuguese "New Christians" comprised "a small, secretly organized presence" in England in the late sixteenth and early seventeenth century.[26] For early modern English culture, this community proved something of a mystery: "Did they consider themselves to be Jews, infidels, renegades, or Christians? Should they be thought of as lapsed Jews or fake Christians?"[27] That England's Jewish communities included a range of affiliations and identities made the situation complex both internally and externally—some were Christians, some practiced Judaism more or less openly. In 1724, Jacob Sarmento was accused of spying for the Inquisition. The charges and his exoneration are described in a brief publication of 1724, *Dr. Jacob de Castro Sarmento, having been proposed to be admitted a Fellow of the Royal Society, and a certain gentleman having industriously propagated a most scandalous report, highly reflecting on the Doctor's character: It is thought proper to publish the following extract, which is a true copy of the Entry of the Registry-book of the Synagogue*. Sarmento was cleared of all charges, but the fact that he was questioned in the first place testifies to the kinds of conflicts that arose around the Sephardic community in the eighteenth century. Jews like Sarmento contributed to the Republic of Letters through his intellectual contributions.[28] But Jewish cosmopolitanism, a central trope of xenophobia then and now, appeared to compromise the possibility of local attachments and the integrity of the body politic.

Sarmento's "general society," both as an instance of religious toleration and cosmopolitan worldliness, is what Richardson organizes around his man of "honour and probity" in *Sir Charles Grandison*.[29] James Grantham Turner suggests that Grandison represents Richardson's "final attempt to balance Enlightenment libertinism and Puritan integrity."[30] The challenge, in the case of the Jewish libertine, is to separate Solomon Merceda from the institution of marriage with which he was closely associated in the controversies over Jewish-Christian unions. From the start, Merceda is singled out by Richardson's narrative from a large cast of secondary characters. He is first introduced by the servant of Harriet Byron's kidnapper, Sir Hargrave, as a libertine whose schemes are more nefarious than those of fellow libertines: "I must say Sir Hargrave is an innocent man to the other two.... Mr. Merceda had a scheme on foot at the same time, which he was earnest to engage me in; but it was too shocking" (184). Presumably, this plan involves a sexual crime of some sort, the seeds, perhaps, of the plot that later unfolds in France. When Grandison meets Merceda, the narrative singles out the Sephardi again, first by his accent and then by his reputation. "[His] being a foreigner, I knew his voice from the rest" (263), Grandison reports. Satirical prints of the day routinely represented Jewish figures mangling the English language in their pronunciation. In *The Grand Conference or the Jew Predominant* (1753), Samson Gideon, who helped restructure British debt in the 1740s, is pictured saying, "Dare [dear] Gentlemens, & my very good Friends, Dis be de Purs collected by our Tribe for de great Favour [of the Jewish Naturalization Act]." Gideon was born and raised in London, and he married a Protestant wife. They baptized their three children in the Anglican Church.[31]

The Naturalization Act, according to the logic of the print, has the potential to taint the British nobility. Henry Pelham and his brother, Thomas Pelham-Holles, are pictured receiving money from Gideon for their part in ushering the act through Parliament.³² How might one distinguish Jews from Christians in this milieu of cosmopolitan capital? When Grandison is introduced to Merceda, he remarks, "Mr. Merceda!—I have heard of Mr. Merceda" (264). It is unclear whether Grandison is referring, here, to the servant's report or to a more established reputation that marks Mr. Merceda as an exceptional rake in the Lovelacean tradition. What is important is that Grandison can distinguish him from the herd. All the better, presumably, to counter the danger he represents.

Every time Sir Charles meets a new character, the narrative asks, Is this person in alignment with the codes that the "good man" embodies? In the particular case of the rakes Bagenhall, Merceda, and Pollexfen, the question is more vexed: Can libertines be recovered from their aggressive, antisocial tendencies and set on the path to civility? Can the social body tolerate their integration? What threat does their absorption into the community through marriage represent to the body politic? The libertines reflect on the pull toward conversion effected by Grandison's character in their first encounter with him:

Louis Philippe Boitard, *The Grand Conference or the Jew Predominant* (1753)

MR. BAG[ENHALL]. See what a Christian can do, Merceda. After this, will you remain a *Jew*?

MR. MER[CEDA]. Let me see such *another* Christian, and I will give you an answer. You, Bagenhall, I hope, will not think yourself intitled to boast of your Christianity?

MR. BAG. Too true! We have been both of us sad dogs. (270)

Here the epithet "dogs" signals that Bagenhall's and Merceda's immoral conduct ranks them among the uncivil, but we should also remember its common usage as an anti-Semitic slur.[33] Later in the conversation, Bagenhall reveals a further compromising detail—his Catholic identity:

MR. BAG. But, Sir Charles, you despise no man, I am sure, for differing from you in opinion. I am a Catholic—

SIR CH. A *Roman* Catholic—No religion teaches a man evil. I honour *every man* who lives up to what he professes. . . .

MR. JOR. The Truth is, Mr. Bagenhall has found his conveniencies in changing. He was brought up a Protestant. These *dispensations*, Mr. Bagenhall!—

MR. MER. Ay, and they were often an argument in Bagenhall's mouth, for making me his proselyte. (282–83)

Bagenhall converted to gain access to dispensations—allowances for his sins—and has tried to persuade his Jewish friend to do the same.[34] Charles links this disposition back to the Vatican, associating libertine self-interest with papal greed. *Roman* Catholicism is mere "*Court*" (283) religion so long as it attends to the self and its violent passions: "No [true] religion teaches a man evil" (282). Grandison observes further that institutional religion breeds hypocrisy when it winks at the illicit behavior of men like Bagenhall. True Christianity is marked by its transparency: "I honour *every man* who lives up to what he professes."

By this account, conversion to "true religion" requires, first, a naturalization from the particularities of nation—Portugal, Italy—to the universalism of Christian doctrine and, second, a recalibration of the heart from hypocrisy to sincerity. The third challenge is a temporal one: how to make conversion *stick*. Seventy years earlier, Gilbert Burnet, future archbishop of Canterbury, remarked on the timing of the libertine Earl of Rochester's conversion, which occurred shortly before his death: "I am apt to think that the Divine Goodness took pity on him, and seeing the sincerity of his Repentance, would try and venture him no more in Circumstances of Temptation, perhaps too hard for Humane Frailty."[35] In *Grandison*, Bagenhall's question as to whether Merceda will "remain" a Jew is complicated by his own "changing" ways. Which is worse? To remain steadfast in a faith that is wrong or to inhabit one so lightly it comes and goes? A conversion is not a true conversion if undertaken for the wrong reasons, or compelled—as was the case for the Portuguese *conversos* of the late fifteenth century. Further, conversion becomes problematic if it has to be repeatèd, over and over. "I had rather be Sir Charles Grandison in this one past hour, than the Great Mogul all my life," declares Sir Hargrave (268). The desirability of Grandison—one hour inside his skin trumps the whole life of a Muslim emperor—registers the difficulty of achieving his standard. Perhaps one can perform "Grandison" *only* for an hour. Any longer is unimaginable. The libertines conclude as much after Grandison's departure: "Yet his maxims, they said, where confoundedly strange; impracticable for such sorry dogs as them (that was their phrase) to practise" (285). A sincere and lasting conversion, by this account, might be too high a bar to set, at least for some.

In this first meeting, Grandison sets his sights to the much nearer target of politeness. Achieving this standard means renouncing violence. When Bagenhall attempts to line up dueling with Catholic doctrine, Grandison quickly corrects him, pointing out that the defenses he references originate not in doctrine but in the writings of "*Sir Ch. Bannes and Catejan* . . . one a Spaniard, the other an Italian" (283). Dueling has no Christian authority, Catholic or Protestant. The Christian subject, properly socialized, renounces the violence of passions in favor of the rationality of a public sphere that extends beyond national self-regard. But the libertine stubbornly clings to the desires of the local and of the body, which wants what it wants. Bagenhall ends the conversation about dueling by reverting back to the only subject that interests him, Harriet Byron: "She *must* be mine" (283). Later in the narrative, Sir Charles reflects on the discipline required to avoid this relentless falling back into particularity, which allegorizes the failure of civility as he defines it. Having spent a "riotous day" with the libertines, he remarks, "It is not indeed agreeable to be the spectator of riot; but how easy to shun being a partaker in it! How easy to avoid the too freely circling glass, if a man is known to have established a rule to himself, from which he will not depart" (773). The "rule" protects the self from violation by transforming him into a spectator who stands outside or above the vicissitudes of the body, he maintains. Sir Charles adopts this disinterested position in the circles of intimacy sustained not only by libertines but also by other small groups—groups of women, in particular—a subject to which I will return below.

Instead of rehabilitating Merceda, the narrative kills him off. Bagenhall, Merceda, and Sir Hargrave receive rough justice at the hands of the Frenchmen who chase them down after their attempts on the women of Abbeville. The Frenchmen were hoping, as they tell Grandison, "to give them [the libertines] reason to remember their villainy as long as they lived; and to put it out of their power ever to be guilty of the like" (951)—that is, they planned to castrate the would-be rapists. But only one libertine suffers the wished-for punishment. Sir Charles notes that "Mr. Merceda had been treated more severely... than the other; for he, it seems, was the greatest malefactor upon the Lady" (953). "He has, it seems, a wound in his thigh... which, but for his *valiant* struggles against the knife that gave the wound, was designed for a still greater mischief" (964). Here the threat of circumcision to the Christian body, so common to anti-Semitic polemic, is turned against the Sephardi.[36] As a wound, it serves as a reminder to Englishmen that their masculinity is at stake in the protection of Protestant interests—interests put at risk by men such as Pelham-Holles, who is willing to "convert" by way of circumcision to increase his wealth. (The inscription above his head reads, "It [the bribe] comes seasonably to me at this juncture/Circumcision or anything."[37])

The wounding ensures that the problem of belief that the Sephardic Jew poses for Protestant nationalism becomes legible. His body, having attempted to escape its religious specificity through assimilation into an English code of libertinism, now finds itself made vulnerable once again: "His recovery is despaired of; and the poor wretch is continually offering up vows of penitence and reformation, if his life may be spared" (964). Bonnie Latimer claims that Merceda "tries to convert again in exchange for his life" but Richardson is not specific as to what kind of reformation—Jewish or Christian—Merceda promises.[38] Instead of pressing home the conversion narrative, in other words, Richardson defines religious ambiguity as wounded masculinity. The assimilation project—the desire to bring the libertine back into the fold of polite society, the Jew into the embrace of Christian culture—ends, finally, with failure and a death full "of horror and despair" (1358). Richardson could not be sure Lovelace's death marked the end of the libertine tradition. Indeed, his readers' responses to the character suggested his charms remained a draw. In this case, however, the libertine's death is attended by the revival of his religious difference. His second "circumcision"—marked as castration—

Anon., *Vox Populi Vox Dei, or The Jew Act Repealed* (1753)

brings his Jewishness back into focus. Richardson draws on his readers' anti-Semitism, in the last instance, to keep his libertine in the grave.

But not without cost to his Good Man, as we shall see. Solomon Merceda reveals the limits of civility, its instantiation of white Protestant masculinity as the English standard. He also shows the instability of the conversion plot as a species of *Bildung*. Instead, he represents a more porous subjectivity, whose development reveals the vicissitudes of identity as it is sustained, or not, by a larger community. Richardson recasts the stories of Anglo-Jewish interfaith marriage circulating in mid-century England as a libertine narrative. In doing so, he foregrounds the extent to which the companionate marriage plot consolidates its authority through the creation of scapegoats.

The Taming of the Inquisition

Where the portrait of the Portuguese Jew employs religious difference to contain the risks associated with Anglo-Jewish libertinism, the portrait of the Catholic Clementina works in a different but related direction, using sexual difference to manage the threat of religious freedom. Like Solomon Merceda, Clementina della Porretta allows Richardson to engage alterity in order to contemplate, if not finally embrace, a species of toleration that moves beyond the limits imposed by political theory. The sincerity crisis posed by the Jew is made legible by externalizing religious identity as a wounded subjectivity. In Clementina's case, the narrative moves away from the body into a linguistic register, disciplining language as the corrective to too much, rather than too little, sincerity. That is, the narrative of female spiritual independence is overwritten by plain speech and common sense. But here, too, the case cannot be made without cost to Harriet Byron's story.[39]

The story begins when Sir Charles takes up residence in Bologna to attend the recovery of Jeronymo della Porretta (struck down by assailants, from whom he is rescued by Sir Charles) and passes his time in the sickroom teaching English to the Porrettas. Where Solomon Merceda's limitations are marked by his foreign accent (and, by extension, his displacement from a home country that does not want him), here language acquisition signals an atypical Italian cosmopolitanism. The love relationship between tutor and student presents itself immediately, a recasting of the transgressive Abelard-Heloise story, first in the guise of a respectable marriage plot authored by Clementina's brother Jeronymo. Sir Charles writes of the affair, "The younger brother, unknown to me, declared that he thought there was no way of rewarding my merits to the family, but by giving me a relation to it" (628). Grandison admits that "it was impossible . . . that my vanity should not sometimes be awakened, and a wish arise, that there might be a possibility of obtaining such a prize: But I checked the vanity, the moment I could find it begin to play about and warm my heart" (628–29). Capable of repressing them, Grandison nonetheless acknowledges the feelings that Clementina elicits, not least as a result of her sharp intelligence: "Tho' she was not half so often present at the lectures as they [her brothers] were, [she] made a greater proficiency than either of them" (628). The scene is set for an Italian Heloise, passionate and intellectually precocious, to take center stage.[40]

The Porrettas' absolutism on the article of religion prevents them, initially, from respecting Clementina's feelings for Grandison: "She is the first woman, that ever I heard of, who fell in love with a Philosopher: And she must, I think, take the consequence of such a peculiarity," the General remarks (704).[41] But if, initially, we blame the Porretta family for the failure of the interfaith marriage plot, we have intimations early on of the refusal that will eventually come from Clementina herself. For Clementina dreams of conversion, not compromise: "Let me beseech you, Sir . . . to hate . . . the unhappy Clementina . . . but, for the sake of your immortal Soul, let me conjure you to be reconciled to our Holy Mother Church!" (719). She assumes that Sir Charles might as easily convert to her faith as she to his: "I really look upon you . . . as my *fourth* brother: I should be glad that *all* my brothers were of one religion" (660). In a conversation with her mother she asks, "Might I not have had as great a chance of converting him, as he could have had of perverting me?" (715). Here, the lack of conviction that Richardson feared in the case of Jewish-Christian marriage is replaced with the vision of an interfaith marriage as a covert operation to prompt a Catholic conversion. Clementina's unwillingness to entertain an interfaith union stems, in part, from a recognition that, in the eyes of the world, marriage requires the subordination of a wife's interests to those of her husband, even if she manages to secure her rights by contract, as Sir Charles proposes.[42] Clementina reflects on the sexual double standard that pressures women to convert to the religion of their husbands: "I believe, you men think, it is no matter for us women to have any consciences, so as we do but study your wills, and do our duty by you" (713). Indeed, Sir Charles insists, as a condition of marriage to Clementina, that her religion remain strictly private: her confessor and servants must conform to the rules of his home and nation, and his sons, who will inherit his estate, must be raised Protestant. Liberty of conscience for Clementina takes precedence over the social identity marriage will confer on her.

From the start, both Clementina's love and her Catholicism express themselves in the form of cultural and linguistic exchange. Upon hearing the news of the Jacobite Rebellion in England, she contemplates the Roman Catholic Church's reestablished authority there: "And Clementina particularly pleased herself, that then her *heretic tutor* would take refuge in the bosom of his holy mother, the church: And she delighted to say things of this nature in the language I was teaching her, and which, by this time, she spoke very intelligibly" (629). Linguistic skill provides the mask behind which Clementina can hide her desire, even as she takes pleasure in the intimacy it promotes between her and her love object. Her mother remarks, "She was never chearful but when she was taking lessons for learning a tongue, that never . . . was likely to be of use to her." Where Solomon Merceda's libertinism consigns him to a world of bodily appetites and literal significations, Clementina's linguistic virtuosity allows her to protect her interiority from prying eyes. When questioned by Grandison about the melancholy into which she sinks as her love takes hold, Clementina speaks in her "newly-acquired language" in response to his questions, which he poses in "Italian or French" (630). Grandison moves between languages in search of the one that will unlock the secrets of Clementina's heart. Clementina blocks access by insisting on keeping the focus on the tutor/student relationship marked by her use of English. When Sir Charles brings up Count Belvedere, Clementina admonishes him, "Next time I am favoured with your lectures, it shall be upon Languages, if you please; and not upon Lovers" (653). For Clementina, cosmopolitanism grants access to a wider world upon which to stage an identity that reaches beyond the familiar and the familial, while remaining very much her own. And so, when Sir Charles makes his first departure, Clementina steps forward to receive his compliments "with a polite French freedom" (631).

Sir Charles criticizes Clementina's impatience to learn English quickly as a form of ambition, a desire to be "every-thing at once" (650). Indeed, Clementina's dream of mastery shapes not only her language lessons but her relation to her tutor more generally. Clementina's fantasies entertain only winners and losers, victors and vanquished. As a result, when talks between Sir Charles and the Porrettas falter over the article of religion, Clementina reads the failure of the marriage plot as a personal attack: "*To be despised! . . . To be despised!*—And by an English Protestant! Who can bear that? . . . [H]e has refused me, you know: . . . I never was refused before: . . . Don't let it be told abroad, that a daughter of that best of mothers was refused by any man less than a Prince!" (692, 710, 713). The narrative of defeat and rejection confirms Clementina's sense of her own importance, if only as a scorned object. Tita Chico suggests that "Richardsonian community in this final novel endorses modes of suffering and humiliation purportedly in the service of moral and social improvement," but it is important to note that the meaning of suffering is context specific.[43] Here, it bolsters rather than diminishes Clementina's understanding of herself as a tragic figure locked in struggle against her opponent. Clementina feels compelled to teach her tutor the lessons she learns from her suffering: "What a vain thing is this world! ... And so I shall tell the Chevalier! ... He has been my tutor, and I want, methinks, to return the favour, and be his tutress; ... Now I am sorry that you are an obstinate man. You *know* better, Chevalier. I think you *should* know better. But you have been my tutor. Shall I be yours?" (710, 712). Clementina's ensuing madness moves us into a linguistic register reminiscent of Clarissa's post-rape letters. Talking to her closet door, quoting Shakespeare (significantly, Ophelia's lines), citing the Latin Bible (632, 698, 756), speaking English to an invisible interlocutor (632, 756, 764), Clementina communicates in new ways. For Diderot, the breakdown of reason allows Clementina's moral sense to emerge more clearly: "But why is this Clementine so interesting in her madness? ... [S]he says not a word but that shows candor and innocence, and her condition leaves no room for doubt as to what she says."[44] Without romanticizing Clementina's madness, as Diderot does here, we can note how her compromised reason helps to secure the integrity of her speech acts by removing them from the realm of social hypocrisy into the transparent register of feeling.

To what extent does Clementina's style emerge as a universal grammar that has an affective, as well as a communicative function?[45] When Sir Charles returns to Italy, Clementina notes the change in herself: "Chevalier, I have quite forgot my English. I shall never recover it. What happy times were those, when I was innocent, and was learning English!" (1004). But if Clementina has lost her innocent relation to her tutor, she has gained a new perspective on the politics of exchange. Out of the linguistic madness emerges the pointedly sane refusal of Grandison's second marriage proposal, a refusal Clementina communicates, significantly, in a textual form: "*Read my paper.* ... *Read it*, I again say. ... I never can be happy with a man whom I think a heretic" (1125). At the same time as it announces her refusal to marry a heretic, Clementina's writing authorizes epistolary desire. "I was the more willing," Clementina remarks in the letter she writes to Sir Charles when he retreats to Florence, "to become your correspondent, as I thought I could write to you with greater freedom, than I could speak. ... My heart shall be open to you, as if ... you could look into every secret recess of it" (1139). Like Heloise before her, Clementina appears ready to move into a new phase of her relationship with her lover, one organized not around the sociability of marriage but around the loneliness (and independence) of disappointed love.[46]

Like Solomon Merceda, Clementina is finally subjected to a narrative arc that limits her ability to challenge Protestant imperatives. When Clementina appears in England, having fled Italy and her family's desire that she marry Count Belvedere, she hopes to say no to Count Belvedere and yes to religious vocation. Her long-standing desire to retire to a convent—"it was with utmost difficulty they [her parents] could restrain her from assuming the veil" (629)—reminds us of the Continental alternative to marriage. Clementina identifies the veil as a manifestation of her heart's desire: "Fain, very fain, would I take the veil. My heart is in it. . . . Indeed, indeed, I cannot be easy, if I am denied the veil" (1145, 1158). But for those around her, Clementina's desire suggests a dangerous tendency to imagine that the heart represents a law unto itself. By setting Clementina's desire against the property interests of her family, Richardson reminds us of the Harlowe disputes that set the stage for Clarissa's tragedy. In this case, however, the convent poses a threat not only of an individual woman's desire to contravene her family's wishes but of the Roman Catholic Church's collective interest in providing an alternative life story to that sustained by the marriage plot. In the face of this threat, Richardson insists that religious vocation can only represent a retreat from *all* social imperatives, a singular pathology at odds with the requirements of civility. Elsewhere, the novel reflects positively on the idea of a Protestant monastery for women in which, Sir Charles remarks, "single women of small or no fortunes might live with all manner of freedom" (867). The security of the British model is guaranteed, however, by the fact that the sanctuary is controlled by family, rather than church, interests.[47]

Sir Charles represents Clementina's desire as a form of narcissism: "Shall I say, there is often cowardice, there is selfishness, and perhaps, in the world's eye, a too strong confession of disappointment, in such seclusions?" (1148). Clementina must learn to measure her emotions on a scale set by him—or rather, by "the world's eye." What emerges is a struggle between Sir Charles and Clementina for the right to author her story.[48] The contest shapes itself around linguistic mastery. In England, Clementina falls from the grandeur of her Continental, multilingual negotiations with Sir Charles into an abject, vulnerable foreigner. Writing of her flight from Italy, her brother exclaims, "To what insults may she be exposed! So little as she knows of the English tongue!"

(1547). Reflecting on her dependence on an English-speaking (male) servant, Clementina notes, "My page he was called in the days of my state, as I may, comparatively, call them; but now [he is] my every-thing" (1554). In a language reminiscent of Clarissa's letters from prison, Clementina writes to Sir Charles from her hiding place in London: "Don't disgrace yourself in acknowledging any acquaintance with a creature who is poor and low; and who *deserves* to be poor and low" (1556). "A woman wants a protector," Clementina remarks when she finally agrees to meet with him—a remark we can hardly imagine her making in Italy (1563). Passive and fearful in London, Clementina devolves from the heroine of a plot of refusal to a more common French literary figure: the powerless, suffering woman, whose vulnerability appears as a feature of her sexed nature.[49] "She is every hour more and more sensible of the danger she has run; and censures herself very freely for the *rash* step, as she calls it herself," writes Sir Charles (1568). Sir Charles, meanwhile, assumes omnipotence by presumably speaking Italian and translating for those who don't.

Sir Charles agrees to serve as her protector on the condition that Clementina "promise to lay aside all thoughts of the veil" (1563). The plot of refusal that she has entertained until this point must suddenly submit to an English narrative of protective paternalism. Authored by Sir Charles, a contract that guarantees Clementina's protection from familial harassment also requires that she relinquish her dreams of the convent not only in the present "but [also] for all future time" (1599). Significantly, the language of property and contract bridges the Italian-English divide. Sir Charles respects the Porrettas' desire to protect the estates that will come to the family only if Clementina marries and urges her to contemplate the social good her wealth can effect: "You have virtues which cannot be exerted in a convent; and you have *means* to display them for the good of hundreds" (1660). From the abstractions of the "heart" and "virtue," we move to charitable donations: look how far Clementina will be able to spread her money as a wealthy and generous property owner. "Are not the conjugal and maternal duties . . . of higher account, than any of those can be, which may be exerted in the sequestred life?" asks Sir Charles (1660), translating a Protestant social vision into a transnational standard of virtue.

Unsurprisingly, contract and property hold little appeal for Clementina. Instead, she obsesses over breaches her parents make of the contract Sir Charles has drawn up, threatening with each perceived encroachment to resume her quest for the veil even as she settles into life at Grandison Hall (1641). Having no faith in the family, Clementina appears content to inhabit the blank page of social narrative. That this blank page might, in fact, have secret desires written on it in invisible ink prompts the narrative to invoke the world's regard once more in its efforts to move Clementina forward into marriage. Responding to news from Italy that people are beginning to reflect on her desire to linger at Grandison Hall, Clementina remarks, "My eyes are now open to the impropriety I have been guilty of in taking refuge in England. . . . The world has begun to *talk*" (1653). The "world" signals here a universal language of reproach that can be countered, as in Harriet's case, only with the positive affirmation of social mores that marriage upholds. "It behoves you to consider," remarks Mrs. Beaumont to Clementina, "that the husband of Lady Grandison ought not to be so much the object of any woman's attention, as to be an obstacle to the address of another man really worthy" (1641). The conjugal imperative requires Clementina to stand alone, not in the cloister, as a religious subject, but in the marriage market, as a sexual object.

In between discussions of Clementina's need to marry, the novel pauses to comment on the plot of refusal with explicit reference to *The Princess of Cleves*. Reflecting on her own prudential marriage, Mrs. Shirley remembers wise Mrs. Eggleton's castigation of that novel's heroine: "That princess, my dear, was a silly woman. Her story is written with dangerous elegance; but the whole foundation of her distresses was an idle one. . . . Let us take our rules, my dear, from plain common sense, and not from poetical refinements" (1626–27). "Plain common sense" defies Clementina's linguistic and emotional excess. Clementina must resume the marriage plot, if only tentatively, to meet the requirements of narrative, which, with the eradication of alternate traditions, take on a global dimension: "Leave her sea-room, leave her land-room, and let her have time to consider; and she will be a Bride," Lady G. opines (1633). Clementina's willingness to be repatriated to Italy, with no hope of entering a convent there, signals the internationalization of the marriage plot, an overwriting of the French novel tradition by the English.

Of the ending of Clementina's story, Richardson could only write, "What is done, is done."[50] The flat footedness of this response reveals how the story moves from a cosmopolitan dance of linguistic and religious difference to an English literalism that maintains male authority over female speech by the fiat of contract and common sense. Clementina's dreams of spiritual independence must give way to a narrative organized around family and property relations. As Richardson anticipated, many readers objected to the idea of Clementina's marriage. Writing to Lady Echlin after the publication of the novel's final volume, Richardson notes, "I have half a dozen of my female Correspondents, who (sweet Romancers, as they are, yet know it not) cannot bear the Thoughts of that Noble Lady's resolving to reward the Count for his persevering Love."[51] In attributing childlike and unconscious motivations to Clementina's champions, Richardson dismisses the desire for an alternate outcome as the romantic imaginings of the immature.

But for the century and a half that followed *Grandison*'s publication, readers challenged Richardson's insistence on the efficacy of the marriage plot and Harriet's preeminence as a literary heroine. Again and again, critics granted the laurels of aesthetic excellence to Clementina and her desires. "As the character of Sir Charles is the most instructive, that of Clementina is the highest effort of genius in this piece," claimed Anna Laetitia Barbauld in 1824. Sir Walter Scott concurred: "The real heroine of the work, and the only one in whose fortunes we take a deep and decided interest, is the unhappy Clementina." William Hazlitt, reflecting on the "peculiarity" of Richardson's mind, observed the author's tendency to value his "his most insipid characters" over his finest: "Thus he preferred the little, selfish, affected, insignificant Miss Byron, to the divine Clementina." In a journal entry of November 18, 1841, John Ruskin wrote: "Read the Clementina part of *Sir Charles Grandison*. I never met with anything which affected me so powerfully."[52] These readings attest, I believe, to Richardson's endeavor to accommodate the authority—both linguistic and religious—that Clementina's story maintains. If, in the final instance, he chose to subordinate her story to Harriet's, it is not without an acknowledgment of the possibilities that lay beyond the conventions of companionate marriage and nationalism.

Clementina della Porretta, like Solomon Merceda, reminds us of the perils and possibilities of interfaith marriage and the casualties arising from the imposition of sexual and religious conformity on the social body. After spending time with Solomon Merceda and Clementina della Porretta—as I have purposely done first—we see what the model of community Richardson establishes must exclude.[53] Most immediately, these characters show us how the imperatives of the marriage plot work against those of an expansive toleration. But they also remind us of Richardson's efforts to imagine a new aesthetics of narrative sociability.

Harriet Byron's Rule of Love

Harriet Byron responds to her accidental introduction to the Grandison family by committing herself to its interests and by falling in love with the man of the house. We discover that Sir Charles compels love in all who meet him, but Harriet proves to be unique in the conviction that arises from her attachment.

That is, while we know that several other young women will be disappointed in their expectations—after all, not everyone can marry this paragon—we don't hear any accounts that would suggest they are inclined to adopt the idealist stance that Harriet assumes: "Since I have seen and known Sir Charles Grandison, I have not only (as before) an *indifference*, but a *dislike*, to all other men" (233). As a young girl, Harriet was identified as "an enthusiast" (191), and she tenaciously defends her right to remain true to her attachment to the active exclusion of anyone who might compete for her affection. She writes to Charlotte, "He was my first Love; and I will never have any other" (1067). The zealotry of Harriet's love marks her as an independent thinker whose belief in the freedom of conscience, here shifted into an affective register, grants her the liberty to pursue truth as she defines it.[54] Zealotry, that is, guarantees the disinterestedness of Harriet's claims, for it sets her affect apart from pragmatic and material concerns. The excessiveness of her pronouncements guarantees the quality of their content, for it manifests a feeling heart.

The language of the "whole heart," to which the novel returns over and over again, shores up our sense that Harriet's intentions are always complete and uncompromised. Early in the narrative, Harriet asserts that she will marry only on the condition that her "whole undivided heart" fix itself on a suitable object (18). Interrogated by Sir Hargrave about her willingness to marry, Harriet replies, "Perhaps I may, if I meet with a man to whom I can give my whole heart" (120). Having met and fallen in love with Sir Charles, she admits, he "has possession of my whole heart" (450). Harriet claims the value of the whole heart as a universal principle of affective relations; the whole heart must meet its identical, and mutually engaged, mate for marriage to meet the standard of integrity she maintains. Harriet takes her affair public, defending her love of Sir Charles as a subject larger than a mere *"hopeless passion"* (232). To Sir Rowland Meredith she writes, "If you knew him, you would love him yourself, and own him for a son. . . . Enquire about him. His character will rise upon you from every mouth. . . . [M]y esteem for this noblest of men is of such a nature, that I cannot give my hand to any other" (923–24). Defending her passion to Lady G., Harriet stresses, again, that her love meets a public standard and therefore merits her commitment: "Love merely *personal* . . . may, I believe, and perhaps *generally* ought to, be subdued. But Love that is founded on a merit that every-body acknowledges—I don't know what to say to the vincibility of *such* a Love" (1237).

The moral integrity of Harriet's attachment allows her to imagine love as an ethical imperative. In her willingness to defend her right to love on her own terms, Harriet anticipates the heroines of later eighteenth-century narratives, including those feminists who populate the Jacobin novels of the 1790s. To the proposal of marriage to the Earl of D., Harriet replies, "I would not, for twelve times my Lord's 12,000*l*. a year, give my hand to him, or to any man, while another had a place in my heart; however unlikely it is, that I may be called by the name of the man I prefer" (330). As a quality of character linked to a moral standard, Harriet's commitment becomes part of who she is, not just in the moment of courtship, but forever. When invited to move forward in the wake of news regarding Sir Charles's Italian connection, she writes, "[My heart] is *already* a wedded heart" (799). Confronted with the possibility of Sir Charles' alliance with Clementina, Harriet resigns the world of marriage rather than break the tie her love has forged: "His I cannot expect to be: I must then of necessity be a single woman as long as I live" (417). In this register, Harriet's love takes on a timeless and abstract quality, even as it generates our desire for the marriage plot that will allow for its realization as a lived practice.

Harriet laments, in the wake of learning Sir Charles's Italian affair, "Now my ambition has overthrown me: Aiming, wishing to be every-thing, I am nothing. If I am asked about him, or his sisters, I shall seek to evade the subject; and yet, what other subject can I talk of? . . . And what indeed but Him and Them, since I have known this family, have I wished to see, and to know?" (688). Harriet's language of ambition adds a new dimension to her affective zeal. The political content of Harriet's passion appears explicitly when she links her affective claims to debates concerning women's place in society:

> [Love] which is founded on interior worth; that blazes out when charity, beneficence, piety, fortitude, are signally exerted by the object beloved; how can such a Love as that be restrained, damped, suppress'd? How can it, without damping every spark of generous goodness, in what my partial grandmamma calls a *fellow-heart*, admiring and longing to promote and share in such a glorious philanthropy?
>
> *Philanthropy!*—Yes, my uncle: Why should women, in compliance with the petulance of narrow-minded men, forbear to use words that some seem to think above them, when no other single word will equally express their sense? It will be said, They need not *write*. Well then, don't let them *read*: And carry it a little further, and they may be forbidden to *speak*. And every lordly man will then be a Grand Signor, and have his mute attendant. (415)

Love that has its roots in a conviction of the love object's public worthiness seeks to unite itself to that object in order to expand the scope of activity for "philanthropy." The union of two ethically committed hearts, that is, obviates the division of labor that designates only men as philanthropic agents. Harriet does not focus merely on the practical side of things (i.e., that two hands are better than one) but elevates her claim to a more abstract level, whereby women's use of the term "philanthropy" marks the necessity of their inclusion in a common effort of bettering the world. Against this vision of sociability she pits the Ottoman master and his "mute attendant," the arbitrary tyrant who imposes silence on his subjects.

Harriet's pronouncements set her at odds with her community's commitment to the regulation of marriage, a subject on which the novel dwells at length.[55] Mrs. Shirley provides a long disquisition against romantic love, using her own case as an example of the success of a marriage founded on esteem rather than desire. The sage Mrs. Eggleton, whose wisdom Mrs. Shirley recounts, warns her young protégée against the worship of false idols: "You look upon Love as a blind irresistable Deity, whose darts fly at random, and admit neither defence nor cure.... The passions are intended for our servants, not our masters, and we have, within us, a power of controuling them, which it is the duty and the business of our lives to exert" (1625–26). Romances are singled out as a particularly dangerous contributor to women's delusional thinking, against which common sense and prudence must battle.[56] But Harriet's ability to unite reason and passion challenges the ethics of prudence, exposing their tendency to mask the moral bankruptcy of women and men who allow themselves to be traded in the marketplaces of capital and pedigree. As Wendy Jones notes of the Shirley/Eggleton paradigm, "Although interest is supposedly subordinated to inclination in the companionate marriage, since one should not marry unless a 'preference' exists, this preference, based as it is on balanced and deliberate judgment, is in danger of overvaluing the material or social advantages of marriage."[57] The novel cannot contain the radical import of Harriet's claims by simply asserting the superiority of her love object—that is, by marking her quest as singular. In this very social novel, she strikes an exemplary note.

The novel effectively reroutes Harriet's idealism, which in many ways echoes Clementina's, by harnessing it to a domestic program.[58] Harriet claims that "love is a narrower of the heart" (413) and asserts, after her marriage, that "Sir Charles and his relations and mine, are the world to me" (1501). The expansiveness of her vision, as it turns out, reaches only the horizon of the family unit, protectively closed off from both a larger English social arena and the culture of Continental Europe. Harriet's discovery of a family "that ha[s] no need to look out of itself for entertainments" leads to a larger conclusion—that there is nothing more to the world than this family (589). We are not surprised when a jealous Harriet writes, "I wish this ugly word *foreign* were blotted out of my vocabulary; out of my memory, rather" (610). The whole heart, it turns out, cannot encompass the whole world but only those individuals who seem familiar.

When Harriet thinks of tolerance and difference, she thinks of mediocre marriages—in particular, marriages of convenience, in which "[partners] deal with tolerable honesty with each other. . . . *Tolerable*, I repeat, since, it seems we are to expect that both parties will turn the best side of the old garment outward" (845). The idea of the tolerable defines an emotional compromise that we know Harriet would not apply to her own case, and it reminds us of her earlier pronouncement: "I am in earnest, that I could never be satisfied with a divided heart" (1014). Harriet is not required to think about tolerance in a larger context, in part because the one question that requires a broader frame of reference—the question of religious difference—is one she actively avoids. As a religious subject, Harriet demonstrates both piety and restraint. Early in the narrative, Harriet tells Sir Hargrave that the subject of immortality is "a very material consideration with me, tho' I am not fond of talking upon it, except on *proper* occasions, and to *proper* persons" (103). At the end of the novel, describing the gatherings of the Catholic and Protestant families at Grandison Hall, Harriet notes approvingly that "nothing of religious subjects is ever mentioned among us, but in those points in which all good Christians agree" (1637). The passion of Harriet's affective conviction never threatens to compromise the quietness of her religious life. Indeed, the one guarantees the other.

The fact that Harriet's philanthropic republic, so boldly claimed for women and men alike early in the narrative, ends up restricting itself to conversations in the cedar parlor proves no accident. Richardson insists, finally, that the sexed body, most profoundly expressed in maternity, necessarily limits women's capacity to exercise their intellect. Sir Charles opines, "Supposing, my Charlotte, that all human souls are, in themselves, equal; yet the very design of the different machines in which they are inclosed, is to super-induce a temporary difference on their original equality; a difference adapted to the different purposes for which they are designed by Providence in the present transitory state" (1467). Not only does Sir Charles's assertion of the significance of bodily difference qualify Harriet's earlier assertions; it effectively alters their parameters. Rather than imagining the union of "whole hearts" as its end point, *Grandison* waits on pregnancy to bind men and women in a more compelling fashion.[59]

This trajectory is rather crudely drawn in the story of Charlotte Grandison's marriage, but its more subtle articulation appears again in the representation of Harriet's.[60] Only when her pregnancy is at risk and Harriet is nursed back to health by her husband does she feel secure in his love: "So amiably has he appeared in this new light . . . that tho' I wanted not proofs before of his affection for me, I cannot account my indisposition an unhappiness; especially as it has gone off without the consequences, of which you were so very apprehensive" (1649). Sir Charles, who tends to view women as children—"He treats us . . . as perverse humoursome babies," Harriet observes (781)—can more perfectly recognize his wife when she carries his child. Unlike *Clarissa*, which characterizes the Harlowes' and Lovelace's obsession with the pregnancy as the sign of misogyny and familial oppression in its closing pages, *Grandison* remains confident that women step into full personhood when they become mothers.[61] Affective zealotry, then, emancipates the mind so that it can better find its way home to the body. As it turns out, only in the afterlife will Harriet's unsexed principle of Philanthropy find its realization: "Women will certainly be on a foot with men, as to intellectuals, in Heaven," Sir Charles concedes (1467).

Harriet's embodied vulnerability, I am suggesting, leads not to a kind of porous subjectivity but rather to one summed up by the vicissitudes of maternity. The containment of Solomon Merceda's body through violence here is naturalized as reproductive labor. I return to Chico's claim regarding the relation of suffering to moral and social improvement. These improvements depend, she argues, on "the negotiation of relations—relations that are predominantly affective in nature."[62] What I have argued so far suggests that certain kinds of affective intensities are valued over others, and that the idea of "improvement" becomes increasingly narrow as the novel progresses. The cost of creating social norms organized around the integrity of some bodies rather than others means that certain kinds of cauterization occur to stop the bleeding of edges, to prevent modes of abjection such as those experienced by Merceda and Clementina, that is, from competing with or even appearing in the same category as the vulnerabilities that attend the narrative of Harriet Byron. Nowhere is this cauterization more apparent than in the characterization of the Good Man himself.

Sir Charles, John Bull

Critics routinely note the strange absence at the core of Sir Charles. "Is he a character?" asks Chico. "He is a kind of black hole," Tassie Gwilliam observes, "sucking up the energy of others, producing no light." Eaves and Kimpel state, "Sir Charles cannot write because there is no Sir Charles." "Richardson created a blank where a character ought to be," Jocelyn Harris notes.[63] In what follows, I define Grandison's character as an exaggerated form of the "buffered self" of modernity. Charles Taylor describes the buffered self this way: "As a bounded self I can see the boundary as a buffer, such that the things beyond don't need to 'get to me,' to use the contemporary expression.... This self can see itself as invulnerable, as master of the meanings of things for it." Disputing any nostalgia that we may have as modern subjects for the "porous self" of premodernity, Taylor notes, "the buffered self can form the ambition of disengaging from whatever is beyond the boundary, and of giving its own autonomous order to its life. The absence of fear can be not just enjoyed but becomes an opportunity for self-control or self-direction."[64] Sir Charles Grandison's interest in boundaries and self-control arise directly from the desire for tolerance—of a particular kind.

Early in the third volume, Mr. Deane remarks, "Seas are nothing to him.... [Sir Charles] considers all nations joined on the same continent; and [Dr. Bartlett] doubted not but if he had a call, he would undertake a journey to Constantinople or Pekin, with as little difficulty as some others would ... to the Land's-end" (525–26). Sir Charles's cosmopolitan life provides an opportunity for the novel to reflect on the habits that support toleration. The ease with which Sir Charles travels back and forth across the Channel is matched by a mental capacity that can entertain two religious sensibilities simultaneously. Clementina's brother notes, "It is hard, very hard ... for a man, convinced of the truth of his religion, to allow to another of a different persuasion, what he expects should be allowed for himself. *You*, Chevalier, however, can allow it: and have greatness of mind to judge favourably of those who cannot" (1109). Sir Charles links his tolerance to the expansiveness of Protestantism, writing to Clementina that "the Church of God, we hold, will be collected from the sincerely pious of all communions" (1144). He repeats this refrain to Father Marescotti: "We Protestants confine not salvation within the pale of our own church" (1057). He describes his Protestantism as a personal preference—"the religion of my choice" (660)—and religious experience, more generally, as a private matter: "I would as soon quarrel with a man for his Face, as for his Religion" (1352). But he also requires that his religious sensibility assume a public dimension, demonstrating its charitable nature through civility: "Good manners will make me shew respect to the religion of the country I happen to be in" (660–61). Following Locke, Grandison hopes that differences of private opinion may be subsumed under a higher law—that of politeness, among nations and neighbors.

In her comparison of *Clarissa*'s and *Grandison*'s very different religious sensibilities, Margaret Doody notes that "in *Grandison*, Christianity . . . is objective law, manifested in the outer world of social life and moral behavior."[65] I believe that Christianity, in fact, serves less as an objective law and more as a performative one, brought to life through the enactment of social scripts. When, for instance, Sir Charles concedes, should she marry him, Clementina's right to bring a Catholic priest to England, it will be on the condition that her confessor prove "a discreet man" (702), obedient to the laws of his family and nation. He is even more concerned that the Catholic servants who would attend Clementina recognize his higher authority, superior to that of their priest and mistress: "I must not be subject to the dominion of servants, the most intolerable of all dominion" (1056). His wife's Catholicism, in other words, will never assume any authority in England. Its religious authority means nothing other than what Sir Charles is willing to grant it. Catholicism's minority status is further ensured by the provision that would require sons—that is, heirs to the Grandison estate—be raised Protestant.

These concessions, for Grandison, reflect common sense, against which he contrasts the zeal of the Porretta family: "Religion and Love, Dr. Bartlett, which heighten our relish for the things of both worlds, What pity is it, that they should ever run the human heart either into enthusiasm, or superstition, and thereby debase the mind they are both so well fitted to exalt!" (728). The problem with Sir Charles's religion, however, is that there is no there, there. Precisely to the extent that he empties religious affect of its content, he diminishes his claims to sincerity. Sir Charles's inability to feel passionately, about love *and* religion, registers as a lack in the novel.

The Italian narrative brings the connection into sharp focus. Confronted with the Porrettas' initial intransigence on the subject of a union between their daughter and a Protestant, Sir Charles writes, "I *laboured*, I *studied*, for a compromise. I must have been unjust to Clementina's merit, and to my own Character, had she not been dear to me" (635). The oddness here appears in the equation Sir Charles draws between the labor involved in reaching a compromise and the mental work required to love Clementina. Indeed, Sir

Charles never appears an active agent in that love story except when he is trying to come up with a contract that might contain the dangerous feelings inspired by religious difference. Discussing his return to Italy later in the narrative, he can only say, "The result cannot be in my own power.... I make not any conditions for myself—My reward will be in the consciousness of having discharged the obligations that I think myself under, as a man of honour" (900, 902). If as a civil authority—executor, landowner, broker—Sir Charles wields power absolutely, in the empire of love he proves curiously incapable of lifting a scepter. Reflecting on his condition, Sir Charles describes himself as "a man *divided* ... not knowing what I *can* do, hardly sometimes what I *ought* to do" (901). "The two noblest-minded women in the world, when I went over to Italy ... held an almost equal interest in my heart," he later writes (1215). A divided heart requires discretion to protect its separate loyalties, and Sir Charles maintains his distance from those around him in order to serve the higher principles of honor and justice: "Had I been my own master; Miss Byron, in the first hour that I saw her ... would have left me no other choice" (1260). Even at this later moment, Sir Charles registers a strange passivity: had he not been acted upon by principle, he would have been acted upon by Harriet's beauty. Until he hurls himself into marriage, Sir Charles lives in a state of limbo, writing, in his final narrative to Jeronymo, about the weeks after his first return from Italy: "I thought it became me, in honour, in gratitude, to hold myself in suspense" (1215). Sir Charles imagines his emotional core as an empty space where competing interests must be regulated and supervised by the magistracy of his reason. We are reminded of the distance he assumed in relation to the drinking libertines earlier in the narrative.

In a world where both Clementina's and Harriet's zeal proves so active and compelling, Sir Charles's restraint raises doubts about the man's emotional fitness. Wherein lies the appeal of a heart laboring under a sense of obligation? And who would want to possess such a heart?[66] Harriet indicts Sir Charles's attachment to prudence when she recasts him as Adam faced with Eve's fall, writing to Charlotte Grandison, "Your brother would have had gallantry enough to his fallen spouse, to have made him extremely regret her lapse; but ... he would have done *his own duty* ... and left it to the Almighty, if such had been his pleasure, to have annihilated his first Eve, and given him a second" (1136–37). Insofar as Sir Charles's habit of mind requires self-division, it compromises the idea of one complete mind meeting another, in the mutual recognitions of affective *or* religious alterity. As in affairs of the heart, so too in religious affairs it appears that only a deep attachment produces a truly ethical subjectivity capable of seeing another person clearly. When Father Marescotti bids farewell to Sir Charles, it is the intensity of his Catholic conviction that guarantees the emotional integrity of the moment: "Begging my excuse, he kneeled down at the door of my antechamber, and offered up, in a very fervent manner, a prayer for my conversion. He could not have given me, any other way, so high an opinion of him" (727). Clementina urges Sir Charles to assume a Catholic identity when contemplating her final refusal, if only to see her for who she truly is: "If you cannot be a Catholic *always*, be a Catholic when you *advise* [me]" (1140). When Grandison debates with Clementina, in the closing pages of the novel, her desire to enter a convent, he takes on a Catholic persona: "I argue not as a Protestant, when I address myself to you. . . . [Y]ou see, madam, I address[] myself to you in the catholic stile" (1660). The moments when Sir Charles undertakes these imaginative identifications fill the emotional void we sense at his core.

Richardson admitted to having engaged in cross-cultural identification when he wrote about his Catholic subjects: "[I was] as zealous a Catholic when I was to personate the Lady, and her Catholic Friends, as a Protestant, when I was the Gentleman."[67] The appeal of ventriloquism, of course, was not new to Richardson, who loved to imagine himself as his characters. But in this novel, heartfelt speech takes on a political aspect. To hear the voice of another is to recognize, at some level, her rights. This mode of recognition gives way to Protestant hegemony, I believe, because the idea of religious difference, staged through reflections on interfaith marriage, necessarily returns us to the issue of sexual equality and of the vulnerable body, writ large in Solomon Merceda's destruction. Harriet understands love as an abstraction to which devoted minds aspire, and Clementina imagines religious sensibility to be above social law. But where Harriet's willingness to submerge her affective ambitions in the production of Grandison children appears a natural part of a woman's maturation, the idea of Clementina's conversion more forcefully registers the abandonment of a higher ideal, from the emancipatory vision of two faiths coexisting to the circumscribed—and profoundly gendered—conditions imposed by the marriage that Grandison imagines, including its privatization of women's religious belief. That Clementina is driven to madness because she cannot entertain love and religious attachment simultaneously reveals, on one level, the novel's anti-Catholic sentiment—in this case manifest in Sir Charles's criticism of the Catholic Church's willingness to pervert the "natural" course of a good woman's life by celebrating religious vocation as an alternative to domesticity—and, on another level, the cost of loving a man like Sir Charles.

Peter Sabor claims that "Sir Charles... passes as citizen of the world, but is at heart John Bull."[68] I suggest that Sir Charles becomes John Bull *at heart* only when he marries an English wife. Having landed safely in a Protestant union, Sir Charles can reassure Harriet that "the union of minds between us [that is, him and Clementina] from difference of Religion, could not have been so perfect, as yours and mine must be" (1363). At this point, the novel makes amends for its hero's emotional compromises and attempts to justify Sir Charles's double love retroactively. Sir Charles revises history to emphasize Harriet's superior claim to his affections, mostly by setting his early love for Harriet against a backdrop of pity for Clementina: "Compassion for the one Lady, because of her calamity, might, at that time, I found, have been made to give way, *could those calamities have been overcome*, to Love for the other" (1260–61). We are encouraged to pair Clementina with Sir Charles's charitable mind and Harriet with his heart, so that it is less the good luck and good timing of Clementina's final refusal than the overarching love between Sir Charles and Harriet that motivates the marriage plot. In the present, Sir Charles compensates for the betrayal of his first love another way, by imagining that she lives in Harriet, to whom he observes, "You are Clementina and Harriet, both in one: One mind certainly informs you both" (1404).

But such a claim can only strike us as a palpable, and slightly grotesque, fiction. In a darker register, we know that if Sir Charles loved Harriet from the moment they met, he was capable of entering into a marriage with Clementina harboring adulterous feelings. And if he didn't love Harriet spontaneously but only upon deliberation, then she is, indeed, a second-class citizen in the country of love. Richardson can sustain the integrity of Sir Charles's character only by falling back on the idea of sexual difference. Lady G. notes that "the man who loves virtue for virtue's sake, loves it where-ever he finds it: Such a man may *distinguish* more virtuous women than one" (865). By this account, men's access to a wider range of individuals and experiences means they might meet more than one angel of virtue in their courtship years and thus find themselves drawn, circumstantially, into the dilemma faced by Sir Charles. Richardson frames the topic more abstractly in a letter to Lady Bradshaigh: "The Apostle says, Woman was made for Man, not Man for Woman. It would be the greatest of Indelicacies for a Woman to be thought to love two Men at the same time equally." He then goes on to joke that a bigamous marriage might resolve the question most successfully.[69]

For all that it ushers in a new era of British sociability, then, the marriage of Harriet Byron and Sir Charles fails to answer all the questions raised by the

Clementina plot. Critics have long recognized its limits. Attending to its place in the narrative, John Allen Stevenson observes that "Richardson again brings his central couple together, but his structural decision to put their wedding, as it were, out of place, has the total effect of transforming marriage from an image of harmony and pleasure into one of frustration and sacrifice." Margaret Doody describes the constraints of life at Grandison Hall for its new mistress: "Harriet will always be a guest in her husband's house, the approved conduit for the heir, the wife who cannot disturb her deceased mother-in-law's furnishings."[70] The post-wedding narration drifts listlessly, exhausted after the rush to marriage that consumes most of volume 6, coming to life again only when runaway Clementina appears in England. Toni Bowers suggests that the "hopeful story of Sir Charles and Harriet's appropriate love enacts the growing comfort with the status quo that Richardson himself seems to have felt by the 1750s," and I agree. But the novel remains alert to the limits of that status quo, particularly when common sense manifests its xenophobic and misogynous tendencies.[71]

I began this chapter by reflecting on the interfaith marriages of Jews and Christians in eighteenth-century England, marriages that appeared, in the British imagination of the mid-eighteenth century, both as an extension of and an antidote to the perceived problem of Jewish libertinism. The character of Solomon Merceda, I argue, brings into focus the anxiety about conversion and racial mixing that is a central feature of British anti-Judaism, which Richardson figures as a form of failed masculinity. For Richardson, the interpretive problems raised by conversion—how can one guarantee its authenticity?—interrupt his desire to render visible a communal standard of sincerity. This desire to abstract religious interiority into a sociable ethics leads Richardson to insist on the companionate marriage as a space where difference maps onto the complementarity of sexed bodies. Clementina's spiritual autonomy, like Solomon Merceda's libertinism, marks her as an unfit social subject for the community Grandison and Harriet labor, in their different ways, to unite.

During the year he was completing the first six volumes of *Grandison*, Richardson reflected on writing his first ventriloquized letter as a child: "I was not Eleven Years old, when I wrote, spontaneously, a Letter to a Widow of near Fifty, who, pretending to a Zeal for Religion, & who was a constant Frequenter of Church Ordinances, was continually fomenting Quarrels & Disturbances, by Backbiting & Scandal, among all her Acquaintance. I collected from [the] Scripture Texts that made against her Assuming the Stile and Address of a Person in Years, I exhorted her; I expostulated with her. But my Handwriting was known."[72] Religious difference expresses itself here not in the lament of a young Catholic woman but in the voice of an evangelical "Widow of near Fifty," whose zeal the young Richardson corrects by mustering all the rhetorical and scriptural authority gleaned in his eleven years. Richardson's fear of women's claims to religious authority appears again in his description of an early marriage proposal: "A pretty ideot was once proposed. . . . A violent Roman Catholic lady was another, of a fine fortune, a zealous professor, whose terms were (all her fortune in her own power—a very apron-string tenure!) Two years probation, and her confessor's report in favour of his being a true proselyte at the end of them."[73] Here, the scandal is deepened by the Roman Catholic lady's attachment to both her fortune and a man other than her intended, namely, her confessor. Clementina's threat contains itself, almost, in the immaturity of her character and in the pathos that Richardson evokes when narrating her story. But in the novel's anxiety about the possibility of servant insubordination and the presence of Catholic priests in England, we glimpse the larger challenge posed by a woman whose faith challenges her spouse's prerogative.

In the final instance, Richardson could not entertain a compelling solution to the inequalities of religious and sexual difference without undermining his commitment to the cultural authority of paternalist governance. I return, here, to Richardson's response to the anti-Semitic backlash against the Jewish Naturalization Act. In a letter to Elizabeth Carter, Richardson suggests that individuals in favor of the act might be better off letting political sleeping dogs lie. Jews ought to go along with the movement to repeal the act, he writes, because it serves no practical end for English-born subjects, only inciting hatred against them in a country "which they honour for the Liberty of Conscience and the Safety of Property given them in it."[74] This logic echoes that of the novel. On the one hand, England stands, abstractly, for the principles of liberty of conscience and safety of property; on the other hand, those principles are protected only when individuals maintain their belief in them privately rather than agitating for their security in the public sphere, where the gendered and racial limits of liberalism's universality are more plainly viewed. What we don't encounter is the means by which the private conviction of equality might find security in the law. In the novel, sexual difference, as framed by the companionate marriage plot, minds the gap. Harriet embodies private conviction, which Grandison secures as landowner and citizen, and together we imagine they will preside over their estate harmoniously and set an example to the larger public. Harriet's private zeal is worthy because she is a woman and proper love is her proper subject; Sir Charles's white cosmopolitanism, unlike that of his Sephardi counterpart, allows his estate, writ large as the nation, to imagine itself a partner among equals in Europe. Charlotte's description of the happy couple's performance of the wedding service sums up the difference neatly: "Sir Charles seemed to have the office *by* heart; Harriet *in* her heart" (1441).

The novel, I believe, attempts more than it achieves; its shadow narrative maintains an alternative ethics and aesthetics of sociability. Richardson translates the Lockean paradigm of toleration into narrative and, in doing so, reveals its limitations as well as its alternatives. Of the possibility of an alternate history, "in which Clementina accepts his proposal, and Sir Charles accepts Catholicism as a religion fit for his modern English family," Geremy Carnes writes, "such a thing cannot, or must not, be imagined."[75] But I'm not so sure. When confronted by his readers about the dangers of entertaining a union between Sir Charles and Clementina, Samuel Richardson took their concerns seriously. "Sir Charles," he wrote, "is sensible of imperfections, . . . and many there are, who look upon his offered compromise of with the Porretta family, in allowing the daughters of the proposed marriage to be brought up by the mother, reserving to himself the education of the sons only, as a blot in the character" (1695). While not conceding the point, he allows the criticism to stand. At the same time, he is at pains to model, in his responses, the very tolerance that his critics decry: "I have, as Editor, further endeavoured to obviate the apprehended Mischief, *by not contending with such of my Readers*, whose laudable Zeal for the true Faith, led them to consider this Compromise as a Blemish in Sir Charles's Character."[76] This willingness to allow for the zealots' feelings leads us back into the novel. Richardson suggests that closer attention to Grandison's feelings reveals an alternative perspective on the question of the compromises he makes with the Porretta family than the one that critics describe: "If his Distress, in different Scenes of the Story, were duly attended to . . . together with his Stedfastness in his Faith, I presume, that he would be thought a Confessor for his Religion, in the whole Affair between him and Clementina."[77] Here we discover that the reader who has the capacity to *feel* the affective arc of the narrative, rather than simply grasping the ideas that it communicates, will arrive at a different conclusion regarding Grandison's religious values. "Distress" and "Stedfastness" are twinned: our hero's ability to withstand the Porretta family's pleas for conversion in the face of his love for Clementina marks him as a true Protestant "confessor," rather than a compromised shirker. But as a confessor, he contemplates marriage to a Catholic despite the pain the idea of the union causes and the struggles it will entail. Pain, in fact, allows tolerance to appear. Toleration emerges not as an abstract principle but rather as an embodied practice, something that engages the reader and the character together in a moment of shared affective experience. It does not require that individuals produce their sincerity credentials, but rather trusts that social networks fostered by narrative exchanges can sustain new configurations of religious tolerance.

CHAPTER 3

Frances Brooke's Civil Disputes

> It is much to be lamented indeed, that on the continent of America, unfortunate civil disputes have raised difficulties in the way of our endeavours.
> —*Brownlow North*, A Sermon Preached Before the Incorporated Society for the Propagation of the Gospels in Foreign Parts *(1778)*

Frances Brooke, like many others, credited Samuel Richardson with establishing the novel's moral credentials. Arguing for its didactic value in 1785, she wrote, "In naming Richardson as an illustrious example of my assertion, I silence the voice of prejudice itself."[1] Others placed Brooke alongside Richardson in their reflections on her novels. In its 1763 review of *Julia Mandeville*, for example, the *Critical Review* observed, "She is as sentimental as Rousseau, and as interesting as Richardson, without the caprice of one, or the tediousness of the other."[2] This chapter examines how Brooke navigates the terrain mapped by *Sir Charles Grandison*, expanding the range of possibilities for women as independent subjects, both religious and literary, in her 1769 novel, *The History of Emily Montague*. Sojourns in French Canada in 1763–64 and again in 1765–67, when her husband served as the chaplain to the garrison of the city of Quebec, opened up the marriage plot, for Brooke, to political questions—most immediately, how to effect the "marriage" of French Canada and Britain through the statecraft of religious toleration.[3]

In *Emily Montague*, I argue, Brooke's representation of the lives of Catholic and, to a much lesser extent, Indigenous women in the colonies shifts her understanding of religious toleration beyond the limits of her conservative Anglicanism toward the more radical view articulated by her contemporary, Baptist Joseph Fownes, in 1772: "There is room to think . . . that [toleration] is considered by many as a matter of mere grace or favour, which government has a right to withhold, grant, abridge, or resume at pleasure. But, if the arguments, which have been advanced, are conclusive, it stands on a totally different foundation. It is the acknowledgement and confirmation of a right."[4]

This language of rights and religious freedom intersects, in *Emily Montague*, with a feminist discourse Brooke had established in earlier work on the question of women's independence. *Emily Montague* thus exposes the limits of Grandisonian paternal governance as a guarantor of marriage and religious community and expands on the vision of sociability Richardson gestures toward.[5] As in Richardson's novel, the interfaith marriage plot both tests the limits of religious and sexual citizenship and intimates an alternative model.[6] In the final instance, Brooke goes only so far in her re-visioning of Richardson's politics. She, too, brings her characters home from their travels to a country estate, where alliances organized around the principle of religious, racial, and sexual likeness root themselves in domesticated landscapes and the conventions of the realist marriage plot.[7] But, like *Grandison*, *Emily Montague* rests uneasily with the closure it effects.[8] In its counterfactual imagining of the union that could have been, Brooke's novel suggests how the politics of feminism and tolerance might align.

In his insightful reading of *Emily Montague*, Stephen Carl Arch describes the novel as an "interregnum" text: "Metaphorically, the concept of an interregnum recurs throughout the novel. . . . We are introduced to the trope of interregnum in the realm of politics, then, but it quickly takes on spatial, temporal, and social dimensions."[9] Most immediately, the term "interregnum" designates the transfer of power between Governors Murray and Carleton that took place in Canada as Brooke was writing her novel. But, as Arch observes, the idea of hiatus circulates much more widely in the novel, signaling an opening of narrative horizons to new worlds, both real and symbolic. It also returns us to the seventeenth-century conflicts with which this study began, signaling rising tension around competing religious and state imperatives that would culminate in the Gordon Riots of 1780 and the Priestley Riots a decade later. In its exploration of interfaith marriage, I argue, Brooke's novel reveals how deeply questions of toleration and empire concern private as well as public interests.

I begin by analyzing Brooke's early representations of single women and the problem of "unequal marriage" in *The Old Maid* and *The History of Lady Julia Mandeville* to situate *Emily Montague* as part of longer career *durée*. The disparity of economic resources between spouses that results in "unequal marriage" poses a particular danger to women's status as marital subjects, Brooke maintains. Brooke's awareness of the importance of financial questions confirms Susan Lanser's thesis that economic agency serves as "the linchpin of liberty" for eighteenth-century women.[10] The marriage plot, Lanser notes, marks the space in which women lose any economic power they might have had, securing their subordination under the sign of love. The plot's attempts to paper over this loss, Lanser observes, "rests on another silence: the axis of colonialism, enslavement, and class exploitation that underwrites European wealth and by extension the prosperity of [the] fictional couple."[11] In the Canada that Brooke describes, Indigenous women threaten to break this silence. This is not to say that the novel gives voice to the Indigenous women but rather that their representation raises a number of questions. For instance, What does the mobility of Indigenous women point toward? What is the significance, for the realist novel, of the mixed marriages between Indigenous women and French Catholic men that it recounts?

Emily Montague leaves unanswered the challenges posed by Indigenous women, and the novel, as a whole, reinforces an emergent racism toward First Nations peoples. But the questions Indigenous women raise in the narrative reemerge in the love story between French Catholic Madame Des Roches and Edward Rivers that the novel more directly addresses. Here, a counterfactual narrative of interfaith marriage appears, one that identifies women's independence with Brooke's claims to literary authority. As in *Grandison*, we see the contours of an alternative narrative of sociability. The novel's attempt to imagine the interfaith marriage of a French Canadian and a Protestant Englishman reveals the fault lines in the logics of conversion and assimilation that govern both the defeat of the French and the colonization of Indigenous lands. Even as it gives voice, in various moments, to an Anglican and white dream of comprehension, *Emily Montague* starkly reveals the inability of that vision to account for the varieties of religious experience and mixed unions in the colonies—and, by extension, in England.

Being Mary Singleton

The weekly publication of *The Old Maid* over the course of several months in late 1755 and early 1756 allowed Brooke to entertain, in the characters she introduced to her readers, a range of ideas and identities, laying the groundwork for her epistolary fictions.[12] The figure of the "old maid" encompasses not only Mary Singleton, the periodical's "editor," but a variety of interlocutors, including "Virginius," who writes, "I am an old Fellow of a College; or in other words, *an Old Maid of the masculine gender*; . . . there being no character generally *the same*, and concerning which the opinions of mankind do so perfectly agree, as that of an *Old Maid*, be the *gender* what it will."[13] For Brooke, the sexless character of the "old maid" represents freedom from the constraints of gender in general and from the burden of marriage carried by women in particular. "Abigail Easy" writes, "I fled from marriage when I was young with more fear than prudence, but again resuming the latter for my companion, and growing daily more in love with that *liberty* and *independency* I had made my choice, I am as chearful and happy a creature as yourself" (*OM* 192). Against the narrow pursuit of marriage and a settlement, the single woman lines up her identity with a larger principle: freedom. Mary Singleton recounts a dream in which she is given the choice of following Marriage or Celibacy. "I was already inclining to enlist under [Celibacy's] banners, when, on waving her hand, a youth approached, lovely as the blush of morning . . . and the rod of manumission in his hand, discovered him to be *Liberty*" (181). Rather than apologize for her failure to adhere to normative standards, *The Old Maid* identifies the single woman with a larger cultural project whose political consequences are aligned, symbolically, with those of emancipation.[14]

Repeatedly, Mary Singleton returns to liberty as a key principle governing both the British nation and the lives of women who choose not to marry. As Betty Schellenberg observes, "Mingled assertions of female citizenship and of English liberty imbue *The Old Maid* from its first number."[15] The two ideas come together as self-sovereignty in the figures of Queens Elizabeth and Anne: "It indulges my pride as a woman to reflect, that the two bright Æras of wit and learning were female reigns; reigns . . . when arts, arms, and liberty were in their highest perfection" (*OM* 17). Art emerges as the third term that links liberty and women to the progress of civilization. Men have excluded themselves from the civilizing project in recent times, Mary Singleton argues, by their attachment to commercial culture: "The other sex are, in general, so devoted to the sordid pursuit of interest that I give them up" (18). The identification of men with mercenary pursuits leaves the cultivation of the arts to women like Mary Singleton. In the absence of queens, each woman becomes what Catherine Gallagher calls the "moi absolu." For Tory feminists, Gallagher argues, this designation enables self-sovereignty, bypassing the liberal model of the subject in favor of an independent absolutism.[16] For the woman artist, this sovereignty appears as female rule in the alternate worlds the imagination sustains.

In *The History of Lady Julia Mandeville*, published several years later in 1763, the idea of female independence is represented by the character of a young widow, Anne Wilmot. Anne's early unhappy marriage allows her to refuse the idea of a second union: "Have not I been married already? And is not once enough in conscience, for any reasonable woman?" (*JM* 68). The language of "conscience" here registers her protest as an ethical stance; no woman is required to give up her right to happiness *twice* to cultural expectations. Of all the characters who populate the novel, Anne exercises the most freedom, both in terms of her actions and, importantly, her writing: "I early in life discovered, by the meer force of genius; that there were two characters only in which one might take a thousand little innocent freedoms, without being censured by a parcel of impertinent old women, those of a Belle Esprit and a Methodist; and, the latter not being in my style, I chose to set up for the former."[17] I will return to the Methodist below. My interest here lies in the connection Brooke makes between rhetorical freedom of the *belle esprit* and the single life. Anne Wilmot spends most of the novel exercising her considerable wit, which she uses to decipher the various plots unfolding around her. The novel draws a clear line between the openness of communication and understanding that Wilmot enjoys and the opacity and subterfuge to which the novel's heroine, Julia Mandeville, is subjected.

The novel's central plot recounts the story of two young people who love, they think, illicitly, and yearn for a romantic union. The fathers of Henry and Julia have contrived to make it appear as though there are obstacles to the union so as to author a love story in the place of the more familiar story of family alliance. The fathers are committed to the idea that young people should choose their own partners. They have planned to let their children fall in love "naturally," and then to remove the obstacles so that the marriage can proceed, driven by love rather than paternal oversight. Henry's father writes to Julia's, "The alliance your Lordship proposes, if it ever takes place, will make me the happiest of mankind: having, however, observed marriages made by parents in the childhood of the parties to be generally disagreeable to the latter. . . . [I] will intreat our design may be kept secret from all the world, and in particular from the young people themselves" (*JM* 104).

Julia and Henry, having imbibed their family's lessons regarding the evils of unequal marriage, can only imagine their love story as doomed—and then take steps, inadvertently, to ensure that it is. Brooke had written against unequal marriage years earlier in *The Old Maid*: "Marriage, where the disproportion of rank and fortune is very great, especially if the disadvantage is on the woman's side, seldom turns out happy. There is so much delicacy required on the obliging side, to lessen the pain of receiving a benefit; and so much circumspection on the part of the obliged, to prevent suspicion of interestedness, that it is next to impossible that their lives, can be passed agreeably" (*OM* 53). In *Julia Mandeville*, Anne Wilmot writes, "I know Lord Belmont's sentiments on this head, and, that with all his generosity, no man breathing has a greater aversion to unequal marriages: the difference is so immense in every thing but birth and merit, that there remains not a shadow of hope for her [Julia]" (*JM* 62). Brooke's discomfort with unequal marriage confirms what Schellenberg calls her "feminist Country ideology,"[18] an ideology that adheres to conservative class politics while recognizing women's vulnerability as objects of trade in the marriage market. Mary Singleton warns women to guard themselves against the idea of economic gain through marriage: "I would advise my female readers, who may be less obliged to fortune than to nature, rather to endeavor the making themselves acceptable to men of worth in their own rank of life, than to lay snares for men of superior condition, who from thence are so apt to suspect them of being governed by views merely mercenary, that they think every art justifiable on their side" (*OM* 52). Brooke questions the cliché that women's power lies in their ability to trade beauty for wealth, arguing that these transactions render women more, rather than less, vulnerable to ill treatment in marriage. "Unequal marriage" ends up encompassing more than just a difference of material wealth, signaling a larger concern that *all* marriage plots contain the seed of exploitation.

Lorraine McMullen claims that *The Old Maid* supports "a happy medium" between love matches and marriages arranged by parents, warning against the risks of the one and the tyranny of the other.[19] But *Julia Mandeville* strikes a darker note. On the one hand, it adheres to the conservative proscription against unequal marriage. But, on the other, it exposes the limits of its corrective—that is, of paternalism. As the narrative unfolds, the arbitrary and coercive nature of the fathers' actions becomes increasingly apparent. Henry's father goes so far as to send his son to Europe so that he might fall in love with a family friend, be disappointed, and come home single. He writes to the woman he hopes will teach him the ways of love without threatening the family's role in choosing its appropriate object: "To you, Madam, I shall make no secret of my wish, that he may come back to England unconnected.... [T]he charms of the Lady cannot fail of attaching a heart which has no prepossession, from which, I conjure you, if possible, to guard him. I should even hear with pleasure you permitted him, to a certain degree, to love you, that he might be steeled to all other charms" (*JM* 110). His son is to be affectively trained without courting the risk of attachment before being released back into the carefully controlled environment of the family. Even as it attempts to balance the competing epistemologies of parental wisdom and youthful sensibility, Brooke's narrative exposes the larger forces at work. The fathers' surveillance evolves into a species of sexual control. Economic inequality appears less threatening, in the final instance, than the inequality of knowledge as it is distributed between adult children and their parents.

One secret begets another, leading to violence and the deaths that close the narrative (Henry dies in a duel provoked by ill-founded jealousy; Julia dies of grief soon after). It is not clear how the tragedy could have been avoided, given the fathers' commitments both to authoring the marriage plot and to rendering their hands invisible in its writing. Brooke makes it clear that everyone's intentions are good, heightening our sense that the problems are structural, not personal. Unsurprisingly, critics were confused and objected to the ending. "We cannot recommend the catastrophe," wrote the *Critical Review*.[20] Anne Wilmot, like Anna Howe before her (to whom she was compared),[21] sounds the conciliatory note by moving (perhaps) toward marriage without the interference of parents in the novel's closing pages. But the uncertainty that attends the novel's conclusion prevents it from achieving either the clarity of *Clarissa*'s tragic individualism or the consolations of *Grandison*'s sociable community. Instead, we are left contemplating the limits of the marriage plot as it is imagined by parents and children alike.

Written during the six years that followed the publication of *Julia Mandeville*, *The History of Emily Montague* sets the questions raised by the earlier novel against a colonial backdrop and by doing so brings the question of religious difference—the problem of being "unequally yoked"—into focus. We see also how the question of religious difference becomes, as it is in *Grandison*, part of a larger conversation about intermarriage, including mixed-race marriage, shaped here by the British conquest of French Quebec and its subsequent attempts to negotiate the cultural practices it found there, including marriages between French fur traders and Indigenous women, themselves active economic agents in the northeast. The mobility of Indigenous women that Brooke's novel documents references the transnational trade network they had built by the time the British took over from the French and speaks directly to Brooke's interest in women's independence, which becomes, in this novel, part of a larger global conversation.[22] In *Emily Montague*, the politics of "home" are set against those of the new colony—but the narrative invites an interrogation of this opposition.

The novel tells the story of a group of young correspondents across the Atlantic, with intermittent political discourses by one of the characters' fathers, William Fermor, writing to the Earl of—from Quebec. Its epistolary form sustains multiple perspectives on events unfolding in the colony and mingles accounts of public and private affairs refracted through the lenses of the various characters' preoccupations, political and personal. The novel styles its English characters as amateur ethnographers observing and reflecting on the habits and customs of French Canadians and the Indigenous peoples they encounter during their sojourn abroad. The ethnographic model brings into sharp focus the insights of Brooke's earlier work concerning women and the marriage plot. As Barbara Benedict observes, "The most cogent critique of sentimentalism and society . . . comes from the persistent comparison between the native Canadian Indians, the Canadian French, and the newly arrived English colonials."[23] The novel opens up the landscape of narrative possibilities in the attention it pays to alternative traditions and the arguments made on their behalf.

The novel begins with the challenge of unequal marriage. Emily Montague's first engagement, to George Clayton, becomes unequal when Clayton receives a large inheritance, one that places him economically in a position of superiority over his fiancée. Emily writes, "I now see faults in him which were concealed by the mediocrity of his situation before, and which do not promise happiness to a heart like mine."[24] Emily echoes Mary Singleton writing against unequal marriage: "Marriage is seldom happy where there is a great disproportion of fortune. The lover, after he loses that endearing character in the husband . . . begins to reflect how many more thousands he might have expected" (*EM* 62). Her ability to extract herself from her engagement appears as a bid for freedom, rather than a loss. Arabella notes, "My Emily is now free as air; a sweet little bird escaped from the gilded cage" (110). Women's liberty depends on their ability to refuse marriage as a pathway to social advancement.

But Emily's struggle with unequal marriage does not end with the termination of her engagement to George Clayton. Her love for the novel's hero, Edward Rivers, immediately runs into money problems. She writes, "It is not in his power to marry without fortune, and mine is a trifle: had I worlds, they should be his; but, I am neither so selfish as to desire, nor so romantic as to expect, that he should descend from the rank of life he has been bred in, and live lost to the world with me" (*EM* 120). Emily's lack of wealth, relative to Edward's status, creates an insurmountable barrier to their union in her mind. And everyone else agrees. Mrs. Melmoth, Emily's guardian, notes, "It is impossible he could have thought of a woman whose fortune is as small as his own" (142). Arabella writes to her friend Lucy, "I am only sorry they are two such poor devils, it is next to impossible they should ever come together" (145). Edward's relative lack of wealth does not mark him as an inappropriate partner, but Emily's does. Emily can marry up, but Edward cannot marry down, economically. The "English privilege" of choosing husbands that Arabella celebrates extends only to women who are able to consolidate the social standing of the men they love.

Emily and Edward could unite, were they to marry in Canada: the space of the colony expands the marital horizon by creating economic opportunities for men.[25] But the choice to stay in Canada or return home reveals that cash is not the only concern. To stay in Canada will compromise Edward's masculinity, Emily believes: "He must return to England, must pursue fortune in that world for which he was formed: shall his Emily retard him in that glorious race? . . . shall she suffer him to hide that shining merit in the uncultivated wilds of Canada?" (*EM* 180). Katherine Binhammer points out that Canada is revealed to be too "barbarian and masculinized" an economic space for the likes of Edward Rivers, a man of refined sensibility.[26] The integrity of Edward's character depends, then, not only on his income but on the relational context that shapes its meaning. The way that Emily frames the conflict—"shall his Emily retard him . . . ?"—reinforces the expectation that women, as wives, should secure the private foundation of men's public merit by subordinating their interests to their husbands'. Emily recognizes that the shrinking of women's interests creates space for the expansion of men's. The colonies strip the veneer of culture away from the economic terms governing this private/public division, demystifying the patriarchal sex right that subtends it.[27]

Indigenous women become the litmus test for Brooke's understanding of women's rights, and Brooke appropriates their stories to frame her main characters' ideas.[28] For Edward Rivers, Indigenous women reveal the lie of liberalism's sexual contract; in stark contrast to British practice, marriage expands, rather than restricts, a wife's political powers. Edward writes with admiration of Indigenous women who "acquire a new empire in marrying; [they] are consulted in all affairs of state, chuse a chief on every vacancy of the throne, are sovereign arbiters of peace and war" (*EM* 9).[29] He makes explicit the contrast between their authority and the political subjugation of European women: "The sex we have so unjustly excluded from power in Europe have a great share in the Huron government" (27). For Edward, the example of Indigenous governance reveals the limits of Anglo-European standards. The discourse of British women's "native" liberty is challenged by the proximity of Indigenous women to a more fundamental natural law. Uncorrupted by discourses of civility, they practice the equality to which England pays only lip service.

Arabella Fermor maintains the counterargument, one that identifies the progress of civilization with its cultivation of feminine sensibility in the private sphere. In her version of the life story of Indigenous women, their lack of choice in marriage partners proves the salient issue: "In the most essential point, they are slaves: the mothers marry their children without ever consulting their inclinations, and they are obliged to submit to this foolish tyranny.... They may talk of the privilege of chusing a chief; but what is that to the dear English privilege of chusing a husband?" (46). Without the right to choose husbands for themselves, the political emancipation Rivers celebrates proves merely a consolation prize that obscures a more fundamental injustice. Arabella dreams of a "commonwealth of woman" whose empire extends only over "hearts" (82). Her views rehearse the Enlightenment commonplace, that women gain authority in their capacity as cultivators of sensibility.[30] For Arabella, the separation of private and public spheres allows women full control over the only event of any significance in their lives, marriage, and she limits the role of female intelligence to the task of pleasing and amusing men, "the employment for which nature intended [women]." She deems Indigenous women "vile" in their contravention of European norms (231).

The opposing views of how women gain authority represent two poles of an argument about marriage. But an alternative account of women's authority appears in the story Arabella tells of Indigenous women's freedom of movement: "Never was any thing so delightful as their lives; they talk of French husbands, but commend me to an Indian one, who lets his wife ramble five hundred miles, without asking where his wife is going" (*EM* 40). This species of liberty is realized in the distance women can put between themselves and the domestic sphere, a freedom symbolized by the vastness of the landscape through which Indigenous people move. This freedom is both inviting and threatening, insofar as it refuses the boundaries of English political and cultural norms. As the narrative looks outward, it encounters an increasing number of subjects who threaten British claims to authority. What follows traces how these claims are undermined by the cultural engagements of the colonies and the mixed unions they make possible.

Siting Toleration

The end of the Seven Years' War in 1763 forced Parliament to devise a plan of governance for its new Catholic subjects in Canada living in territories ceded by the French. The Royal Proclamation Act of that year established the Test

Act and eliminated the tithe in Quebec, effectively destroying French political and Catholic ecclesiastical authority. Its goal was assimilation of the Canadian population into Britain's church/state regime.[31] The flaws in the policy of Anglicization became apparent almost immediately. Over the course of the next ten years, Parliament worked its way toward a radically different program, realized in the Quebec Act of 1774, which restored to the Catholic Church limited authority and granted French subjects freedom of worship. Brooke's novel appeared in the midst of this controversy, and although its political representative, William Fermor, makes the case for Anglican establishment in the colonies, the novel's assessment of the situation from the ground reveals a very different understanding of what toleration might look like.

In the moment that Brooke was writing *Emily Montague*, the most immediate danger to British authority came not from their new French subjects but from the American colonies to the south. This danger informs Brooke's preoccupation with Indigenous women and their border crossings, geographic and cultural. In print and visual media, Indigenous women were often used figuratively to represent the American colonies. In a 1774 print titled *The Oracle*, we see Time casting light on a tableau depicting the triumph of peace over conflict for an audience of British subjects: England and Wales, Ireland, Scotland, and the North American colonies. The American colonies are represented by an Indigenous woman seated on a bale of goods, "another bale behind her, representing the commerce of the colonies."[32] Linda Colley suggests that these representations signify a lack in the American colonial subject: "The main reason why an American Indian was used to symbolize the Thirteen Colonies was, of course, that their white inhabitants had yet to evolve a recognizable and autonomous identity of their own."[33] But it seems equally likely that this practice acknowledges the central role played by Indigenous peoples in transatlantic trade. In *Emily Montague*, William Fermor conflates French Canadians, Indigenous people, and Americans who, he writes, are "naturally inferior to the Europeans." Better and more British governance, he believes, will prove a civilizing force in the American colonies: "An equal mixture of mildness and spirit cannot fail of bringing these mistaken people . . . into a just sense of their duty" (*EM* 207). "Dissent" thus encompasses a much broader identity than designated by its original religious signification and association with American Congregationalism.

Edward Rivers provides an alternative reading of the American colonies in his reflections on the rule of law and women's rights: "I don't think you are obliged in conscience to obey laws you have had no share in making," he writes

John Dixon, *The Oracle* (1774)

to his sister. "Your plea would certainly be at least as good as that of the Americans, about which we every day hear so much" (*EM* 27–28). Rivers' observations refuse the idea of both women's and the colonists' "natural" inferiority to British men and bring liberty of conscience into the foreground. The rights of "conscience" recognize the status of those marginalized by institutions of government. Women and colonists have been subjugated by laws they did not make. This injustice is set against the natural law that, according to Edward, guides the political organization of Indigenous communities. Implicit in Edward's critique is an awareness of how British colonialism requires a subjugation of racial and gendered alterity.

Religious toleration, as a state practice, complicates the opposition between natural law and national duty that William Fermor and Edmund delineate. In light of Dissenter activism in the American colonies, the British could not count on Protestant nationalism to secure political loyalty. Indeed, Protestant radicalism came to pose a greater challenge to monarchical authority than did Catholic interests. As Heather Welland has observed, "For those concerned with American dependence, Dissent was a dangerous breeding ground for sedition.... Undermining supremacy, once the preserve of popery, was now potentially Protestant—Catholicism was no longer a special threat."[34] This made religious toleration, for the Whig regime governing from London, attractive as a means of securing the loyalties of the Canadian colonies against the American insurgents. That is, religious toleration became an extension of monarchical prerogative, rather than a challenge to it. Liberty of conscience is not the goal of toleration, in this instance, but a way of containing its revolutionary potential.

For Brooke, religious toleration represented the starting point for a project of Anglican assimilation in the colonies.[35] As Mary Singleton, Brooke gives thanks for having received an education "under an establishment, where we are taught by the very terms in which our common devotions are offered up to heaven, that all acts of religion are designed to improve us in good affections and habits, all piety to God, to make us more happy in ourselves and with each other" (*OM* 184). In the same essay, she sets the benevolence of "reasonable faith" against the enthusiasm of evangelical Protestantism: "As nothing ... strikes so much at the root of all private and social good, as a superstitious and enthusiastic persuasion of religion, so on the contrary, there is no armour against the frailty of human nature, nor any thing which makes for the perfecting human happiness in all states and circumstances, like the reasonable faith and service of Christianity" (190–92). The language of "superstition" identifies Methodism as a form of Catholic thinking, which undermines the project of human happiness "in all states and circumstances."

In *Julia Mandeville*, Lord Belmont traces a narrative arc for the newly acquired colony:

> Canada, considered merely as the possession of it gives security to our colonies, is of more national consequence to us than all our Sugar-islands on the globe: but if the present inhabitants are encouraged to stay by the mildness of our laws, and that full liberty of conscience which every rational creature has a right; if they are taught by every honest art a love for that constitution which makes them free, and a personal attachment to the best of princes; if they are allured to our religious worship, by seeing it in its genuine beauty, equally remote from their load of trifling ceremonies, and the unornamented forms of the dissenters: ... we shall find it, considered in every light, an acquisition beyond our most sanguine hopes. (*JM* 84–85)

Lord Belmont's advocacy of toleration—"that full liberty of conscience to which every rational creature has a right"—is premised on the idea that it serves as a means to an end, which is membership in the Church of England. Assimilation is the goal, brought about by the cultivation of a taste for Anglican worship, neither so baroque as Catholic traditions, nor so stark as Dissent's. In *Emily Montague*, William Fermor writes from Quebec on the same subject to the Earl of—:

> Till that time, till [French Canadian] prejudices subside, it is equally just, humane, and wise, to leave them the free right of worshiping the Deity in the manner which they have been early taught to believe the best, and to which they are consequently attached.
>
> It would be unjust to deprive them of any of the rights of citizens on account of religion, in America, where every other sect of dissenters are equally capable of employ with those of the established church; nay where, from whatever cause, the church of England is on a footing in many colonies little better than a toleration. (178–79)

The liberty of conscience Lord Belmont promotes as an ethical principle here is blended with realpolitik. In light of the freedoms already enjoyed by American Dissenters, Quebec Catholics cannot be forced into conformity. The goal in Canada, most immediately, is to foster loyalty in the interest of securing the new colony against the dangerous wave cresting farther south. But the larger goal is the establishment of Anglican hegemony, with the American situation serving as a warning, rather than as an example to follow: "Had all prudent means been used to lessen the number of dissenters in our colonies, I cannot avoid believing, from what I observe and hear, that we should have found in them a spirit of rational loyalty, and true freedom, instead of that factious one from which so much is to be apprehended" (179). Had efforts to convert Dissenters to the Church of England been initiated earlier, Fermor maintains, the current political crisis could have been avoided. Fermor can only hope that, in Canada, a desire for prosperity will lessen the number of Catholics over time, as they come to identify English interests with their own: "It is scarce to be doubted . . . that these people, slaves at present to ignorance and superstition, will in time be enlightened by a more liberal education, and gently led by reason to a religion which is not only preferable, as being that of the country to which they are now annexed, but which is so much more calculated to make them happy and prosperous as a people" (178).

The Church of England attempted to naturalize itself both as the custodian of everyday communal and spiritual life in England, and yet it could never, as Mark Canuel has observed, "seem entirely natural enough."[36] Betty Schellenberg notes that Brooke's own Anglican community was less secure than the image projected by the author: "The subculture of traditional country clergy families was a site of instability, where self-interest and principle mingled in competition for livings, under pressure from Catholics, Dissenters, and then Methodists, and accompanied by debate over the function of an Established Church in an era of growing nationalism and colonial expansion."[37] In *Emily Montague*, we see that the Fermors' hopes that French Canadians will gravitate toward the Church of England, whether in the interests of expediency or through the cultivation of a more refined religious sensibility, are not likely to be realized.[38]

The history of conversion was already written by the time Frances Brooke arrived in the Quebec—by the French. The novel uneasily recounts this history. William Fermor notes that "the Jesuit missionaries still continue in the Indian villages in Canada; and I am afraid it is no less true, that they use every art to instill into those people an aversion to the English; at least I have been told this by the Indians themselves, who seem equally surprized and piqued that we do not send missionaries amongst them." Here, engagement with Indigenous communities contributes to the formation of important alliances, and the English are missing out. Behind the "aversion" toward the English that Fermor worries will result from Catholic proselytizing, however, lurks a fear of contact. As Cecily Devereux notes, *Emily Montague* worries that "the effect of the church upon the French in Canada has been in part to bring them into too close contact with native North Americans."[39] For it is evident that the habits of the Indigenous have come to shape the culture of the French Canadians. Fermor reports, "There is a striking resemblance between the manners of the Canadians and the savages; . . . the peasants having acquired the savage indolence in peace, their activity and ferocity in war; . . . their love of a wandering life, and of liberty" (*EM* 232). Native Americans, by contrast, seem impervious to European influence: "Nothing astonishes me so much as to find their manners so little changed by their intercourse with the Europeans," Edward remarks of the Indigenous peoples he meets (31). The Jesuits boast of their conversions, but, Edward suggests, "[I] find they have rather engrafted a few of the most plain and simple truths of Christianity on their ancient superstitions, than exchanged one faith for another" (26). Evidence suggests, then, that the kind of assimilation William Fermor hopes will transpire is unlikely to occur, either among the Indigenous peoples or among the French, who, after decades of contact, bear a close resemblance to the communities they've attempted to convert.

As in *Sir Charles Grandison*, concerns over conversion inform suspicions about mixed marriage.[40] From the lessons of the French, the British can imagine how their own proximity to the "other" might lead to the kinds of mingling documented with such concern in these accounts of Indigenous/European contact. The novel records the commonplace occurrence of marriage between Indigenous women and French fur traders. Ann M. Little notes that "the economy of New France was famously dependent on intermarriage with Native families in the *Pays d'en Haut* for its lucrative successes in the fur trade."[41] J. M. Bumsted observes the family systems that resulted from these marriages: "Both because the vast majority of mothers (rather than fathers) were Indian and because many Indian tribes were matrilineal, most mixed-bloods were raised as natives, not as Europeans."[42] Mixed marriage, then, points toward the possibility of conversion but conversion that moves the spouse away from, rather than toward, the dominant culture. William Fermor must confront the possibility of communities with blended cultural traditions, communities who practice tolerance from the ground up, rather than from the top down.

This history of Indigenous-French engagement informs the stories of adoption and captivity that Brooke recounts in the novel: "Many of the [French] officers," Edward notes, "have been adopted into the savage tribes" (*EM* 233). Early in the novel, we hear the true story of Esther Wheelwright, mother superior of Hotel Dieu, captured as a child and then turned over to the French, who placed her in the Ursuline convent. Arabella writes, "The superior is an English-woman of good family, who was taken prisoner by the savages when a child, and plac'd here by the generosity of a French officer" (11). Brooke leaves out one important detail in translating the story from fact to fiction: that Esther Wheelwright declined the offer of a reunion with her white, Protestant family in the American colonies.[43] Her "good family," as Arabella tells the story, guarantees her "civility." But this mother superior was a product, in fact, of the education she received in the Catholic Wabanaki community where she spent her formative years from age seven to twelve, not of her birth family.[44] As Little observes, Wheelwright's Wabanaki girlhood "was foundational to her chosen vocation as a religious woman in Quebec."[45] She was placed in the Ursuline convent at twelve for reasons that are unclear—including, possibly, the death of her Wabanaki family as a result of the diseases and starvation ravaging that community in the early eighteenth century.[46]

Leonard Tennenhouse and Nancy Armstrong argue that the captivity narrative of Mary Rowlandson, which they read alongside Richardson's *Pamela*, anchors the history of the English novel: "The voice of someone captured by Indians speaks with authority because it . . . testifies to the individual's single-minded desire to go home. . . . The captive's ability to return . . . depends entirely upon qualities of mind that resist illegitimate forms of domination."[47] By this account, the authority gained by marginalized voices such as Rowlandson's is founded on an ability to withstand the sufferings of captivity. In England, this narrative authorizes the nonaristocratic woman to assert herself against the predations of a libertine predator who holds her captive in his home. They write, "We have focused on the captivity narrative as the means of individuating consciousness and of placing such consciousness in a position of mastery over all that it surveys—including an alien landscape, the Indigenous peoples of the Americas, other Englishmen, and even one's own body." Armstrong and Tennenhouse's thesis confirms the novel histories that place *Pamela* at their center. But in their effort to theorize the Anglo-American novel as a "creole" genre,[48] they miss an opportunity to consider how non-British content informs the new cultures of the eighteenth-century novel.

What about, for instance, the captive who is never reintegrated into her Protestant community—who, when offered the chance to return "home," refuses it? Gayle K. Brown notes that "if, on one level, captivity represented a spiritual test, then those who stayed in Canada, converted to Catholicism, intermarried with the French and even entered convents had surely failed that test."[49] A willingness to leave the Protestant standard behind challenges the ideal as one to which individuals "naturally" gravitate when offered the opportunity. The mother superior whose story captures Arabella Fermor's attention reverses the terms of the captivity narrative, suggesting an alternative model of authority to that of the "self-important woman" who comes to stand for "the virtue of the English."[50] Like the European man who marries an Indigenous woman, Esther Wheelwright marries the Catholic Church—that is, she marries out of Protestantism and into its rival. The threats that captivity and conversion represent to Brooke's Anglicanism return us to the fears of Richardson's reader, who, having read *Sir Charles Grandison*, imagined British wives held hostage by Catholic priests in Protestant households.

For Arabella, all of the nuns in French Canada are captives in the same way that their mother superior was as a child: "Could any thing but experience, my dear Lucy, make it be believ'd possible that there should be rational beings, who think they are serving the God of mercy by inflicting on themselves voluntary tortures, and cutting themselves off from that state of society in which he has plac'd them, and for which they were form'd? by renouncing the best affections of the human heart, the tender names of friend, of wife, of mother?" Arabella imagines women as bearers of religious interiority and key agents of Enlightenment progress, writ large in marriage and civil conversation. The interiority that renders women rulers over "the empire of the heart"— champions of marriage and childbearing—is akin to the interiority that defines religious faith, in Arabella's mind. The nuns suffer a species of "slavery," she claims, which in turn transforms their private sphere into a carceral one, "a more irksome imprisonment than the severest laws inflict on the worst criminals" (*EM* 12). Anglicanism, by contrast, represents a form of religious experience that enables women's progress as Enlightenment subjects. She describes Anglicanism as "the peculiar mode of [Christianity] established in England [that] breathes beyond all others the mild spirit of the Gospel, and that Charity which embraces all mankind as brothers" (199). In Arabella's world, religion is a feeling, one she associates with female sensibility: "You must know, I am extremely religious; . . . I think infidelity a vice peculiarly contrary to the native softness of woman" (89). Religious feeling arises not from "principles" but from an "elegance of mind, delicacy of moral taste" that circumvents the need for "all the tedious reasonings of the men." For Arabella, tolerance simply extends that sensibility into a principle of universal benevolence: "All good minds in every religion aim at pleasing the Supreme Being; the means we take differ according to the country where we are born, and the prejudices we imbibe from education; a consideration which ought to inspire us with kindness and indulgence to each other" (89). Good religious taste can build communities, despite its subjective quality, through the practices of conversation and exchange.

But, as we have seen, colonial realities expose the limits of this kind of thinking. In Quebec, the practices of Catholic women reveal the idea of religion as a species of interiority to be a Protestant construct, rather than a psychological truth. Their religious principles are maintained not as an internal quality of mind but rather as a communal standard upheld in the public sphere. Jessica L. Harland-Jacobs notes the efforts of General Murray (whom Brooke eventually sought to depose) to protect "both the female and male orders, including the Jesuits," having observed that the female orders, in particular, "were much esteemed and respected by the people."[51] When Arabella and Lucy Temple compare the conditions of an unhappy marriage and the convent, they reflect that the two male-controlled institutions differ inasmuch that nuns, at least, have their personal independence. "Certainly, my dear, you are so far in the right," Arabella concedes to Lucy, "a nun may be in many respects a less unhappy being than some women who continue in the world; her situation is, I allow, paradise to that of a married woman ... who dislikes her husband" (*EM* 203). The nunnery can function as a refuge from, rather than an extension of, those spaces where women may find themselves subject to male control. When Arabella objects to religious vows as a life sentence, a French woman asks her, "And is not marriage for life?" (204).

Neither in her life nor in her novel could Brooke find a way to secure a foothold for the Anglican Church in Canada. In her novel, at least, she could restore its integrity by repatriating her characters to England, where their marriage plots could allegorize the next generation of church-state harmony. But the young peoples' departure from the colonies leaves unfinished the story of religious and sexual difference that Quebec sets in motion. In particular, it leaves unfinished the counterfactual interfaith marriage plot, one that takes up the challenge posed by the women of Canada and the religious and cultural alterity they represent.

"A Widow Extremely to My Taste": Mme Des Roches's Sexual Aesthetics

The narrative of the European woman left behind in Canada, Madame Des Roches, explores the possibility of interfaith marriage as a species of deep tolerance. Mme Des Roches effectively triangulates the allegorical marriage of Quebec and England to include France, the displaced mother country. Brooke's investment in French culture, and in the literary women who maintain it, creates an alternative standard to that of the English companionate marriage. In *The Spread of Novels*, Mary Helen McMurran draws a portrait of "cross-channel cosmopolitanism" between English and French traditions as "the possibilities for and practices of cultural mixing across the Channel, the ethical tolerance of each other's difference, and at the same time, the kind of Enlightenment humanism and universalism that fortifies their sense of culture as civilization."[52] In *Emily Montague*, Mme Des Roches reroutes this cross-Channel connection through Quebec. By hanging around the marriage plot long enough, Mme Des Roches creates a shadow plot, one that maintains both the self-sovereignty of women and the possibility of an interfaith marriage between Catholic and Protestant cultures.

As a translator of Riccoboni (1760), De Framery (1770), and Millet (1771), Brooke had close ties to the world of French letters. *The Old Maid* upbraids

British women who don't read, noting their inferiority to their counterparts across the channel: "A French woman of distinction would be more ashamed of wanting a taste for the Belles Lettres, than of being ill dressed; and it is owing to the neglect of adorning their minds, that our travelling English ladies are at Paris the objects of unspeakable contempt, and are honored with the appellation of handsome savages" (18–19). Brooke contributes to a larger cultural dynamic identified by Harriet Guest, who analyzes how eighteenth-century British women authors viewed their French peers, concluding that "competition with France . . . seemed to be a spur to the recognition and celebration of learned British women in the mid-century."[53] Guest's and McMurran's analyses of English participation in the Enlightenment's Republic of Letters complicates the story told, most influentially by Linda Colley, about British anti-Catholic sentiment. In response to Colley's *Britons* and its characterization of Francophobia as a defining feature of British identity in the eighteenth century, Robin Eagles identifies the importance of the English elites who "thoroughly identified with the French. . . . [P]ublic entertainment in theatres and in novels owed much to the influence of these people, over and above that of the patriot Protestants."[54] In the case of Frances Brooke, a deep investment in French culture as integral to her English literary identity complements and complicates the religious allegiances she describes in her novels.

Emily Montague's linguistic virtuosity extends beyond Europe to include North America. As McMurran points out, "The letters include a rendering of an Indian song, . . . as well as translated conversations with francophones, Iroquois, and the Huron."[55] Among the various characters who write letters, Arabella Fermor most closely resembles the figure of the woman author: "she is central to Brooke's exploration of the possibilities for literary creativity in the new world."[56] Like Anne Wilmot in *Julia Mandeville*, Arabella styles herself a wit, critical of the vapidity she finds in social milieu of French-Canadian women and attentive to what she can learn and transmit on the subject of Canada: "Are you not all astonishment at my knowledge?" (*EM* 52). Her education in French is evidenced by her bon mots, her literary references and the translations she undertakes, and the freedom with which she moves through French Canadian society. Ann Messenger has analyzed Brooke's decision to name her heroine after the historical figure who served as the occasion for Pope's "Rape of the Lock," concluding that Pope's Belinda serves as a warning, in a novel of sensibility, of the perils of "triviality and narcissism."[57] The Catholic identity of Pope's Belinda, writ large in the cross that "*Jews* might kiss, and Infidels adore," should also be kept in mind.[58] Faye Hammill observes that

"Arabella's adaptable voice is strengthened and liberated in North America, [while] Emily's rather reticent one remains within the conventions of English sentimental fiction."[59] Only Arabella can imagine the life she might have enjoyed in Canada had she and her friends remained there: "We should have been continually endeavoring, following the luxuriancy of female imagination, to render more charming the sweet abodes of love and friendship" (231).

Edward Rivers finds his complementary match in Emily Montague, and together they author an English sentimental story, replicating in many ways the story of Sir Charles and Harriet Byron.[60] The match that would more closely correspond to Rivers's tastes, however, lies outside of his intimate circle, and Brooke's interest in this figure signals a key difference between her agenda and Richardson's. The opening pages of the novel reflect on Edward Rivers's sexual history, which takes as its objects French women and widows: "Such is the amazing force of local prejudice, that I do not recollect having ever made love to an English married woman, or a French unmarried one." "Local prejudice" dictates marriage conventions, including the French custom of unions "made by the parents," which, in the absence of "inclination," allows partners sexual freedom after marriage: "gallantry seems to be a tacit condition" (*EM* 70). Widows prove even more appealing to Edward, since they obviate the need to justify adultery: "That I have amused myself a little in the dowager way, I am very far from denying; . . . Widows were, I thought, fair prey, as being sufficiently experienced to take care of themselves," Edward remarks (69–70). His advocacy for women's rights elsewhere in the narrative here corresponds to an appetite for independent women who like to roam, as he does. He leaves a relationship behind when he departs for Canada. From England Jack Temple reports, "I have seen your last favorite, Lady H—, who assures me . . . that, had you staid seven years in London, she does not think she should have had the least inclination to change: . . . I am told, you had not been gone a week before Jack Willmott had the honor of drying up the fair widow's tears" (68–69). The kind of sexual freedom Richardson identifies in *Grandison* as a degraded masculinity here appears to be the purview of women. The insouciant sexuality of the women Rivers loved does not register as libertine, exactly, but more as an instance of sexual autonomy made possible by very specific cultural circumstances.

Rivers's attraction to widows speaks not only to their sexual liberty, however, but also to their maturity of mind and feeling. He observes, "Women are most charming when they join the attractions of the mind to those of the person, when they feel the passion they inspire" (*EM* 71). Rivers desires women who desire, and whose desire is combined with powers of discernment. These features are epitomized in the figure of Mme De Maintenon (mistress and later wife of Louis XIV), who, Rivers argues, "must be allowed to have known the heart of man, since, after having been above twenty years a widow, she enflamed, even to the degree of bringing him to marry her, that of a great monarch" (174). We are a long way from Richardson's characterization of Madame de Maintenon, in *Clarissa*, as a sexual predator passing as a virtuous woman—the most dangerous instance of self-interest he can imagine. Here the famous widow's powers manifest themselves in a perspicacity borne of self-possession.

It is not surprising to discover, then, that the most significant relationship of Rivers's adult life involved a foreign widow: "I have, once in my life, had an attachment nearly resembling marriage, to a widow of rank, with whom I was acquainted abroad; and with whom I almost secluded myself from the world near a twelvemonth, when she died of a fever, a stroke I was long before I recovered" (*EM* 270). Stephen Arch finds the inclusion of this episode "surprising"—"how can one have a 'true love' twice?"—before going on to identify its place in the bildungsroman of Edward's sexual history: "The widow lures him into a dangerous asocial seclusion from the world and then she dies of her own hot-blooded nature."[61] I see no evidence in Brooke's characterization of the attachment that supports these conclusions. Rather, I'm reminded of Sir Charles Grandison—he, too, loved twice. As we saw in the previous chapter, this kind of self-division complicates the logic of romantic love and replaces it with a more complex understanding of how sexual relations fit into an affective network. Here, Edward measures his emotional maturity in relation to having loved before—unlike his friend Temple, who has only ever formed fleeting attachments as a libertine. No moral impropriety attaches itself to either Rivers or his lover, nor does the attachment stand in opposition to marriage. Rather, it provides credentials for Rivers's readiness as a partner, in contrast to Jack Temple, who, we suspect, will make Lucy Rivers unhappy, sooner rather than later.

Were Rivers the hero of a French novel, the obvious choice of partner for him would be Madame Des Roches. Indeed, she marks the irruption of French literary impulses in Brooke's novel, as Clementina does in *Grandison*. Dermot McCarthy argues that "while the aspect of her identity that derives from her race places her among the conquered and inferior, . . . her sexual identity as woman and widow . . . empowers her with a subversive energy that Brooke barely manages to control."[62] But what if Mme Des Roches's nationality completes, rather than competes with, the story of her sexuality? That is, if we think of her as the bearer of French literary culture, she appears not as the "conquered and inferior" but rather as an alternative plot. When we meet Mme Des Roches, she appears wholly self-sufficient: "She is very amiable; a widow about thirty, with an agreeable person, great vivacity, an excellent understanding, improved by reading, to which the absolute solitude of her situation has obliged her" (*EM* 76). Like the nuns, she lives apart. Her isolation from social intercourse fosters, rather than limits, her intelligence. Throughout the narrative, we witness the widow moving freely in the public sphere, securing property rights, settling tenant farmers on her land, and traveling widely. She never seems far from the action in Quebec.

Edward loves Emily, who herself has attractive French qualities, having been raised in a convent on the Continent: "She has all the smiling graces of France, all the blushing delicacy and native softness of England" (*EM* 47). Mme Des Roches forms a third party as the courtship narrative unfolds. Edward writes, "I am determined to pursue Emily; but, before I make a declaration, will go to see some ungranted lands at the back of Madame Des Roches's estate" (153–54). The news soon circulates that "Colonel Rivers has gone to marry Madame Des Roches" (155), prompting jealousy in Emily. And not without grounds: Edward develops feelings for Mme Des Roches, declaring, "I feel a kind of tenderness for her, to which I cannot give a name" (135). He dreams of settling the lands in Kamaraskas: "I shall not be less pleased with this situation for its being so near Madame Des Roches, in whom Emily will find a friend worthy of her esteem, and an entertaining lively companion" (159). Even as Edward dreams of an inclusive party of three, however, Emily narrows her emotional range in a letter to Mrs. Melmoth: "Without an idea of ever being united to Colonel Rivers, I will never marry any other man" (168). Emily has been trained in the Harriet Byron academy of emotional zeal; exceptional love defines itself by its exclusivity.

"Always Madame Des Roches!" Emily complains of Edward's correspondence (*EM* 167). Arabella queries her jealousy: "If he loves you, of what consequence is it to whom he writes?" (215). But for Emily, the integrity of her love depends on its singularity, a quality that allows her to question Mme Des Roches's emotional fitness: "She has perhaps loved before, and her heart has lost something of its native trembling sensitivity" (219). Mme Des Roches has a history, as does Edward; both are capable of more than one attachment. Even after he decides to keep his distance from the widow—"I am convinced my wish of bringing about a friendship between Emily and Madame Des

Roches... was an imprudent one"—Edward's relation to Madame Des Roches remains complicated (201). He understands that his feelings form part of a larger web of social relations, that they are not stand-alone markers of an isolated heart: "I felt a criminal in the presence of this amiable woman; for both our sakes, I must see her seldom; yet what an appearance will my neglect have, after the attention she has shewed me, and the friendship she has expressed for me to all the world?" The "criminality" is not registered as an illicit passion but rather as a failed obligation (193). His affective range is notably larger than Emily's.

Nor does Edward feel obliged to renounce the warm feelings he continues to have for the widow, although he worries about how they might be read by others: "Gratitude and... compassion give me a softness in my behavior to the latter [Mme Des Roches], which a superficial observer would take for love, and which her own tenderness may cause even her to misconstrue" (*EM* 201). And, indeed, Emily is desirable in part because she resembles her French counterpart. Earlier in the narrative, having heard that she has ended her engagement to Clayton, Edward remarks that "her situation has some resemblance to widowhood" (111). Emily herself declares, "If I was not Emily Montague, I would be Madame Des Roches" (213). Arabella dreams of carrying the widow back to England: "It is a pity such a woman should be hid all her life in the woods of Canada" (304). Like Clementina before her, Mme Des Roches remains close to the marriage plot, even after she has been left behind. We are told that she remains a captive of her love for Edward: "[She] has just refused one of the best matches in the country, and vows she will live and die a batchelor" (405). The single woman's heart, like Clementina's, belongs to a man claimed by another. In this instance, however, we witness a woman who continues to exercise her independence despite her disappointment, rather than retreat into abjection.

Mother(land) Love

Madame Des Roches may be one reason Emily is content to leave Canada, but it is the affective power of another widow who makes the return imperative— Edward's mother. She, too, is both single and attached. But Mrs. Rivers's attachment is maternal rather than romantic. Lucy writes to her brother, after his departure for Canada, "I cannot bear to see my mother so unhappy as your absence makes her" (*EM* 113). Less sympathetically, Arabella remarks, "I wish Mrs. Rivers had born his absence better; her impatience to see him has broken in on all our schemes; Emily and I had in fancy formed a little Eden on Lake Champlain" (224). This dream is death for the mother. Lucy writes, "I am convinced the very idea of a marriage which must forever separate her from a son she loves to idolatry, would be fatal to her" (255). Emily proves her emotional worthiness by initiating the return of the younger generation: "Tell [Edward], I will not marry him in Canada; that his stay makes the best mother in the world wretched; that he owes his return to himself, nay to his Emily, whose whole heart is set on seeing him in a situation worthy of him" (181). She sees a kindred spirit reflected in the "whole heart" of Mrs. Rivers. Where, in Emily, it stands for her sexual attachment to Edward, in the mother it stands as the sign of the phallic mother, a sign that also upholds the imperial project. On the subject of the American colonies, William Fermor writes, "A good mother will consult the interest and happiness of her children, but will never suffer her authority to be disputed" (207). And yet, her authority *is* disputed—and, further, Brooke's novel recognizes the claims of those who dispute it. How does the final volume of *Emily Montague* weigh the competing interests of parents and children? And how does that competition return us to the question of religious toleration and empire?

This English widow, I contend, suffocates plot—in contrast to Mme Des Roches, who energizes it. Stephen Arch attributes the novel's failure to the marriage plot, whose obsession with likeness, he argues, edges the novel "insidiously toward the 'resemblance' of incest at numerous points."[63] Ellen Pollak has shown us how incestuous desire shores up attachments in the eighteenth-century novel, but it also has the ability to mar the novel of sensibility, turning its romance into a maudlin fabula.[64] Emily recounts her first visit with Mrs. Rivers: "She kissed me, she pressed me to her bosom; ... she called me her daughter, her other Lucy" (*EM* 249). Joseph F. Bartolomeo points out that "Emily and Rivers turn out to be related distantly enough to rule out literal incest, but this revelation only reinforces the extent to which their circle remains closed to outsiders."[65] Everyone's desire to be together conflates the characters' closeness and the confining interiors they inhabit, spaces that are too small. In contrast to the excitements and space of Quebec, tedium and claustrophobia are barely held at bay in England. The possibility that cosmopolitan difference could open up the novel's vista fades from view in the narrow confines of "sweet little retreat" to which the family retires (347).

In England, the companionate marriage takes on a recognizable form, far from the vicissitudes of the colonies. Emily Montague's evolution as a wife is marked by her ability to cultivate properly bounded landscapes. Edward writes, "Emily is planning a thousand embellishments for the garden, and will next year make it a wilderness of sweets" (*EM* 342). Both Emily and Edward can distance themselves from the violence of accumulation and dispossession that marks settlement in Quebec. In Emily's case, the garden appears a category of taste, rendering her claim to it less an assertion of property rights than an extension of her sensibility. But the problem introduced in Canada—Emily's relative poverty and the threat it poses to her husband's status—lingers. The difference named "Quebec" returns in the closing pages of the novel as "India," the colonial agent who arrives to solve the problem of the "unequal" marriage between Emily and Edward.

Emily initially describes this family friend as a love object: "There was a gentleman who came with Rivers, who was particularly attentive to me; he is not young, but extremely amiable; . . . I never in my life met with a man for whom I felt such a partiality at first sight, except Rivers, who tells me, I have made a conquest with his friend" (*EM* 340). The "friend," in turn, admires "the easy turn" of Emily's shape; "[he] gazed on her with rapture" (339). As it happens, the gentleman is Emily's father, home from India to find his long-lost daughter and bestow his fortune upon her and the son of his benefactor who turns out to be, conveniently, Edward Rivers. The incest plot, in this instance, serves the double function of securing attachments and financial interests. It also returns us to the question of religious toleration.

In *Emily Montague*, India represents the return of the repressed. Katherine Binhammer explores how the opposition between India and Quebec shapes the novel's representation of imperial economics: "The difference between the imperial riches of the East Indies and Canada is the difference between an old and a new country."[66] I'd like to draw attention to what is linked, rather than separated, by the two spaces in the eighteenth-century imagination, a connection forged by Parliament's attempts to regulate the activities of British merchants. Throughout the 1760s and 1770s, merchants waged a propaganda war against the government, calling out the heavy hand of the British colonial administration in both Quebec and India.[67] Heather Welland documents the fear that "the government was engaged in a systematic plan to extend its patronage and unconstitutional influence through the empire."[68] The question of empire becomes, Who will control its exploitation? In India, merchants objected to government attempts to rescind stock dividends. The author of *A Letter to the Minister on the Subject of the East-India Dividend* (1767) complains, "A free born Englishman will never submit to be controlled in the disposal of his own property, and any attempt to restrain him, by an authority which he does not acknowledge, will be treated with contempt and disdain."[69] In Quebec, the same merchant constituency argued for their property rights and against religious toleration for Catholics, a toleration that, to their mind, demonstrated the government's willingness to bend British law. British liberty, in this instance, was associated with the rule of law—in particular, with the Test Act, which prevented Catholics from participating in public worship or holding government office. In 1782, reflecting on the policies carried out in Quebec over the preceding two decades, government critic and parliamentary journalist John Almon observed that the "acts of provocation passed against the Protestant colonies in America, I shall forbear to mention distinctly, because the word War, which was the *ultimatum*, includes them all."[70] British governance was experienced by the merchants as a form of aggression, its invasive hand manipulating religious cultures and economic markets alike.

Emily's economic independence is secured by a tradesman's ability to withstand the British government's efforts to limit his accumulation of wealth in India. That is, a father's freedom abroad secures her autonomy at home. To establish her heroine's independence as a spouse, Brooke relies on an imperial deus ex machina.[71] Further, the novel's earlier account of Quebec makes the India solution of its closing pages feel not only contrived but out of character. The freedom of India represents the freedom of white men to compete with one another for resources. The story of Quebec, as Brooke tells it, challenges the logic of accumulation and the cultural, sexual, and religious dispossessions it sustains. The mixed marriages realized—between Indigenous women and French Canadian men—and hypothesized—between a French Canadian woman and an English Protestant man—allegorize this alternative to imperial prerogative by refashioning the marriage plot.

Frances Brooke's divided loyalties return us to *Sir Charles Grandison* and the model of paternal governance that Richardson hoped would secure religious sociability. Richardson, I suggested in chapter 2, gives voice to those who challenge the authority of his Good Man but cannot allow the alternative ideas and identities they represent to take a seat at the table of governance. There is room for only one at the head of that table. Brooke, I've argued, *can* represent a mature Clementina but cannot imagine bringing her home to the mother country. Nor can she imagine an Indigenous Clementina, a subject whose freedoms of movement and political authority Brooke both admires and pathologizes. In the final instance, her commitment to securing property for British women restrains the novel's inclusive tendencies, which reach toward both Canada and France in its efforts to encompass a broader range of subject positions for its English characters. As Felicity Nussbaum has demonstrated, the alignment of British women authors with a triumphalist Protestant imperialism would become increasingly important as the empire expanded over the latter part of the eighteenth and beginning of the nineteenth century.[72] In 1775, we find Catherine Macaulay writing against the passage of the Quebec Act as an abridgement of British law: "They have told you that Quebec, being on the other side of the Atlantic, it is of little consequence to you what religion is established there, . . . [but] the establishment of Popery, which is a different thing from the toleration of it, is . . . altogether incompatible with the fundamental principles of our constitution."[73] Even as she asserts her own claims to independent thought, Macaulay silences those of a religious minority with whom Protestants had lived, in her own country, for two hundred years.

Emily Montague expands the sphere of influence for the single woman, arguing for her independence from the English conjugal imperative. I began with Mary Singleton and concluded with Mme Des Roches, figures of female self-sovereignty. A marriage between Edward Rivers and Mme Des Roches, his Kamaraskas "neighbor," would realize an English domestic arrangement outside of the boundaries set by the companionate marriage. The possibility of their union, I argue, allows other stories to come into focus, including a revised captivity narrative. Tolerance happens, in this instance, when alternative plots collide and, in doing so, denaturalize Protestant accounts of religious and sexual difference. In the chapter that follows, we see how a Catholic woman author brings these alternative plots into the English home.

CHAPTER 4

Elizabeth Inchbald among the Cisalpines

> A Roman Catholic writer, attached to his religion, but unshackled in his thoughts, and free in his expressions, is, in this country, rather a new character in the republic of letters.
> —*Joseph Berington,* The History of the Lives of Abeillard and Heloisa *(1793)*

The previous two chapters explored how Samuel Richardson and Frances Brooke shaped the novel of sensibility around Protestant understandings of religious toleration and the sexual politics of interfaith marriage. It is time to consider how the narrative dynamics set in motion by *Sir Charles Grandison* take shape in the hands of a Catholic author. This chapter considers the case of Elizabeth Inchbald, an author whose affiliations with Jacobin writers of the 1790s, most notably William Godwin, have rendered her Catholicism all but invisible as a subject of critical investigation.[1] What do we see when we view Inchbald's work through the lens of her Catholic identity? What does Catholic toleration look like in England? Bringing the Catholic Enlightenment to bear on our reading of the 1790s, I argue, adds another dimension to Laura Mandell's reading of Romantic women writers who, she claims, "queer" Romanticism, "rendering it communal" in their refusal of the heterosexual "*domos.*"[2] Mandell does not include Inchbald in her consideration, for good reason. Inchbald's communal imperatives emerge from a religious context very different from that of her Protestant peers.

The narrative of *A Simple Story*'s first two volumes follows the arc of a Protestant-Catholic courtship that leads to marriage; the third volume begins with an account of its spectacular failure. Inchbald attributes this failure, I maintain, not to the impossibility of interfaith marriage but to the understandings of religious identity that each partner brings to the affair. Out of the ashes of this marriage emerges the possibility of a more successful union. The second half of *A Simple Story*, I argue, shows how a more capacious affective network supports interfaith marriage in the younger generation. In particular, the mixed *household* becomes a space of tolerant attachments. As in Richardson's and Brooke's novels, *A Simple Story*'s interfaith marriage plot complicates the imperatives of the realist novel. The logic of marriage that concludes the novel, I argue, moves in the opposite direction to that of the narrative's first half, away from idea of desire as a species of individual *Bildung* and toward what I call "queer" love, the foundation of an alternative narrative ethics of sociability.

By placing Inchbald's Catholicism at the center of my reading, I hope to revise feminist accounts of *A Simple Story*, which have tended to rehearse the secularization thesis, pitting female agency and desire against the restrictions of church discipline, emancipation with freedom from belief. Barbara Judson, for instance, reads Miss Milner as a Romantic Satan and describes the novel's ambivalence toward obedience as "a fitting requiem for Christianity."[3] I hope to shift attention away from the rebellious Miss Milner as the locus of subversion to a larger social constellation, one that counters the imperatives of both individualism and dogma. My focus on the intersection of religious and sexual difference allows alternative affects to come into view: instead of desire, for instance, gratitude. Inchbald's commitment to the mixed-faith household, I conclude, fosters a feminist epistemology organized around a communal imperative that sustains both religious minorities and women.

"Old English Hospitality": Cisalpine Toleration

I begin with an account of religious toleration as it was defined by the English Catholics known as the Cisalpines, a group of reform-minded gentry and priests who worked together in the 1780s to advance the cause that culminated in the second Catholic Relief Act of 1791. The Cisalpine revolt against the Vatican provided a way of thinking about a more democratic Catholicism, one that could foster feminist, as well as national, interests. Further, in advancing the egalitarian principles of the Catholic hospitality, the Cisalpines provided alternative regulatory principles to those sustained by the Protestant model of family religion, organized around a husband's conjugal prerogative and the family's separation from the public sphere.[4]

"I am a rational Catholic," wrote Joseph Berington in 1785.[5] Berington published works throughout the 1780s that aimed to dispel stereotypes of papist treachery and priestly persecution while advancing the cause of religious emancipation as part of a larger Enlightenment project of reform in England. Even as they forged alliances with reform-minded Protestants, the Cisalpines always swam against a strong tide of anti-Catholic sentiment. Dissenters became more interested in working with progressive Catholics as the decade progressed, but they were not above betraying their new friends from time to time.[6] Samuel Heywood, in 1787, reminded his readers of the continued loyalty of Dissenters since the Revolution of 1688, noting, "Protestant Dissenters should never forget, that they are the descendants of those, who by resisting unto blood, preserved that constitution, to which the nation owes its present share of freedom, and happiness.... Liberty of conscience in religion, without restraint, is our birth-right."[7] Catholics, it went without saying, had to answer for 1715 and the '45.[8] In response, progressive Catholics worked two fronts, arguing that the liberty of conscience was *their* birthright also, while separating themselves from the sins of their fathers. In *The State and Behaviour of English Catholics*, Berington argues, "*Liberty of thought* is essential to human nature.... I chuse my own religion. It is the affair of my own conscience; it is a concern betwixt myself and God; and it belongs to no other to arraign my conduct or to censure my determination.... What has state policy to do with the concern of a man's conscience?"[9] The distinctively Lockean language used by Berington and others allowed Cisalpines to identify with a domestic brand of toleration discourse, part of a larger effort to distance English Catholicism from Rome.

On the subject of Rome, Berington notes, "It has been said—That I generally use the word Catholic without the restrictive term Roman; and that I studiously avoid the words *Papist* and *Popery*.—It is true, I have intentionally done so.... [T]he word Roman has been given to us to intimate some *undue* attachment to the See of Rome."[10] Fellow Catholic reformer Alexander Geddes argued the same point from another angle. If, in the past, both the Stuarts and the pope had manipulated domestic affairs from afar, the English no longer had to fear this particular strand of Catholicism, he claimed. Not only were English Catholics immune to its appeal; Europeans no longer endorsed political interference of any kind. The Catholic discourses that made his English compatriots nervous earlier in the century now belonged to a distant past: "The odious doctrine of deposing power, transferring crowns, and dispensing with oaths, has long since been exploded in every catholic university."[11]

By distancing themselves from *Roman* Catholicism, both past and present, and adopting the universalist language of the Enlightenment, Cisalpines could align themselves with a broader reformist agenda underway in the 1780s. The emancipation declaration of 1789, worked out between William Pitt's ministry and the Catholic Committee in anticipation of the new relief act that passed in 1791, declared all English Catholics to be "PROTESTING CATHOLIC DISSENTER[S]."[12] But once they deployed this language, heavily inflected with Protestantism, the Cisalpines were left having to argue, in public, for the qualities of Catholicism that put conversion out of the question.[13] Cisalpines were not lukewarm or wobbly Catholics, I want to stress, and they address this challenge directly in their writings. Over and over again, they highlight the significance of their communal practices, setting them against the individualism of Protestantism. These communal practices, they claim, laid the groundwork for their expansive view of religious toleration and for their ability to manifest its principles in their everyday lives.

The anchor for Catholic theories and practices of communal living was the family household. Berington, in his preface to *State and Behaviour*, asserts that "*Catholic* is an old family name, which we have never forfeited," identifying English Catholicism as a communal identity stretching back into England's past. His use of "family" is metaphorical but also identifies the loyalty of those particular English families who had suffered persecution since Henry VIII. They never forfeited the family name, "Catholic," placing communal integrity above self-interest.[14] The commitment to community, in turn, served as an ethics of sociability that extended to Protestants. In recounting the practices of peaceful coexistence among English Catholics and their Protestant neighbors, Alexander Geddes focuses his attention on the household: "Were they [English Catholics] known, they would be respected by the people, as they are by their neighbourhoods in the country, who see with their own eyes, and find from experience, that they are sadly injured. . . . Old English hospitality is yet to be found in their families, joined to an almost enthusiastic love for their country and constitution; which no foreign education, nor penalties, nor premunires have been able to alter or abate."[15] If all English Protestants were to spend time with Catholics, they would empathize, as their local friends already have, with the suffering caused by penal laws. They would also discover Catholics' commitment to opening their homes, creating an alternate public sphere by linking one household to the next. The nation, by this account, becomes a network of interdependent households. Each has many rooms and enough space for Catholics and Protestants to live together peaceably. There are no secret closets or hiding spaces for spies.

Mark Goldie has noted that the Cisalpines were as "anti-episcopal or anti-clerical as they were anti-papal, and inclined to a Catholic presbyterianism or even congregationalism."[16] This congregationalism had its seat in the Catholic household of which the lay gentry, not their chaplain clergy, were the head.

The practice of communal decision making allowed the Cisalpines to endorse the authority of rules, rather than of individual conscience, without invoking papal infallibility. The Cisalpines returned repeatedly to the importance of an authority outside the self as a way of emphasizing the dangers of Protestant subjectivism. Berington remarks, "The *instability of belief* is another strong objection to the Protestant communion; yet this again is an immediate consequence from its first principles. If I may form my faith as I will, surely I may change it as I please."[17] Arthur O'Leary makes the same observation from an anthropological standpoint: "Let the right of private judgment be painted as the offspring of Heaven; on earth, individuals must assimilate its features to the judgment of the societies to which they belong."[18] Humans make meaning in their engagements with one another, not in isolation, O'Leary argues.

O'Leary uses this interdependence to argue for the integrity of Catholic ecclesiastical authority: "If he [the Catholic] submits to authority, he is not in a worse condition than any other Christian, who submits to the authority of that collective body of which he is a member." There is no meaningful religious identity outside of the community that fosters it, and no religious discourse that can maintain itself without regulation. Berington asks, "Will you allow that religion is a matter of some concern; and that unity in belief would be preferable to variation?—He is no Christian who denies the first; but if you grant the Second, you overthrow the Reformation.—We must have a guide."[19] The Reformation was doomed to failure because it imagined that belief could retain its integrity with only the solitary heart to guide it. An external principle must be in place to maintain collective identity of a faith; without one, there is no possibility of building a larger structure capable of housing two faiths, or more. Individualism, the Cisalpines argue, must always end in selfishness and intolerance.

The fear of a house divided was a mainstay of Protestant discourses, as we saw in chapter 1. The uniformity of religion in the Protestant household serves as a counterweight to religious pluralism in the public sphere. For the Cisalpines, however, religious identity looks outward, rather than inward, moving from the household into the larger community. Uniformity of belief among Catholics provides a social fabric that binds households together, but not so tightly as to preclude the engagement of other faiths. Hospitality becomes the means by which others may be included in the household, which expands, rather than contracts, its boundaries in the face of religious alterity.

Cisalpine controversy filled the years when Elizabeth Inchbald was drafting *A Simple Story*.[20] Michael Tomko has documented Inchbald's connection to various members of the Cisalpine movement, as well as her religious turn after the death of her husband in 1779: "After the spring of 1780, her attachment to her Catholic identity seems to have become more prominent. She made two extended visits to her hometown near Bury St. Edmunds in Suffolk, where she regularly attended Mass, said prayers, and read religious material. From June 1780, she was in touch with her closest Catholic contacts."[21] Inchbald never remarried. She lived alone, moving frequently in London until 1819, when she settled in a Catholic community for women, Kensington House, where she died two years later.[22] Inchbald's freedom as a single woman allowed her to circulate among the households of various families and friends. One of those friends was John Kemble, a fellow actor and, perhaps, love interest, who some have speculated shaped the character of Dorriforth in *A Simple Story*. John Kemble and his sister Sarah Siddons were raised in an interfaith household. Their parents, Roger Kemble, Catholic, and Sarah Ward, Protestant, agreed to raise their five children in both faiths, the sons raised in their father's, the daughters in their mother's. Such a marriage would not have been unfamiliar to Inchbald. As Francis Young observes, "Mixed marriage was not a novelty in Bury's community."[23]

Before turning to the story of interfaith marriage recounted by *A Simple Story*, I want to examine, briefly, how Cisalpine ideas about religious toleration intersect with the sexual politics in Inchbald's 1787 play, *Such Things Are*, staged while Inchbald was working on the novel.[24] The opening of the play introduces us to a sultan who (before the action of the play) converted to Christianity when he married Arabella, "a lovely European."[25] He has forgotten his Christian duty since becoming a sultan and now rules Sumatra with an iron fist, selling his political opponents into slavery or consigning them to years of imprisonment.[26] Having lost his wife in the chaos of the rebellion that made him ruler, the Sultan's self-pity closes his heart to the suffering of others. The violence of his emotions leads him to rule with "unsparing justice" (35). Haswell, the English protagonist of the play, notes how the Sultan's selfish cruelty has robbed him of the object he has been seeking for so long: "Your wife you will behold—whom you have kept in want, in wretchedness, in a damp dungeon, for these fourteen years, because you would not listen to the voice of pity.— ... [W]hile your selfish fancy was searching, with wild anxiety, for her *you* loved, unpitying, you forgot others might love like you" (66). Loving immoderately leads to persecution because "selfish fancy" dictates both heart and mind—the same "selfish fancy" that led the Sultan to pursue the rule of his nation under false pretenses in the first place.

Haswell's integrity has its roots in religious principle. He directs the Sultan to "the Christian Doctrine" to explain his own benevolence: "There you will find all I have done was but my duty," he notes (34). The difference between the two men is that one directs his Christianity outward, the other inward. The reformist translates Christianity into the practice of justice. The outcome of Haswell's intervention on behalf of the prisoners, in the play, is both political and domestic security. Arabella is restored to her husband, her only criterion for "liberty" from bondage. The hardness of the political rebel Elvirus is sufficiently softened by Haswell's spirit of forgiveness to enable marriage with his lover. In each case, Haswell's performance of his "duty" puts the welfare of the collective, rather than the individual, first. The collective imperative provides stability in both domestic and political arenas.

Such Things Are links the habits of mind that foster bigotry to violations of marriage. Individualism—as an expression of obsessive love—is set against a communal standard of care and obligation. This communal standard has particular significance for women, insofar as it represents a species of obligation that exists outside the purview of the law. In her reading of Inchbald's comedies, Misty Anderson notes that "suspicious of contract, Inchbald instead reaches toward a model of community and relationship . . . that can keep women safe when the law denies them a place as agents and subjects."[27] As the Cisalpines argued in their political commentary on toleration, community is achieved when the individual's capacity for empathy is mapped onto a program of religious sociability that binds itself to an authority greater than that of the individual heart. In Inchbald's work, that sociability appears only when women and religious minorities are fully seen by the communities to which they belong. As we shall see, prose narrative provided Inchbald with the space to develop her vision of religious sociability more fully in relation to the imperatives of the marriage plot, which was fast becoming the sign of the novel.

The Politics of Vows

In a 1994 essay, Ian Balfour observes that *A Simple Story* "revolves around a series of promises, vows, and oaths made and broken."[28] Inchbald's preoccupation with failed promises, he argues, reflects a Jacobin suspicion of social contracts and serves as a precursor to William Godwin's work later in the 1790s. The narrative's rehearsal of one broken vow after another teaches us "not to promise in the present" when we can't know what the future holds.[29] The only answer is to refuse vows altogether and to anchor claims "in nothing less than the truth."[30] Balfour's account of *A Simple Story* follows a Protestant logic, one that echoes Dissenting appeals for emancipation from the Test and Corporation Acts in the 1790s. These acts, the Dissenters argued, undermined individuals' freedoms of conscience and their pursuit of truth. As we have seen, the Cisalpines' defense of conscience moved in the opposite direction to the Dissenters', away from the individual's pursuit of truth toward collective engagement. Inchbald's novel, I argue, expands this interest to include the rights of women, whose recognition requires practices that support them, rather than vows that bind them. Truth, however, is not the goal. Rather, it is how stories contextualize the meanings of speech acts that Inchbald wants to foreground.[31]

At the end of the courtship plot stands the vow that brings marriage into being. The distance Inchbald maintains from the conventions of an emergent realist tradition can be measured by the precarious nature of this performative speech act in *A Simple Story*. The first wedding party says their vows precipitously; the second never says them aloud. Inchbald's ambivalent relation to vows, I suggest, takes its cue from the Cisalpine controversies of the late 1780s. While Inchbald drafted her novel, British politicians formulated the oaths of allegiance and abjuration to be included in the Second Relief Act of 1791. The Catholic Committee and its conservative Catholic opponents, the vicars apostolic, lobbied hard to have their wording included.[32] We see, in this intra-Catholic conflict, a return to the concerns governing Cisalpine responses to Protestant polemic earlier in the 1780s. The Catholic Committee argued for a language that would signal English Catholics' independence from papal authority, which the vicars vigorously defended. Alexander Geddes argued, "We absolutely deny that the Pope has any sort of temporal jurisdiction, out of his own dominions; and the spiritual supremacy, which we allow him, as bishop of Rome, affects no more the government of this realm, than the primacy of Canterbury that of the Grand Mogul."[33] In the first version of the oath, drafted in consultation with William Pitt over the year 1788–89, the committee refuted four more points that had long buttressed anti-Catholic sentiment: that princes excommunicated by the pope could be deposed by their subjects, that the pope could absolve subjects of their allegiance to a ruling monarch, that the pope was infallible, and that Catholics were not required to honor promises made to heretics. The vicars immediately declared the oath, as the Catholic Committee had drafted it, "unlawful to be taken."[34] Of the name for English Catholics, "Protesting Catholic Dissenters," proposed by the committee, Charles Plowdon wrote, "the new title ... is a monster ... produced in all its deformity in the oaths."[35]

The larger concern attending the controversy around the wording of the new relief act involved the appointment of Catholic bishops in Ireland and the United Kingdoms of Scotland and England. The Cisalpines wanted local elections, rather than papal appointments. In *A Letter Addressed to the Catholic Clergy of England on the Appointment of Bishops*, John Throckmorton claims that "the oath taken by Bishops at their consecration, is a violation of the freedom of the Church, and of the duty they owe to Society."[36] The bishops' allegiance to Rome, the Cisalpines maintained, compromised the autonomy of the English church and its members. The vicars, in response, reminded the Catholic Committee that "the episcopal authority is an emanation of the divine authority which Christ has over his church transmitted through a continued succession of pastors from the time of the apostles."[37] The universal Catholic Church, in other words, cannot be divided into autonomous regional parts. This problem had far-reaching implications. When they refused the authority of Rome, the Cisalpines had to rewrite the history of the apostolic tradition without repeating the terms that governed the Reformation. Vicar John Milner pointed out that the Cisalpine position took them close to Protestant territory, that the refusal of papal rule sounded a lot like Protestant claims about the authority of private judgment. When we cut ourselves off from Rome, we have nothing more than our "own passions" to guide us, Milner argued.[38]

The Cisalpines were aware of this challenge and shared the vicars' belief that the British obsession with oath taking reflected the larger problem of Protestant belief—its failure to stabilize any point of authority outside the individual. In a letter to John Hawkins, who had recently converted to Protestantism, Joseph Berington wrote, "In no country under heaven is to be found that multiplicity of oaths, which are at every turn administered in Great Britain. It should seem as if the legislature had discovered something so infamously base in the character of an Englishman, that nothing but the most extraordinary ties could bind him to his duty."[39] Duty should be a habit, not something individuals take up or lay down as they see fit. The Protestant subject requires constant reinscription into a larger collective through the act of oath making because he believes in neither service nor a larger common good: "He, whom a simple oath of allegiance cannot bind, will be tied by nothing. But rather let there be no oaths at all.— . . . However, some of them serve to keep the papists in a state of bondage, and the views of legislators are thus fulfilled.—We want a treatise on this business of oaths."[40] The habit of oath making seems to *invite* that persecution of others—as had been true in

England—for it stands in place of a social order that secures the trust of its members through an external authority rooted in the community. The difference between the Cisalpines and the vicars was only in what constituted that authority—should it be housed in a local community or framed by the universality that "Rome" signified?

The first two volumes of *A Simple Story* use the representation of oaths and vow making to frame questions central to the debates surrounding religious toleration in the 1780s: What is the connection between identity politics and vow making? How is the success or failure of vow making linked to the presence or absence of communal standards? Built into these questions are larger philosophical and ethical concerns framing the making and breaking of oaths: Can individual conscience provide a stable epistemological ground from which to speak and act? To what extent, as a corrective to the limits of self-knowledge, should we rely on the authority of others? In answering these questions, Inchbald challenges the orthodoxies of both conservative Catholicism and Protestantism. Indeed, Protestant liberty and Catholic absolutism end up becoming versions of each other as the novel's characters retreat into the corners of their minds in the first two volumes of the novel.

In the novel's opening sentence, we learn that Dorriforth, our protagonist, has received a training at St. Omer's, a Jesuit college.[41] Dorriforth's vows direct him to the project of "reforming mankind."[42] His willingness to serve as the guardian of his friend's daughter speaks to this mandate. While asking that his friend to refrain from questioning Miss Milner's Protestant education, Mr. Milner hopes nonetheless that the priest will make his daughter good "by choice rather than by constraint" (5). The widow with whom Dorriforth lives translates this moral imperative back into the household's Catholicism: "I am sure Mr. Dorriforth, you will convert her from her evil ways" (10). The question of personal reform, from the outset, is bound up with religious affiliation.

Miss Milner, upon meeting her new guardian, takes her own vows: "[She] promised ever to obey him as her father" (13). But we soon learn the impracticality of Miss Milner's promise, given her personality: "From her infancy she had been indulged in all her wishes to the extreme of folly, and habitually started at the voice of control" (15). Dorriforth and Miss Milner find themselves constantly negotiating the boundaries of restraint and freedom, organized around promises made and broken. Miss Milner's Protestant identity asserts itself in the freedom of speech she assumes as her prerogative. As Geremy Carnes has noted, she maintains an attitude of casual disrespect for the Catholic sensibility of the household. "As a Protestant," Carnes observes, "she makes an unconscious assumption that she may mock Catholicism without consequence."[43] The limits of her Protestantism are not restricted to anti-Catholic prejudice. Rather, Inchbald uses Miss Milner's fierce individualism as a means of reflecting on the tension between private judgment and the communal standards. Miss Milner's sense of independence makes it impossible, finally, for her to realize a life beyond the limits of her immediate appetites, so closely does she associate their indulgence with the exercise of liberty. Inchbald identifies Miss Milner's anti-Catholic sentiment with a larger cultural venality that expresses itself as Protestant triumphalism. The libertine who eventually ruins the lives of Miss Milner and Dorriforth, Sir Frederick Lawnley, makes explicit the pleasure he takes in the idea of Catholic sacrilege: "Monastic vows, like those of marriage, were made to be broken" (21).

The various vows characters make underwrite their dreams of agency and authority, even as their repeated failure suggests that personal convictions mask epistemological blind spots. The exertion of will and the making of vows inform how individuals understand themselves—or rather, how they fail to do so. Mr. Sandford, Dorriforth's priest and mentor, is a case in point. The narrator tells us, "Mr. Sandford, although he was a man of understanding, of learning, and a complete casuist; yet, all the faults he himself committed, were entirely—for want of knowing better.—He constantly reproved faults in others, and he was most assuredly too good a man not to have corrected and amended his own, had they been known to him—but they were not" (142–43). This lack of insight renders characters oddly passive in relation to their words; as Ian Balfour points out, "Characters operate as much as victims as they do makers of their own speech acts."[44] The more individuals appear certain in their judgments, the more likely they are to be governed by forces larger than themselves, including their own vows.

A lack of self-awareness on the part of characters is coupled, in *A Simple Story*, with a narrative practice that refuses to provide the missing information regarding its characters' internal states. As Emily Hodgson Anderson notes, Inchbald "refuses to specify or delimit her characters' emotions."[45] This withholding alters the narrative principles of formal realism, to the extent that, as Dianne Osland points out, no character seems to manifest the psychological complexity we attribute to the novel at this stage of its development.[46] Inchbald breaks the link between interiority and plot maintained by realism, and by doing so, she registers her suspicion of Protestant claims regarding the efficacy of self-examination. In this novel, characters who think they know what they are about tend to fare worse than those who don't.

In what narrative world do we not value self-reflection? For Inchbald, the problem with self-reflection is that, in the absence of verification by an external standard, it only reinforces what individuals believe about themselves. In the case of Dorriforth and Miss Milner, religious difference exacerbates the contest of wills. Each wins battles but neither can win the war. Nor can they negotiate peace, because they can't view the conflict from a position outside of themselves and no one is available to mediate between them. The marriage plot becomes implicated in the fight when their feelings turn to love. When Miss Milner confesses her love for her guardian to her confidant, Miss Woodley, we are told by the narrator that "that passion, which had unhappily taken possession of her whole soul, would not have been inspired, had there not subsisted an early difference, in their systems of divine faith—had she early been taught what were the sacred functions of a Roman ecclesiastic ... education would have given such a prohibition to her love, that she had been precluded by it, as by that barrier which divides a sister from a brother" (74). It may be tempting, here, to read this passage as a condemnation of the interfaith marriage of Miss Milner's parents—a marriage that allowed Miss Milner to be raised in her mother's Protestant faith. But the problem lies not so much in Miss Milner's lack of a specifically Catholic education as in the failure of an education that allows for the faith of only one parent, rather than both, to be taught to a child. The boundary that is maintained around Miss Milner's Protestantism ensures that her father's Catholicism remains invisible to her; the prohibition around any discussion of it leads to a profound ignorance.

The same prohibition governs the rules of religious toleration in the household she shares with her guardian. Early in the narrative, Dorriforth declares, "Let not religion ever be named between us" (17). Ostensibly a means of respecting privacy and maintaining peace, this silence allows Miss Milner to remain oblivious to the effects of her words.[47] Isolated in the bunkers of their individual faiths and identities, the characters have no means of listening to each other. The privacy of belief, in this novel, creates the conditions for the possibility of conflict. Indeed, the isolation of individual minds accounts for the alacrity with which reason and conscience succumb to the more powerful forces of passion and self-interest as the narrative unfolds, making it impossible for characters to fulfill their Christian obligations to others.

The alternative to Protestant individualism is not the authority of the pope, however. When his cousin Lord Elmwood dies, Dorriforth must give up his religious vows in order to marry, have children, and so keep his property in

Catholic hands. Geremy Carnes claims that "Inchbald does all she can to draw attention away from the fact that her plot hinges upon Rome's interest in engineering a continued succession of English Catholic earls."[48] But I believe the opposite is true, that Inchbald places Rome's authority in the foreground to make explicit the compulsory elements of the marriage plot and what that compulsion reveals about the making of promises—namely, how they can be governed by forces external to us, even when we make them ourselves. No one consults Dorriforth as to his preference for marriage or celibacy. More importantly, the novel never suggests that he has any wishes of his own, either way.

When it finally appears, Dorriforth's desire for Miss Milner seems, like the obligation to marry, introduced from outside himself. After Miss Woodley confesses the secret of Miss Milner's desire to her employer, without naming its object, we read this description of Dorriforth's thoughts: "He ran over instantly in his mind all the persons he could recollect . . . [T]he object was presented, and he beheld *himself*" (130). The mind, here, seems to function separately from Dorriforth's consciousness. Only after seeing himself as the object of Miss Milner's desire does he announce a desire of his own. We never hear a confession that this desire predates the moment of Miss Woodley's confession. Rather, her confession seems in and of itself to spark the desire, one mixed with equal parts passion and dread: "I am transported at the tidings you have revealed; and yet, perhaps, I had better never have heard them" (131). Dorriforth's transport signals the anxieties and appeal of the dangerous liaison, of yoking the sacred and the profane. The narrative pauses for a moment to consider the quality of Dorriforth's affect: "[Miss Woodley] wished him to love Miss Milner, but to love her with moderation.—Miss Woodley was too little versed in the subject to know, that had not been love at all; at least not to the extent of breaking through engagements, and all the various obstacles, that militated against their union" (130). This particular love—the love that violates the taboos surrounding interfaith unions—constitutes itself in relation to the prohibitions it must overcome. In this context, moderation would prevent that love from realizing its goals. But to the extent that Dorriforth's amatory language reproduces the zeal of his attachment to authority, both his own and that of the church, we recognize the dangers as Miss Woodley does. As Eun Kyung Min observes, "Dorriforth's habit of submission to the Church renders him equally incapable of finding a vantage point from which to view his conduct. Dorriforth's lack of self-knowledge, his inability to read beneath the surface . . . are all of a piece with his religious vows, his insistence that words conform to some prior truth and guarantee future facts."[49]

Bridget Keegan argues that the Jesuit teachings around "indifference" serve as the antidote to emotional excess in the novel. But indifference, I suggest, is not what Inchbald is after. Indeed, when it appears in the novel, indifference proves entirely unappealing. Miss Fenton, Lord Elmwood's first fiancée, receives news of both her acceptance and then her rejection "with the same insipid smile of approbation, and the same cold indifference at the heart" (137). Miss Woodley's moderation provides an affective middle ground, I suggest, between the ardencies of submission and rebellion modeled by Lord Elmwood and Miss Milner. But moderation is a less an attempt to think reasonably, for Inchbald, than a feeling that attends to difference. The question is, then, What conditions can make moderation seem like a "real" feeling to those who are isolated in the prison house of their own selfhood? Miss Milner and Lord Elmwood trust the knowledge of their hearts, but this trust guarantees, rather than prevents, the failure of their marriage, for it rests on the securities of individuals who have neither learned how to respect difference in principle nor developed habits of living to accommodate it.

In Search of a Proper Education

The final sentence of *A Simple Story* sums up the moral of the novel thus: "And Mr. Milner, Matilda's grandfather, had better given his fortune to a distant branch of his family—as Matilda's father had once meant to do—so he had bestowed upon his daughter A PROPER EDUCATION" (338). For Gary Kelly, the sentence points directly to the novel's Jacobin political agenda.[50] For feminist critics, it suggests the victory of disciplinary regimes, a bad faith gesture toward the normative, or both.[51] But when we attend to the conversation about education taking place among English Catholics in the 1780s, different questions appear. How do the politics of "home" shape educational practice? What regulatory principles can sustain communal ties without sliding into authoritarian rule? How is religious duty best inculcated? What kind of education might foster better relations between Protestants and Catholics?

A key element in the negotiations leading up to 1791 Relief Act was the right of Catholics to educate their children at home.[52] After the Reformation, formal education for Catholic children had to be undertaken abroad, and even then Catholic families could find themselves subject to severe penalties in the event that they were caught sending their children out of the country. In 1781, Joseph Berington pointed out the unfairness of this policy: "It was surely a stretch of cruel despotism, thus to subject those who should send their children abroad, to hard penalties, and, at the same time, not to allow them to be educated at home, unless they took oaths, which in their consciences they thought unlawful!" He goes on to reflect on what is lost by the English policy, particularly in relation to young Catholic women: "At this day, English Nunneries abroad are no less than twenty-one.... It is a misfortune, that England should be deprived of so many fair examples of virtue: Their presence would surely be productive of more real advantage, than their absence."[53] Alexander Geddes notes the related malaise attending the exclusion of young Catholic men from English universities: "They have neither the means of improving their talents, nor an opportunity of exerting them. Useless to themselves, and useless to the common weal, they are, if they have any spirit, obliged to seek abroad what they cannot find at home."[54] The nation loses every time one of its young citizens is deprived of an English education, by this logic.

More immediately, of course, Catholic families lost someone they loved every time a child was sent abroad, and this separation, too, had lasting effects. As Eamon Duffy observes, "To send a child to Douai was to accept a separation of years, to send a daughter to a convent, that of a lifetime." He continues: "No other dissenting group in England experienced this sort of separation as a matter of course—and it is not too fanciful to suggest that the dispatching of the sons and daughters of the gentry to foreign colleges and convents must have acted as one of those religious 'rites of separation' of which Professor Bossy has written so eloquently."[55] This repeated fracturing of families signaled, for English Catholics, an internal division of the body politic. The domestic education of children helped in the forging of a nation capable of maintaining religious toleration, Catholic activists argued. Berington did not stop there. Anticipating Maria Edgeworth's programs, he looked to interdenominational education as a way of ameliorating "religious animosity":

> I think the Sunday schools may be made to answer to this great design. Why then should it not be done? Hitherto it has not, and only partial good has been obtained—Where the members of the Church have established them, either the children of the Dissenters have been excluded, or the rules of the institution served as an exclusion. They are compelled to attend the service, and to learn the catechism of the Church. This surely is unreasonable. The Dissenters, on their side, have not always been more liberal. The tendency of such an arrangement is evident. Not only does it keep alive an opposition spirit among the leaders, but it also gives birth to it in the unsuspecting minds of the children. Party names are given, and prejudices are formed....
> *Where schools are established, let children of all religions be invited to enter.*[56]

Berington traces the "opposition spirit" prompting religious conflict to the corruption of the "unsuspecting minds" of children. Teachers responsible for instructing a "mixed" class would be required to foster Christian values shared by all: "But then it will be necessary that elementary books of instruction be prepared, which shall contain nothing contrary to the particular tenets of any Christian society.... When we have separated from each society its distinctive opinions, which are mostly speculative will be left a great mass of Christian doctrine, and the whole system of moral duties."[57] Sounding like Locke, Berington argues that shifting attention from theology to morality fosters religious tolerance. But, importantly in this case, the children learn not only about Christian morality in this pedagogical experiment, but also what religious toleration looks like in practice: "The effect on their minds must be pleasing, when they begin to reflect, that they who from pure benevolence became their benefactors, were men of different persuasions."[58] Here, the tolerance described in Cisalpine accounts of Catholic hospitality are modeled by teachers sharing the space of the classroom.

When the narrative of *A Simple Story* resumes in the second chapter of volume 3, a scene of interdenominational community greets the reader: "In one corner of the room, by the side of an old-fashioned stool, kneels Miss Woodley, praying most devoutly for her still beloved friend, but in vain endeavouring to pray composedly—floods of tears pour down her furrowed cheeks, and frequent sobs of sorrow break through each pious ejaculation" (199–200). As Miss Woodley prays for the dying Protestant, Lady Elmwood, the Catholic priest Sandford performs last rites over her: "By that sincerity which shone upon your youthful face when I joined your hands; those thousand virtues you have at times given proof of, you were not born to die *the death of the wicked*." The scene is remarkable for the distance it measures between the earlier household, divided by young Miss Milner's xenophobic Protestantism and the Catholic strictness of Mrs. Horton and a younger Sandford. Now, the narrator remarks of the priest, "Compassion changed his language, and softened all those harsh tones that used to denounce resentment" (200). Time and a shared life have fostered mutual regard and trust.

This is the household in which Miss Milner's daughter, Matilda, has been raised and educated. In describing her education, the narrative moves back and forth between its content and the affective contexts that shape it. Matilda's education contains two streams, informal and formal. Her informal education has attended to the moral lessons provided by Lady Elmwood's example: "Matilda (with an excellent understanding, a sedateness above her years, and early accustomed to the most private converse between Lady Elmwood and Miss Woodley) was perfectly acquainted with the whole fatal history of her mother; and was by her taught, that respect and admiration of her father's virtues which they had justly merited" (216). The intimacy of the circle of women allows for the relation of the sexual content of Lady Elmwood's "fatal history," its erotic charge neutralized by the pedagogical use to which it is put. We learn, further, that Matilda is "accomplished in the arts of music and drawing, by the most careful instruction of her mother." Art creates a space of growth and expression for the young girl. The second strand of Matilda's education is provided by Sandford: "As a scholar she excelled most of her sex, from the great pains Sandford had taken with that part of her education, and the great abilities he possessed for that task" (221). Kaley Kramer argues that "if Matilda is an example of a properly feminine character, it must be remembered that her education resembles her Catholic father's—not her Protestant mother's."[59] But it is not clear that Matilda is schooled exclusively in one tradition or the other. I would argue that she inherits her mother's Protestantism as her "family" religion but receives, at the same time, a Catholic education. And it is clear that the education Sandford provides has, like Lady Elmwood's, not only a religious but also an affective component: "[Matilda's] forlorn state, and innocent sufferings, had ever excited his compassion in the extremest degree, and had caused him ever to treat her with the utmost affection, tenderness, and respect" (216). Matilda has received a "mixed" education from her Catholic and Protestant interlocutors, one that combines knowledge and feeling.

Matilda has been schooled in the household where her mother and friends live, but, in the absence of a larger community, we can hardly call this space a "home." She is raised in "a single house by the side of a dreary heath," in a "lonely country on the borders of Scotland"—isolated from the neighborly relations that sustain the individual household (199). Later in the narrative, her cousin Harry Rushbrook describes her as "a wanderer, and an orphan" (290) after her father turns her out of doors, but in fact Matilda has lived in exile since the first time she was ejected, as an infant, from the home where she was born. Indeed, it is as though she has spent her youth in a foreign convent, seeking atonement for the sins of her mother: "Educated in the school of adversity, and inured to retirement from her infancy, she had acquired a taste for all those amusements which a recluse life affords" (221). After her mother's death, Matilda's return to her father's house produces no sense of comfort—only a spectral longing for a childhood that might have been: "As the porter opened the gates of the avenue to the carriage that brought them, Matilda felt an awful, and yet gladsome sensation no terms can describe. . . . 'And is my father the master of this house?' she cried—'And was my mother once the mistress of this house?'" (219). Each space she inhabits registers a loss of some kind, a loss, Inchbald implies, of both intimate and communal ties.

A house divided, as Matilda's new home is, can be experienced only as the uncanny. Inchbald, critics have argued, uses gothic tropes to identify the unconscious desires of Lord Elmwood and his daughter, the sexual underpinnings of patriarchy.[60] But the novel's interest in the gothic lies, I believe, as much in its religious as in its sexual aspect. Where the gothic novels of Ann Radcliffe and others move to link emancipation from patriarchal authority with freedom from religion, *A Simple Story* imagines an alternative trajectory. Indeed, as Michael Tompko observes, "Inchbald's novel connects the rise of Elmwood's dangerous form of fundamentalism not to a religious position but to the abandonment of religious sentiment."[61] When read allegorically, the plight of Matilda and others dependent on Lord Elmwood mirrors, as Carnes has argued, the conditions of a Catholic minority living under siege in a secularized Protestant nation.[62]

The gothic aspect of Elmwood House reflects the restrictions that attended the rise of property rights and the consolidation of the British estate in the eighteenth century made possible by land enclosures, Black laws, and the Hardwicke Marriage Act. Daniel O'Quinn notes that "the reign of George III was arguably the most punitive in the eighteenth century."[63] In Inchbald's novel, the rule of Lord Elmwood's law appears arbitrary and unjust. His attention to "horses, hay, farming, and politics" (225)—to the banality of the everyday—is precisely what allows for the banality of his particular brand of evil, with its homosocial violence and lack of regard for the poor. Striking Lord Frederick, Miss Milner's suitor, fills a young Dorriforth with remorse, but seventeen years later, Lord Elmwood does not hesitate to leave his enemy "maimed, and defaced with scars" in a duel (198). The estate's head gardener, an "elderly gentleman, . . . with a large indigent family of aged parents, children, and other relatives," is turned off the property for merely mentioning Lady Elmwood. In this moment, the narrative pauses to describe what is lost, echoing the language of enclosure's forced displacements of rural populations: "Before the next day at noon, his pleasant house by the side of the park, his garden, and his orchard, which he had occupied above twenty years, were cleared of their old inhabitant, and all his wretched family" (272). Only one day later, confronted with the unconscious body of Matilda in his arms, Lord

Elmwood obliges a servant to disengage him: "Seizing her hand, [Giffard] pulled it with violence—it fell—and her father went away" (274). Lord Elmwood organizes his house around the violence of his resentments, masquerading as household rule.

It is Lord Elmwood, then, who stands in need of a "proper education" such as his daughter has received from her mother, Miss Woodley, and Sandford. At first glance, such an education seems highly unlikely, if not impossible, because Lord Elmwood can love in only one way—the way he loved his former wife: "Love, that produces wonders, that seduces and subdues the most determined and rigid spirits, had in two instances overcome the inflexibility of Lord Elmwood; he married Lady Elmwood contrary to his determination, because he loved; and for the sake of this beloved object, he had, contrary to his resolution, taken under his immediate care young Rushbrook; but the magic which once enchanted away this spirit of immutability was no more—Lady Elmwood was no more, and the charm was broken" (251). In Lord Elmwood's mind, love is a species of magical thinking, conjured up by a genie in a bottle—in this case, Lady Elmwood. Romantic love makes possible a concern for others—in this case, his orphan nephew—but only as long as the primary love object remains in place.

A more durable love requires a different disposition, and here we return to Miss Woodley and her advocacy of moderate love.[64] As Matilda's companion and teacher in exile, Miss Woodley knows best the affective gap between "before" and "after." Upon hearing they will be living with Lord Elmwood after the death of his wife, "Miss Woodley . . . smiled at the prospect before her . . . picturing . . . a thousand of the brightest hopes, from watching every emotion of his soul, and catching every proper occasion to excite, or increase, his paternal sentiments" (218). Miss Woodley's proximity does, indeed, generate feelings in Lord Elmwood, who uses her as a stand-in for his daughter. We learn, for instance, that after a dangerous illness, that "there was no one person he evidently showed so much satisfaction at seeing, as Miss Woodley." Sandford makes the connection explicit when he sees Lord Elmwood respond warmly to her: "Sandford was present, and ever associating the idea of Matilda with Miss Woodley, felt his heart bound with a triumph it had not enjoyed for many a day" (269). Miss Woodley's life in the home of Lord Elmwood makes the idea of his daughter tolerable. That is, Miss Woodley becomes, herself, the space where moderate love is fostered.

To learn how to tolerate his daughter's existence, Lord Elmwood must let go of the obsessions that organized his love for Lady Elmwood in favor of a different affect, one that can stand divisions and pluralities. The second agent in Lord Elmwood's education is his nephew, Harry Rushbrook. Like Matilda, Rushbrook is an orphan—and he is also the child of an interfaith marriage. Unlike Matilda, Rushbrook enjoys every privilege afforded an adopted son of Lord Elmwood: "Rushbrook had been a beautiful boy, and was now an extremely handsome young man; he had made an unusual progress in his studies, had completed the tour of Italy and Germany, and returned home with the air and address of a perfect man of fashion—there was, beside, an elegance and persuasion in his manner almost irresistible" (230). Although he is his heir, Rushbrook has none of his uncle's qualities but is rather "youthful, warm, generous, grateful" (291). "Grateful," here, is the key word. For, unlike his uncle, Harry Rushbrook has not forgotten how to love Lady Elmwood. He has practiced loving her since childhood, when she rescued him from his status as an orphaned foster child and gave him a home. The practice of gratitude allows him to maintain divided loyalties, as he tells his uncle: "'I feel gratitude towards you, my lord,' continued he, 'gratitude is innate in my heart, and I must also feel it towards her, who first introduced me to your protection.' . . . 'It was the mother of Lady Matilda . . . who was this friend to me'" (290). Harry's heart is capable of feeling gratitude and love for two objects, despite their differences.

In a recent essay, Colin Jager reflects on the relationship between gratitude and tolerance. The violence of the French Revolution stemmed, he suggests, from an inability to imagine divided loyalties—in the instance he describes, to both nation and church. The affect that enables loyalty to more than one thing, Jager writes, is gratitude, "a word that preserves the affective weight of love while also opening up its potential range. . . . Gratitude, in fact, may be the affect most nearly allied to tolerance precisely because it is directed outward."[65] Here, Rushbrook draws the connection between his divided love and social justice, telling his uncle, "Nor will I ever think of marriage, or any other joyful prospect, while you abandon the only child of my beloved patroness, and load me with the rights, which belong to her" (290). Lord Elmwood is forced to hear from his nephew the lesson his household has been trying to teach him by example.

Lord Elmwood, we are told early in volume 3, is "by nature, and more from education, of a serious, thinking, and philosophic turn of mind" (201). Rushbrook, by contrast, has an "unthinking mind" (241). But his capacity for gratitude renders him the superior ethical subject. Reflecting on Lord Elmwood's failure as a father, Rushbrook "gazed with wonder at his uncle's insensibility to his own happiness, and longed to lead him to the jewel he cast away" (241). Matilda, too, proves herself superior to her father in her willingness to honor Lady Elmwood. Like Rushbrook, Matilda keeps her mother alive in her memory. At one point, she speaks to her dead mother: "For your sake I will bear all with patience" (244). Matilda and Rushbrook, as well as Miss Woodley and Sandford, provide alternative models of loving to those sustained by Lord Elmwood's romantic attachment and resentment, both fostered by the secular world. By contrast, the religious sociability of Matilda's childhood home advocates communal interdependence as a principle of ethics, rather than property. The question, for Matilda's story, is how those ethics will translate into a marriage plot.

Queer Matilda

In *Born Yesterday: Inexperience and the Early Realist Novel*, Stephanie Insley Hershinow describes how the adolescent, in eighteenth-century fiction, functions "as a site of *suspended possibility* rather than as a catalyst for development."[66] Inexperience, she observes, allows characters to create parallel universes in which the "merely possible" exists alongside the real.[67] The adolescent's alternative visions complicate an emergent realist tradition that claims to capture truth, showing us what is both "descriptive and conjectural" in the eighteenth-century novel. The stories that the adolescent tells herself confront the facts of the world with a counterfactual logic.[68] The imperatives of plot are defied when the social push toward mature personhood (paradoxically, for women, identical with the non-personhood conferred by marriage) comes up against the perversity of an *in*-experiential mode that the adolescent seems unable or unwilling to relinquish.

Hershinow identifies the gothic as the mode best able to measure the distance between the novice's fantasies and the "the grounding objections of the real world."[69] In *A Simple Story*, the gothic generates affects capable of sustaining a beleaguered community, as we saw above. It also enables Matilda to swerve away from the *Bildung* of the marriage plot entered into by her mother before her.[70] This alternative plot is made possible by Matilda's powers of fabulation, harnessed to the sociability sustained by the household of Miss Woodley and Sandford. In an early scene in volume 3, Sandford intimates that her father seems happier with his daughter in the house, despite his strict prohibition of any acknowledgment of her presence. Sandford highlights the dangers of this happiness—its potential, if fully recognized, to trigger a backlash: "If he is in spirits that you are in this house—so near him—positively under his protection—yet he will not allow himself to think that, is the cause of his content—and the sentiments he has adopted . . . will remain the same as ever; nay, perhaps with greater force, while he suspects his weakness" (225). Here, Sandford imagines Lord Elmwood using the law of his prohibition to discipline any feelings he may sense lurking in his heart. (As we saw earlier in the narrative, a tendency toward self-reflection does not, in this novel, produce good outcomes.) But Matilda translates this garbled language of lurking love and violence into a meaningful engagement between father and daughter:

> "If he does but think of me with tenderness," cried Matilda, "I am recompensed."
> "And what recompense would his kind thoughts be to you," said Sandford, "were he to turn you out to beggary?"
> "A great deal—a great deal," she replied.
> "But how are you to know he has these kind thoughts, while he gives you no proof of them?"
> "No, Mr. Sandford; but *supposing* we could know them without proof." (225)

Matilda's *supposing* allows her father's tenderness to override the facts of her banishment. Matilda is right in thinking that Lord Elmwood may have thoughts that no one knows about, despite Sandford's insistence that there is no proof of their existence. Since no one knows what goes on inside the head of another, Matilda's guess is as good as anyone else's. And the idea of the kind thoughts' existence compensates for the threat of beggary Lord Elmwood holds over her. Matilda refuses the abjection of the real, choosing instead to tell a story that answers her emotional needs.

Matilda's conjectural thinking allows her to go further still, to put herself in her father's presence: "'How strange is this!' cried Matilda, when Miss Woodley and she were alone, 'My father within a few rooms of me, and yet I debarred from seeing him!—Only by walking a few paces I might be at his feet, and perhaps receive his blessing. . . . [T]o entertain the thought, that it is possible I could do this, is a source of great comfort'" (226). Matilda soothes her wounded heart by way of the counterfactual: she will not try to meet her father, but she takes pleasure in the imaginative staging of that meeting. Over and over again, we see her fantasizing dramatic scenes of encounter: "She would rush boldly into the apartment where he was, and at his feet take leave of him for ever.—She would lay hold of his hands, clasp his knees, provoke him to spurn her, which would be joy in comparison to this cruel indifference" (244). But she never moves toward transforming her thoughts into action, because she does not need to: the imaginative act of storytelling is sufficiently solacing.

It is entirely fitting that Matilda, when she finally does meet her father, faints: "She gave a scream of terror—put out her trembling hands to catch the balustrades for support—missed them—and fell motionless into her father's arms" (274). Unconscious Matilda does not have to witness the scene that follows, with her father naming his daughter "Miss Milner" and a servant tearing her hand from its grip on her father's coat. When she awakens, she remembers a love Lord Elmwood will not own: "I thought he held me in his arms, she replied, I thought I felt his hands press mine—Let me sleep and dream it again" (275). Unconsciousness allows love to override the actions that betray it. Here, I suggest, Matilda occupies the space of "suspended possibility" that Hershinow foregrounds, a space in which mental states are held separate from the empirical world.[71] That is to say, Matilda's fantasy of paternal care does not encourage her to mistake abusive treatment as love. Rather, it fosters a belief in her own worthiness, that she deserves to *be* loved.

For Harry Rushbrook, the appeal of the conjectural, rather than the real, would seem to be less powerful. He is heir to Lord Elmwood's estate, enjoying all the freedoms and privileges that identity entails. But he, too, learns to defend himself against his uncle by resorting to the conjectural. In the face of Lord Elmwood's demand that he marry a woman chosen for him by his uncle, Rushbrook equivocates:

> "I have only to say, my lord," returned Rushbrook, "that although my heart may be totally disengaged, I may yet be disinclined to the prospect of marriage."
>
> "May! May! Your heart *may* be disengaged," repeated his lordship. "Do you dare to reply to me equivocally, when I have asked a positive answer?" (253)

Later, when the subject of the earlier conversation comes up, Rushbrook misremembers it, prompting Lord Elmwood's angry response: "What, equivocating again, sir?—Do you remember it, or do you not?" (287). Rushbrook refuses to engage Lord Elmwood's either/or logic that can lead to only one conclusion: an arranged marriage. He does so by countering his uncle's demands with demands of his own, evoking the sanctity of promises to gain a footing with Lord Elmwood:

> "My lord—waiving for a moment the subject of my marriage—permit me to remind you, that when I was upon my sick bed, you promised, that on my recovery, you would listen to a petition I had to offer you. . . ."
>
> "You promised to hear me, my lord," cried Rushbrook, "and I claim your promise." (289)

The promise here takes on a very different form than those exchanged in the earlier volumes, pointing only to the possibility of listening, rather than to particular content. Rushbrook is able to hold his uncle to his promise, but he is not able to protect himself from the violence that unfolds when he speaks. When he advocates for Matilda's rights, his uncle responds with rage.

It is Sandford's touch that saves Rushbrook from banishment: "[Sandford], for the first time in his life, took hold of him by the hand. . . . Rushbrook made an effort to go, but Sandford still held his hand; and said to Lord Elmwood, 'He is but a boy, my lord, and do not give him the punishment of a man'" (291). As Matilda's relation to her father is mediated by Miss Woodley's presence, so Rushbrook is able to take shelter in Sandford's touch, a very different touch from the rough grabbing of hands that united Miss Milner and Lord Elmwood at the conclusion of volume 2. The combination of embodied affect and imaginative thinking proves more powerful than Lord Elmwood's literalism, grounded in the facts of property and patriarchal authority.

Rushbrook wants to bring a new household into existence, a household founded on reciprocal regard that properly acknowledges each of its members. "'How hard is it to restrain conversation from the subject of our thoughts,' Rushbrook declares to Sandford, who reminds him, in turn: 'you have made pretty free with your speech to-day, and ought not to complain of the want of toleration on that score.'" But Rushbrook wants to unshackle tolerance from the status of an indulgence, "If toleration was more frequent, the favour of obtaining it would be less," he notes (295). He seeks, in other words, a leveling of distinctions among members of the household so that its minority—that is to say, its youth—may gain full and equal rights. Significantly, when Rushbrook speaks to his uncle of marriage, he turns immediately to the question of rights: "Nor will I ever think of marriage, or any other joyful prospect, while you abandon the only child of my beloved patroness, and load me with the rights, which belong to her" (290).[72] Gratitude, tolerance, and love organize themselves around questions of justice, and it is this configuration that sets the stage for the marriage between Rushbrook and Matilda.

The marriage plot, such as it is, is precipitated by Matilda's banishment from her father's house. Lord Elmwood's casual disposal of his daughter allows for the narrative's second gothic villain, Lord Margrave, to act: "As he was no longer fearful of resentment from the Earl, whatever treatment his daughter should receive, he was determined the anger of Lady Matilda or of her female friend, should not impede his pretensions" (299). Like Lord Elmwood, this tyrant represents not the old dispensation of Catholic oppression but the new dispensation of the secular. Merely a "rustic Baron," Lord Margrave nonetheless understands the language of paternal property. The idea of rape occurs to him only when it has become clear "from the behavior of Lord Elmwood to his child, [that] it was more than probable he would be utterly indifferent to any violence that might be offered her" (249). The ease with which Lord Margrave moves between the marriage plot—which he entertains when Lord Elmwood factors into his consideration—and rape—when Lord Elmwood does not, suggests a continuum made possible by a world in which sexual ethics have been translated into property laws.

When Matilda is kidnapped, the family she remembers does not include her father: "The memory of Sandford with all his kindness, now rushed so forcibly on Matilda's mind, she shed a shower of tears, thinking how much he felt, and would continue to feel, for her situation.—Once she thought on Rushbrook too, and thought even he would be vext for her.—Of her father she did not think—she durst not—one single time the thought intruded, but she hurried it away—it was too bitter" (328). As Miriam Wallace notes, "The narrator makes clear that Elmwood risks the cultural capital he has in his daughter's chastity because of his own actions, while Matilda performs no actions which would either cause or prevent her own abduction and rape."[73] Matilda's eventual rescue brings the homosocial relations governing the whole affair into sharp focus: "The law shall be your only antagonist," Lord Elmwood tells Lord Margrave (329).

Upon returning to Elmwood House, Matilda longs for her true family: "She seemed to be at that summit of her wishes which annihilates hope, but that the prospect of seeing Miss Woodley and Mr. Sandford, still kept this pleasing passion in existence" (331). Matilda's sense of family, organized around their shared experience of precarity, sets the stage for her acceptance of Rushbrook's marriage proposal. Her father is on the verge of banishing his nephew for disobedience when Matilda, like Sandford before her, intervenes: "I cannot see him turned out of your house without feeling for him, what he once felt for me." The shared experience of persecution prompts Matilda's generosity. When asked whether she would grant him what he asked for, she replies, conjecturally, "Most willingly—was it in my gift" (336). Her generosity, writ large in her acceptance of Rushbrook's proposal, consolidates the family that Lord Elmwood has repeatedly threatened to destroy. As Eun Kyung Min argues, "What is clear is that her final gift overrides her father's denial and threat, to give in the place of a prohibition."[74]

Matilda, the narrator tells us, does not consider Rushbrook in the light of a romantic partner: "She loved him as her friend, her cousin, her softer brother, but not as a lover.—The idea of love never once came to her thoughts; and she would sport with Rushbrook like the most harmless child" (334). So how does Matilda get from "softer brother" to "husband"? The narrative does not tell us, but it does invite us to think as she has, throughout the narrative—that is to say, conjecturally: "Whether the heart of Matilda, such as it has been described, could sentence him to misery, the reader is left to surmise—and if he suppose that it did not, he has every reason to suppose their wedded life was a life of happiness" (337). This conjectural logic mirrors the longings that shape the second half of the novel and the possibilities they have created in the minds of the adolescents oppressed by a tyrannical parent. It also points to the possibility of a counterfactual marriage plot.[75] Most immediately, Matilda is spared the conventions of sentimental love that turn both Harriet Byron and Emily Montague into emotional zealots. Instead, she can extend the "sport" of brother/sister love into the arena of marriage. This bond neutralizes the affective circuitry of heteronormativity, including its vertical power relations.

I call Matilda's love for her cousin "queer" to contrast it to romantic love as it is constructed by the eighteenth-century novel. But I also want to signal its proximity to a minoritized religious sensibility, one that creates a household in which the conjugal unit is only one part of a larger whole. By marrying her cousin, Matilda ensures she will be able to maintain the bonds she has forged with others. The household community that Sandford, Miss Woodley, Harry Rushbrook, and Matilda establish repeals the law of the father. No longer able to divide and conquer, Lord Elmwood will pass his estate to the next generation. The absolutism of his reign of terror is replaced with the democracy of an equal partnership supported by those who protected the young. The religious duties that both Miss Woodley and Sandford exercised in their care of Matilda demonstrate an obligation that represents a higher law than Lord Elmwood's. Both Matilda and Rushbrook were schooled in those ethics, and we can anticipate they will pass them along to their children. In the constitution of this interfaith home, we see how Inchbald reimagines the novel form to encompass a model of sociability that recognizes English Catholic hospitality as the grounds for an alternative community. In the final instance, it is Miss Woodley's dream of "moderate love" that the narrative realizes, and this love, I suggest, encompasses the model of tolerance promoted by Cisalpines in the 1780s, including what Joseph P. Chinnici has identified as their "attitude of reconciliation."[76] Inchbald's translation of this attitude into a marriage plot that unites the offspring of two interfaith unions enables the representation of a community that, as Tomko shows, "incorporates difference into a common territory without effacing memories of the past."[77]

A year after she published *A Simple Story*, Inchbald wrote another work about religious toleration, *The Massacre*, a play reflecting on the violence in France in September 1792.[78] Inchbald's revisions of her French source, documented in detail by Wendy C. Nielsen, return to the blind spots of liberal political theory: while the male characters debate the merits of religious toleration in a public square, the mob goes about butchering a wife and children in their home.[79] Inchbald changes her source material to include reflections, made by Eusèbe Tricastin, on why he must not arm his wife so that she might protect herself in the case of an attack: "No—by heaven, so sacred do I hold the delicacy of her sex, that could she with breath lay all her enemies dead, I would not have her feminine virtues violated by the act." The precarity of toleration is connected to the gender segregation maintained by the private/public divide, which allows the father to consider the home safe and the mob to use the murder of the trapped and vulnerable as a political weapon.[80]

The Massacre brings the Reformation's religious warfare into the present, suggesting that the question of violence has not been adequately answered by the French Revolution—a reflection that led William Godwin to pressure Inchbald to withdraw the play from circulation. We see, in this moment, how Inchbald's Catholicism took her thinking in a different direction from that of the Jacobins, toward the practices of coexistence that shaped her own community, the daily habits that developed, among the Cisalpines, into a theory of religious toleration. Inchbald and the Cisalpines remind us of the diversity of communal imaginings in the 1790s and how those imaginings could enable a reconfiguration of religious and sexual affiliations into new modes of belonging.[81] Unlike Richardson and Brooke, Inchbald could show how an interfaith household might mitigate the inequalities of companionate marriage and reshape the affects required to sustain it.

CHAPTER 5

Maria Edgeworth's Jewish Enlightenment

> Yet this imaginary Shylock has prejudiced thousands of Christians who never saw a Jew, against the whole tribe of Israel; while those very Christians, who read the story of a certain Duke, who demanded a large sum of money from a Jew, and extorted four of his teeth before he could extort the money, are greatly surprised at the Jew's obstinacy.
> —*William Austin,* Letters from London *(1804)*

In the final pages of Maria Edgeworth's *Harrington* (1817), the sudden revelation that Berenice Montenero, daughter of a Sephardic Jew, is not Jewish but Protestant (having been raised in the faith of her English mother) paves the way to a companionate marriage uncomplicated by religious difference. It has become a critical commonplace to attribute this abrupt revelation and awkward ending to the limits of toleration. Some attribute the failure of the interfaith marriage plot to a latent prejudice in Maria Edgeworth, which her best intentions could not overcome; for others, it reveals toleration's repressive function, the exclusions built into its operating equipment.[1] What these readings obscure, however, is that the interfaith marriage that doesn't happen at the end of the novel is preceded in the narrative by two that do. Yoon Sun Lee has noted how readings of the ideological import of Edgeworth's plots focus on their conclusions, encouraging us to notice "not only what happens to whom at the end, but with how things happen along the way—or even with how things happen to happen."[2] This chapter shows how the things that happen along the way to the union of Berenice and Harrington prove central to understanding Edgeworth's handling of toleration's plot.

This narrative brings us full circle to *Sir Charles Grandison*, a novel that Edgeworth was thinking about when she was writing *Harrington*. In many respects, *Harrington* rehearses the lessons afforded by Richardson's novel, celebrating the virtues of rational self-control and polite sociability. Gentlemanly civility finds expression, as it so often does in *Grandison*, in acts of generosity and care and takes, as its universalized form, the ideal of cosmopolitan disinterestedness. In *Harrington*, Protestant-Catholic relations are addressed in the novel's representation of the Gordon Riots, whose violence Edgeworth deplores. Prejudice appears in stations high and low, and the novel advances a cultural program of education and reform, bracketing politics in favor of morals and manners as the appropriate sites of national reconstruction.

The reflections on Richardson's novel that appear in *Ormond*, the companion tale published with *Harrington* as part of a two-volume set in 1817, suggest that Edgeworth was particularly interested in *Grandison*'s treatment of Clementina's story: "Ormond has often declared, that Sir Charles Grandison did him more good, than any *fiction* he ever read in his life. Indeed, to him it appeared no fiction—while he was reading it, his imagination was so full of Clementina, and the whole Porretta family, that he saw them in his sleeping and waking dreams. The deep pathos so affected him, that he could scarcely recall his mind to the low concerns of life."[3] It's not clear, exactly, where the "deep pathos" of Clementina and the Porretta family lies: is it their internal divisions or their inability to enter into the dream of (Protestant) toleration fostered by Sir Charles? Edgeworth's Anglo-Irish identity afforded her insight into the marginal status of Richardson's Italians. Like Grandison, Ormond must become a man capable of bridging cultural divisions—but he does so from the Irish side. In *Harrington*, the Catholic haunting of Richardson's Protestant marriage plot repeats itself, but this time it is a Jewish bride who lingers over the narrative's ending. The Jewish family narrative that replaces the Porrettas' story does not simply repeat the tale of *Grandison*, however; it also brings us back to the figure of *Grandison*'s Solomon Merceda, used as a foil to the hero in Richardson's novel. Edgeworth's willingness to take on the anti-Semitism that colors Richardson's portrait of the "Portuguese Jew" marks the novel's interest in advancing the project of religious toleration sixty years later. Edgeworth expands the scope of the novel of manners in order to incorporate Merceda's body into its narrative hermeneutics, moving toward, rather than away from, the differences it represents. Edgeworth's attention to how tolerance is made possible only through embodied engagements, I argue, allows *Harrington* to theorize the "radical openness" that Lars Tønder identifies with an experience of pain "that affirms the shared condition of vulnerability and dependency."[4]

Harrington advocates for a cosmopolitan ideal that represents the vision not only of the civil gentleman but of religious minorities and women as well. Interfaith marriage provides a central plank in this platform. I attend, here, to two marriages: one between members of a Jewish family and members of the

Spanish nobility that appears when Montenero tells how it brought valuable paintings into his possession; the second, the marriage of Montenero himself. These marriages, I suggest, represent the possibility of alternative religious affiliations to those defined by English Protestantism. Edgeworth recognizes the significance of maintaining family and cultural allegiances, as the Sephardim did. The story of these Sephardic mixed marriages frames Edgeworth's rewriting not only of *Grandison* but also Shakespeare's *Merchant of Venice*. In particular, by refusing the terms that govern Jessica's conversion narrative, Edgeworth makes room for an alternative model of marriage and, more broadly, familial and religious identity. Unlike Richardson and Shakespeare, Edgeworth advances a conjugal narrative that moves toward what Regina Hewitt calls "the inclusive ideal."[5] The woman author, I argue, appears uniquely positioned to write this new narrative; her art practice mirrors the communal sensibility of tolerance maintained by the interfaith marriage plot.

Pain's Emplotment

In *Harrington*, the problem of pain reminds us why the companionate marriage plot has trouble incorporating religious difference into its narrative.[6] Ostensibly, that plot depends on pain's transmutation from discomfort to pleasure: we move from the erotic pains of courtship to the calm seas of marriage.[7] Harrington's desire initially follows this trajectory. As a young man, he has a young fashionable woman dangled before him as a possible match. The daughter of the antiquated Lady de Brantefield, Lady Ann speaks to a younger generation's commitment to the blank conformity of fashion and politeness—a superficiality that leaves no purchase for sexual attraction:

> I could have turned and moulded Lady de Brantefield, with all her repulsive haughtiness, into a Clelia or a Princess de Cleves or something of the Richardson full-dressed heroine, with hoop and fan, and *stand off, man*! And then there would be cruelty and difficulty and incomprehensibility—something to be conquered—something to be wooed and won. But with Lady Anne Mowbray my imagination had nothing to work upon, no point to dwell on, nothing on which a lover's fancy could feed. There was no doubt, no hope, no fear; no reserve, no woman.[8]

Lady de Brantefield's "repulsive" snobbery serves as the sign of sexual difference for Harrington, here, a difference summarized in the word "haughtiness." This haughtiness sets up a resistance—Clarissa's "stand off, man!"—that triggers desire. "Woman," in Harrington's mind, generates doubt, hope, fear, and reserve, and it sets in motion a plot that resolves itself in the overcoming of difference: pain followed by the pleasure of conquest. In the absence of these feelings, sexual difference fails to appear. Lady Ann registers only as an extension of the shapeless dress she wears, absent hoop and fan, aids to distance and concealment.

Berenice Montenero, by contrast, proves "uncommonly interesting" from the moment Harrington first lays eyes on her (135). Harrington encounters her at a performance of *The Merchant of Venice*, and it is her pained reaction to the representation of Shylock that captures Harrington's attention: "My imagination formed such a strong conception of the pain the Jewess was feeling, and my inverted sympathy, if I may so call it, so overpowered my direct and natural feelings, that at every fresh development of the Jew's villainy I shrunk as though I had myself been a Jew" (137). Here the pain necessary to generate erotic interest comes not from the cruelty of a haughty love, but from pain being inflicted on another. It is not distance, in this case, but proximity that pulls Harrington close, so close that he inhabits Berenice's subject position, feeling the anti-Semitism of Shakespeare's representation as though it were directed at him, rather than her. Importantly, however, this identification does not last. The conventional script dictates that love's emotional transfer can tolerate pain only if it recasts itself as pleasure. Harrington falls in love with Berenice when he assumes a spectatorial distance from her feelings of pain— that is, when he stops identifying with her Jewishness: "During the third act, during the Jessica scenes, I longed so much to look at the Jewess that I took an opportunity of changing my position.... I now saw and heard the play solely with reference to her feelings; I anticipated every stroke which could touch her, and became every moment more and more interested and delighted with her, from the perception that my anticipations were just, and that I perfectly knew how to read her soul and interpret her countenance" (139). Significantly, when Harrington stops identifying with Berenice's Jewishness, he also stops identifying her *as* Jewish. He watches her watch the Jessica scenes in Shakespeare's play, scenes that recount a daughter's renunciation of her father's faith and her conversion to the religion of her husband. Sexual difference emerges to anchor desire in Harrington at the moment when religious difference disappears. On the one hand, it is Berenice's encounter with English anti-Semitism—that is, her experience of pain—that sets her apart as an object worthy of love, a singular subject who stands out from the herd of fashionably indifferent ladies. On the other hand, the Jewish identification that causes this pain translates itself into a sign of availability when the character on the stage assumes her place in the marriage plot as a Christian.[9]

When Harrington contemplates marrying Berenice, his old fear of religious alterity surfaces: "A Jewess!—her religion—her principles—my principles. And can a Jewess marry a Christian? And should a Christian marry a Jewess? The horror of family quarrels, of religious dissensions and disputes between father and child—husband and wife. All these questions and fears and doubts passed through my imagination backwards and forwards with inconceivable rapidity—struck me with all the amazement of novelty—though in fact they were not new to me" (195). Fearful of pain—the "horror" of family dysfunction—Harrington consoles himself with the hope that love will convert Berenice to Christianity after marriage: "Who knows what changes love might produce? Voltaire and Mowbray say 'qu'une femme est toujours de la religion de son amant'" (196). What he can't imagine is the discomfort of living with someone whose beliefs differ from his own. "This difficulty concerning religion increased, instead of diminishing in magnitude and importance, the more my imagination dwelt upon it—the longer it was considered by my reason" (203). Reason does not provide an answer to the challenge posed by interfaith marriage. If the conventional marriage plot subsumes the difficulties of courtship and its erotic alterities into companionate love, a mixed marriage foregrounds the persistence of pain. The discomfort of religious difference, that is, less readily evolves into an alternative kind of feeling through domestic union. It also, in the case of Harrington, suggests that the phobias he claims to have outgrown may linger in his psyche, calling into question the rational self-mastery assumed by the bildungsroman.

For her part, Berenice learns pain management as part of a larger process of cultural assimilation. Insofar as it keeps her attached to her father, Berenice's pain limits her capacity to circulate freely, hampering her assumption of the public identity of an English woman. Her father insists that she suppress signs of her feelings, measuring her maturity according to her ability to prove care-free in the face of anti-Semitic hostility. As she disciplines herself Berenice remarks, "You see, I hope, my dear father . . . that I am curing myself of that *morbid sensibility*, that excessive susceptibility to the opinion of others, with which you used to reproach me" (212). The association of the pain and a "morbid sensibility" makes Berenice responsible for curing herself; having feelings or not having feelings becomes an act of self-will, rather than a reaction to the cues of others.

At the same time, Berenice also learns how to read herself as the potential target of anti-Semitic attacks to prevent impolite gestures appearing in the first place: "As soon as Miss Montenero found that her Spanish dress subjected her to the inconvenience of being remarked in public, she laid it aside. I thought she was right in doing so—and in three days' time, though I had at first regretted the picturesque dress, I soon became accustomed to the change" (210–11). Berenice remains different, but she learns to privatize her difference. Berenice will play Hebrew music, for instance, but only before an intimate audience (189–90). In this way her religious difference becomes irrelevant to the larger community, which can accommodate her family as long as the boundary between public and private is protected.[10]

Edgeworth recognizes, I suggest, that the narrative of pain avoidance embedded in the marriage plot aligns itself with an impetus toward conversion and assimilation. Even as the marriage plot unfolds, however, a counterdiscourse appears, one that moves the novel in the opposite direction. It takes as its starting point aesthetics. Embedded in aesthetic experience, Edgeworth suggests, are those bigotries that, at the level of the bildungsroman, the novel dismisses as childish things. The narrative exposes the limits of rational self-control in its examination of art's production and circulation, using as its central example Shakespeare's *Merchant of Venice*.[11] Edgeworth weighs the bad effects and affects art can produce against the value of aesthetic "genius" and both the national and cosmopolitan ideals it sustains. Art becomes the place where the questions of affiliation and identification are negotiated. It also mediates the relation between taste and pain.

Harrington's kind treatment of Berenice at the performance of *The Merchant of Venice* leads to an introduction to her father and a conversation regarding the merits of Shakespeare's play. Mr. Montenero remarks to Harrington, "No Englishman born can have felt more strongly than I have the power of your Shakespeare's genius to touch and rend the human heart." Harrington's national pride is gratified by the foreigner's admiration: "To an Englishman, what accent that conveys the praise of Shakespeare can fail to be agreeable? The most certain method by which a foreigner can introduce himself at once to the good will and good opinion of an Englishman is by thus doing homage to this national object of idolatry." But Montenero goes on to address the play's anti-Semitism as an instance of injustice: "We poor Jews have felt your Shakespeare's power to our cost—too severely—and considering all the circumstances, rather unjustly, you are aware?" (143). He tells Harrington that the story of the pound of flesh that Shylock wants to take from

Antonio's breast reverses the historical case upon which it is based. Originally, he explains, "it was a Christian who insisted upon having a pound of flesh from next the Jew's heart." Shakespeare exploited his audience's anti-Semitism to heighten their response to his play: "It was his business . . . to take advantage of the popular prejudice as a *power*—as a means of dramatic pathos and effect"; Montenero concludes by observing, "Shakespear was right, as a dramatic poet, in reversing the characters" (144). The problem with Montenero's account is the assumption that all art consumers are as self-aware as he. As Peter Logan notes, "Whereas Montenero differentiates dramatic 'power' from factual 'truth,' society in general does not. When moved by dramatic power, society elevates representation to the status of truth."[12] Montenero is not provoked to hate himself by Shakespeare's representation of Jews, but the majority of theatergoers will take away from the play a bigotry deepened by the affective response elicited by the playwright, as the narrative suggests in its representation of the play's reception in London.

While viewing Montenero's painting collection, Harrington bonds with his host over their shared standards of judgment:

> I was relieved and pleased to find that Mr Montenero had none of the jargon of connoisseurship; while his observations impressed me with a high idea of his taste and judgment, they gave me some confidence in my own. I was delighted to find that I understood and could naturally and truly agree with all he said, and that my untutored preferences were what they ought, according to the right rules of art and science, to be. In short, I was proud to find that my taste was in general the same as his and his daughter's. (161)

Taste appears a natural disposition shared by like-minded people: Harrington's "untutored preferences" align with those of the collector who knows his material. Within this frame of reference, art appreciation appears to move along the same lines as the companionate marriage plot—that is, toward the elimination of difference in favor of universal categories of sameness organized around the eradication of pain: "What pleased me far more than Mr Montenero's taste was the liberality and the enlargement of mind I saw in all his opinions and sentiments. There was in him a philosophic calmness and moderation; his reason seemed to have worked against great natural sensibility, perhaps susceptibility, till this calm had become the settled temper of his soul" (161–62). But immediately this model of affiliation is called into question.

The subject at hand is Alonzo Cano, "the Michelangelo of Spain" (163). Mr. Montenero has Cano's paintings on his wall, prompting Harrington to remember an anecdote recounting Cano's act of defiance in the face of a "tasteless lawyer" who fails to recognize the value of an artwork he has commissioned: "Cano dashed his statue to pieces.... The affrighted counsellor fled ... concluding that the man who was bold enough to destroy a saint would have very little remorse in destroying a lawyer" (163). For Harrington, the salient detail is the assertion of genius. But for Montenero, it's the danger of iconoclasm: "'Happily for Cano this story did not reach the ears of the Inquisition,' Mr. Montenero said, 'or he would have been burnt alive'" (163). The Inquisition reminds us of art's embeddedness, its belonging to the particularities of history and place. A brief reference to Cano's "few peculiarities" and a sigh from Berenice reminds Harrington of the artist's virulent anti-Semitism: "I now recollected having heard or read that this painter bore such an antipathy to the Jews that he considered every touch of theirs as contamination" (163–64). The artist is at once a potential target and an accomplice of the Inquisition. Cano's commitment to art and his own independence put him at risk of censorship, but his irrational phobia, housed in fears of contamination, enables his participation in a national hatred.

Harrington's naive confidence in categorical imperatives is belied by how the art objects he contemplates routinely circle back to the painful localities of the body, starting with Antonio's pound of flesh. Edgeworth underscores this point by housing bigotry in the mouth, beginning with the oral tales told by Nurse Fowler to young Harrington about the murder of Christian children transformed into food for consumption ("at their secret feasts and midnight abominations") and distribution: "There was one story ... about a Jew ... who used to sell pork pies; but it was found out at last that the pies were not pork, they were made of the flesh of little children" (70). The dangers of oral tales—remote from the regulatory space of print culture—is mirrored in their horrific content: Jews eating Christian children.[13] But, as the example of Shakespeare suggests, bigotry doesn't require horrific tales to feed its appetite; it will take anything at hand. A mature Harrington watches his mother absorb the anti-Semitic anecdotes recounted by Mrs. Coates: "She would have scorned on any other subject of human life or matters to have allowed the judgement of Mrs Coates to weigh with her.... Such is prejudice! thought I. Prejudice, even in the proudest people, will stoop to accept of nourishment from any hand. Prejudice not only grows on what it feeds upon, but converts everything it meets with into nourishment" (183). The only antidote is to stop the circulation of both simultaneously: when Harrington wants his father to renounce his anti-Semitism, he tells him, "eat your own words" (287).

Maggie Kilgour's insight into the function of incorporation in the Western literary tradition reveals the larger cultural significance of these moments: "Food is the matter that goes in the mouth, words the more refined substance that comes out: the two are differentiated and yet somehow analogous, media exchanged among men."[14] In the anti-Semitic culture *Harrington* describes, the two are not sufficiently differentiated. Indeed, the novel keeps collapsing the distinction to make its point. Food circulates as an exchange object viewed suspiciously across the religious divide. Mrs. Coates, the novel's representative of garden-variety English anti-Semitism, acknowledges her failure to communicate without inflicting pain—"a hundred times I've hurt her [Berenice] to the quick" (182)—but attributes the pain felt to oversensitivity in her interlocutor: "Miss Montenero . . . is a little touchy on the Jewish chapter" (182). She goes on to complain, in front of Berenice, of having to think of "Jew butchers" when planning dinner for the Monteneros: "One can't have pigeons nor hares at one's table" (182). In response to this casual xenophobia, the Monteneros refuse the Coates family's dinner invitation, a move reminiscent of Shylock's pronouncement, "I will not eat with you!" Mrs. Coates concludes not that she has made a faux pas, but that "the Jews is both a very unsocial and a very revengeful people" (183). She stays on the first level of incorporation—the one closest to the body—in her consideration of social relations, moving from the decline of an invitation to the violence of "revenge" in one easy step. In doing so, she reveals how little the English have progressed beyond tales of Jewish cannibalism. Kilgour notes, "The image of cannibalism is frequently connected to the failure of words as a medium, suggesting that people who cannot *talk* to each other *bite* each other."[15] In this novel, speaking and biting are metaphorically linked in the anti-Semitic jibes and insults Edgeworth represents, rendering Christians, rather than Jews, the instigators of violence and wounding.

The narrative circles back to the mouth in its contemplation of the art that Mowbray, looking to capitalize on his mother's penchant for Jew baiting and paintings, buys in order to sell at auction (to his mother, Lady de Brantefield, for great profit). He describes the painting as a "vile daub" and also a suitable companion piece to the de Brantefields' "old picture," *Sir Josseline Going to the Holy Land*: "Did you ever hear of a picture called 'The Dentition of the Jew'? . . . Only the drawing the teeth of the Jew, by order of some of our most merciful Lords, the Kings John, Richard, or Edward. It will be a companion to the old family picture of the Jew and Sir Josseline" (185). The aesthetic value of these paintings, for Lady de Brantefield, resides in the hatred they depict, a tradition that excites nationalism and family pride: "At the Priory everything attested, recorded and flattered her pride of ancient and illustrious descent" (118). The dentition painting brings anti-Semitism forward, historically, for its reference to King John's torture of a Jew finds echoes in the eighteenth-century practice of extracting teeth from the poor and the dead for consumption as dentures in the mouths of the rich. In Thomas Rowlandson's satiric print, *Transplanting of Teeth* (1787), we see a chimney sweep having his teeth pulled. To the right, a young fashionable woman is having the "live" teeth inserted in her mouth. In a doorway, two young people in tattered clothes leave the office, crying in pain.[16] The practice is referenced in the case of the four Jewish criminals executed in 1771, whose tooth extraction and circulation the *Public Advertiser* reports:

> Two eminent Tooth-Drawers of this Town had a Scramble for the Teeth of the four Jews: One of the Gentlemen, however, stealing a March upon the other, had nearly extracted three whole Sets before the second Operator arrived, who was therefore obliged to content himself with the Teeth of the fourth poor Wretch, (the Doctor) which he soon dislocated, and put into his Pocket, and they will probably ere long adorn the Mouths of some of the *Bon Ton*; a Jew's Eye is proverbially precious—why not a Jew's Tooth?[17]

By way of conclusion, the report observes, "The Curiosity and Impatience of the People to see the dead Bodies of the Jews exposed at Surgeons Hall on Tuesday last was so great that it was with the utmost Difficulty that any Gentleman of the Faculty could gain Admittance; the Mob was never so numerous and unruly upon a like Occasion since the Execution of Lord Ferrars."[18] On the one hand, the scene reports voracious greed, dentists fighting over the mouths of the convicts for the valuable resource they can extract from them. On the other hand, the scene records a more generalized preoccupation with the Jewish body as a physiognomy of difference, a spectacle for the curious spectator contemplating the unknown—even though parts of those alien bodies will end up housed in the mouths of that same public.[19]

Edgeworth highlights this obsession with the Jewish body by including an engraver in the story of Mowbray's purchase of the dentition portrait. Mowbray may hope to sell the painting at auction to his mother, but he also plans to profit from a broader circulation of its image by way of the engraver's reproductions, feeding the public's appetite for Jewish suffering. Montenero ends the art object's participation in a wider economy of hate speech by buying the painting at auction and then destroying it: "So perish all that can keep alive

Thomas Rowlandson, *Transplanting of Teeth* (1787)

feelings of hatred and vengeance between Jews and Christians!" he exclaims (190). We are drawn back to Cano's destruction of his own art object as an assertion of independence from the mediocrity of public standards. Here the independence is marked, more particularly, by the financial power Montenero brings to bear on the exchange of art. It is only because he is willing to pay a large amount of money for a worthless painting that he can exercise this authority over it.

Harrington names the act an "*auto da fé*" (191) by way of reversing the power relations between Jews and the Inquisition, but this is not what fire brings to mind in the moment. Rather, Harrington remembers Mowbray's recent burning of a Jewish business in Gibraltar that had employed Jacob, Montenero's servant: "I supposed that [Jacob] was thinking of the fire at which all he had in the world had been consumed," Harrington concludes (191). While the Sephardic art collector is able to curb anti-Semitic violence through his financial power, his act of burning returns us to persistence of the pogrom. John Plotz argues that Edgeworth establishes, in this scene, stable boundaries between Jewish and Christian households: "Buy Murillos to hoard them, buy hate-art to destroy it: in both cases you have used liquidity to reinforce the dry stability of the safely separate household."[20] But I suggest it more powerfully recognizes the ties between violence, art, and dispossession. Pain is not easily relocated elsewhere when our tastes and possessions are so tightly bound to it.

Montenero's belief that art can overcome the forces of darkness is challenged by evidence to the contrary, as is Harrington's belief that romantic love can overcome all obstacles. Edgeworth is attracted to these beliefs, but she is also aware of their limits. What follows traces the practices of art and marriage that create space for an alternative account of love, aesthetics, and tolerance.

Interfaith Marriage and the Traffic in Art

Montenero achieves the status of "gentleman" in the same way he hopes "genius" can sustain art—by transcending the local: "He had that indescribable air which, independently of the fashion of the day or the mode of any particular country, distinguishes a gentleman—dignified, courteous and free from affectation. From his figure, you might have thought him a Spaniard—from his complexion, an East Indian; but he had a peculiar cast of countenance which seemed not to belong to either nation" (142). His style attaches him to European standards of taste, his skin to an exotic Orient. But his countenance, where temperament and the mind reside, escapes regional description. His "knowledge," Mr. Lyons tells Harrington, "had given a certain suavity and polish to his manners, in which particular *casts* of people . . . are apt to be deficient" (108). Those features that elevate Montenero above the limits of "cast" render him more an observer of the Inquisition he lived through than its victim. Mr. Lyons tells Harrington that "born in Spain, [Mr. Montenero] . . . had early in life quitted that country in consequence of his horror of tyranny and persecution" (108)—a description that registers less an experience of persecution than a formal protest of its principles. Montenero's first conversation with Harrington maintains the same critical distance to its practices: "From *Don Quixote* to *Gil Blas*—to the Duc de Lerma—to the Tower of Segovia—to the Inquisition—to the Spanish palaces and Moorish antiquities, he let me lead him backwards and forwards as I pleased" (148). Here the Inquisition is lumped in with the literature and architecture of Spain, just one more object suitable for contemplation. It is only when Montenero appears as a member of a community that the persecution he has suffered comes into focus. Jacob tells Harrington that "the Manessas had formerly been settled in Spain, at the time Mr. Montenero had lived there; and, when he was in some difficulties with the Inquisition, [they] had in some way essentially served him, either in assisting his escape from that country or in transmitting his property" (159). Persecution becomes real when witnessed by a social collective. The rest of the time it remains a mental obstacle to be defeated by a rational fortitude that fosters social independence.

This independence is writ large in Montenero's art collection. It is a sign of a refined taste that Montenero appreciates the aesthetic value of his Christian art works, even those created by an anti-Semite. But for the larger English community in which he finds himself, the value of the collection registers only in financial terms. No one asks to see his art except Harrington. When Montenero offers to show Harrington's mother an original Murillo, of which she has a print, she replies "in those general terms of acquiescence and gratitude which are used when there is no real intention to accept an invitation" (149). An opening in the wall that separates the Montenero and Harrington families appears only when Mr. Montenero offers to use his art collection as collateral against the risk of bank failure that threatens to ruin Mr. Harrington: "My collection of Spanish pictures ... have been estimated by your best English connoisseurs at £60,000. Three English noblemen are at this moment ready to pay down £30,000 for a few of these pictures. This will secure Mr Harrington's demand on this house" (261). The universal language that breaks down the barriers between the Englishman and Spaniard is the language of commerce, not of politeness or taste. "On hearing the name [Montenero]," Harrington Sr. recounts, "I am sure my look would have said plain enough to any man alive but Baldwin [the banker] that I did not choose to be introduced; but Baldwin has no breeding" (259). Global capital, in the end, forces Mr. Harrington into a relationship with a Jew, whose generous terms provide a starting point for a new attitude toward Berenice: "I now for the first time understood that the daughter was in the house; and I certainly felt a curiosity to see her" (262). She appears a possible gift in the economy of marriage exchange: "If there was any chance of the girl's conversion, even he would overlook the father's being a Jew, as he was such a noble fellow" (263).

Montenero's art collection is valuable because it is rare, and it is rare because Spaniards do not like to share their art with the world: "Few of Murillo's paintings had at this time made their way out of Spain; national and regal pride had preserved them with jealous care" (148). The Spaniards' attachment to their paintings shows the same national pride in their art that Harrington earlier displayed when Montenero praised Shakespeare. But this pride is excessive; "jealous care" suggests an irrational possessiveness that exceeds art appreciation. The attachment to visual objects, further, registers differently than does an attachment to Shakespeare, whose texts can circulate widely in a print economy, regardless of national origin. Paintings, by contrast, lend themselves more readily to hoarding, and intimations of Catholic iconophilia here color the Spaniards' relation to art.

The Montenero family found a way to bring the Murillos out of Spain: "Mr. Montenero had, from an intermarriage in a noble Spanish family, inherited some of Murillo's masterpieces, which, with a small but valuable collection of Spanish pictures he had been many years in forming, he had brought with him to England" (148). To be a cosmopolitan is to circulate art in a global arena, to remove paintings from the clutches of the Spanish so that the wider world can see them. It is also, in this instance, to marry across religious lines—someone in the Monteneros' Jewish family married into the Catholic Spanish aristocracy. Here we return to the history that we examined in chapter 2. Jerome Friedman references the frequency of intermarriage between "Old Christians" and *conversos*—Jewish converts to Christianity—in early modern Spain: "Many, if not most, mixed freely in society and were evidently well enough accepted into the noble and wealthy merchant families intermarrying with them."[21] The *converso* marriage to a Spanish "Old Christian" was always, categorically, an interfaith marriage, since the distinction between "Old" and "New" remained in place regardless of the particular faith or cultural practices of the convert. But the evidence suggests that *converso* marriages often *were* mixed in practice—not just categorically. According to Yirmiyahu Yovel, before 1492 "it was an open secret that many *conversos* continued, in some degree, to practice their religion" in ostensibly Christian households; likewise, in some Jewish homes, "one spouse was Jewish and the other Christian."[22] The hybridity of the *converso* subject was a common focal point for anti-Semitism. Friedman notes that "in the minds of many Spaniards, many if not all Marranos (converts to Christianity) were crypto-Jews performing Jewish ceremonies at home while outwardly conforming to Christian demeanor."[23] In the 1480s, after Isabella assumed the throne, the Spanish Inquisition took the *converso* community as its particular target, fearing hybridity more than Judaism itself before the expulsion of the Jews in 1492.[24] Ironically, the expulsion decree led to a new wave of conversions: "Although something like 175,000 Jews left Spain in the spring and summer of 1492, another 100,000 chose to convert during those last final months of panic."[25] For the next three hundred years, there were no Jews in Spain, only *conversos*.

It is not clear that Edgeworth was aware of the history of the Sephardim. When we first hear of Montenero, he is introduced as "a Jewish gentleman born in Spain, who had early in life quitted that country, in consequence of his horror of tyranny and persecution" (108). Later, he tells the Harrington family that he married Berenice's mother, the Protestant daughter of a British diplomat posted in Spain. But, historically, he could not have been living in Spain as a Jew in the time period the novel describes, nor could he have married a Christian woman there unless he were a *converso*. Other British writers were aware of *converso* culture. Richard Cumberland devotes three stories in the *Observer* to Nicholas Pedrosa, a crypto-Jew who finds himself in front of an Inquisition panel after his donkey tramples some priests: "He was not long to seek for the cause of his misfortune: his adventures with the barefooted friars was a ready solution of all difficulties of that nature, had there been any; there was however another thing, which might have troubled a stouter heart than Nicholas's—he was a Jew—."[26] It is possible that Edgeworth was aware of this history but decided to telescope it to reference, more simply, the Inquisition and the forced migrations of Jews throughout early modern European history. Within this frame of reference, "Spanish Jew" identifies Montenero as a member of a cosmopolitan, wealthy community. Interfaith marriage represents the tolerance of this community, which, in the case of the Montenero family, extends back into earlier generations.

The story of the paintings suggests that interfaith marriage does not, in Edgeworth's mind, lead to conversion and assimilation. We know, from the narrative, that the Catholic Spanish nobility keep their paintings close to home; we also know that the Jew who married into that nobility bequeathed the art to his or her Jewish family. The art takes on new meaning when it leaves the country. Its expression of Spanish national "genius" becomes part of a global art market when the paintings constitute the moveable wealth of a displaced people. The secrecy of the paintings' export mirrors the secrecy of the modern banknote, whose history Montenero explains to his daughter: "The tyranny which drove us from place to place, and from country to country . . . compelled us by necessity to the invention of a happy expedient by which we could convert all our property into a scrap of paper, which could be carried, unseen, in a pocket-book, or conveyed in a letter, unsuspected" (179). In the case of the paintings, an interfaith marriage allows a Jewish spouse to smuggle art out from a Christian family; an interfaith marriage, in other words, creates the conditions for the emergence of a global art market.

Aesthetic genius, rather than standing apart from practices of cultural exclusion, turns out to be embedded in them. In his reading of *The Merchant of Venice*, James Shapiro notes the ironic inflection that adheres to the dictum that Shakespeare's plays "were not of an age, but for all time" in light of the persistence of anti-Semitism across the centuries.[27] In *Harrington*, interfaith marriage gives the lie to the image of the detached, disinterested man of taste. "Follow the art," we might say, and the particular configurations of xenophobia that shaped its making and circulation will come into view. More immediately, marriage brings into focus those aspects of Montenero's singularity that remain necessarily untranslatable, speaking, as they do, to the persistence of a religious affiliation understood as private in one register and as veiled in secrecy in another.

John Plotz has argued that the reserve of the Montenero family represents a "domestic insularity" that would go on to define Victorian bourgeois ideology: "It has often been said that Napoleon made the British nation; it has less often been argued that the British middle class was made by Jews."[28] He identifies Berenice as part of a Jewish collection of precious objects, properly preserved in the domestic sphere until ready for circulation.[29] Indeed, Harrington considers Berenice a "great object": "Here was a woman who could fill my whole soul; who could at once touch my heart and my imagination" (165). He associates her "picturesque and graceful" (210) Spanish dress and veil with "painting and poetry" (209). Her reserve constitutes part of this appeal: "There was a timid sensibility in her countenance when I spoke to her which, joined to the feminine reserve of her whole manner, the tone of her voice and the propriety and elegance of the very little she said, pleased me inexpressibly" (160). Harrington dreams of converting Berenice, a conversion that would render her reserve a sign of a properly Christian religious interiority. Like Harrington, Mowbray considers Berenice a "great object." But unlike Harrington, he remains indifferent to her content. He looks at her in the same way the bank views Mr. Montenero's paintings, as capital: "Two hundred thousand pounds, Miss Montenero is, I think they say" (200). The proper circulation of capital, in this instance, requires an emptying of religious content. Mowbray entertains the possibility of conversion to Judaism for convenience—"I should make it a point of conscience to turn Jew, to please the fair Jewess, if requisite" (202). Mowbray's indifference to religious identity renders him part of the blank fashionable society that Harrington earlier juxtaposed to the particularities of an older generation in his description of Lady Anne and Lady de Brantefield. The absence of faith renders him a cipher.

Berenice gives nothing away to either man, and, when we read her reserve against the backdrop of the Inquisition, it sets her against both Mowbray's religious indifference and Harrington's dream of conversion. We learn, late in the narrative, that she has been hoarding a secret shared only by her father—the secret of her (maternal) Protestant identity. Her secret keeping, I suggest, can be considered a Sephardic legacy, transmitted paternally. In this register, conventions of sympathetic identification take on an additional aspect. We read, "When her father spoke, it seemed to be almost the same as if she spoke herself, her sympathy with him appeared so strongly." The closeness of father and daughter represents a correspondence in feeling here. When read alongside other moments of exchange, however, it becomes part of a larger system of communication that facilitates the transmission of private knowledge to a select interlocutor. Montenero registers the anti-Semitic rudeness of Mrs. Harrington, for instance, only through small, barely perceptible gestures: "Mr. Montenero bowed his head courteously, removed his eyes from my face, and glanced for one moment at Miss Montenero with a look of regret, quickly succeeded by an expression in his countenance of calm and proud independence" (160). These secret engagements link the cosmopolitan gentleman and his daughter to a network of communications established over generations of persecution.

So far, I have shown how the novel's representations of the companionate marriage as a form of pain management and its endorsement of cosmopolitan disinterestedness are complicated by Edgeworth's awareness of the body's proximity to taste and bigotry. The companionate marriage will not prove painless should it take on religious difference. Interfaith marriage brings the novel's discussion of art and marriage together in the story of the Sephardim and the Spanish Inquisition, gift exchanges and global economies. Men approach both women and art as "great objects"; how they define that objectification marks the difference between proper and improper modes of appreciation. Finally, we have seen how Berenice lives the history of her Jewish family in her negotiations, with her father, of British anti-Semitism. The interfaith marriages that have brought the Sephardim into alliances with Catholic and Protestant families have not resulted in the eradication of Jewish identity. To the contrary, they create a way of protecting that identity by foregrounding the obligations of the conjugal unit to sustain and protect the vulnerable members of a family. Edgeworth's admiration for the politeness and cosmopolitan aesthetics of the Sephardim, I am suggesting, points to the intimacy of marriage as a starting point for an embodied form of tolerance. But interfaith marriage requires a larger community to sustain this ethics. That community, in *Harrington*, is imagined through the Jewish Enlightenment rooted in the philosophy of Moses Mendelssohn.

Ashkenazi Enlightenment

Alexandra Walsham identifies the shift in Hanoverian England to a focus on the "social exclusiveness and foreignness" of religious minorities: "Less attention is paid to their theological error than their political orientation and their association with 'strangers' and 'aliens.'"[30] This shift coincided with an influx of Ashkenazi Jews into London between 1700 and 1835.[31] Although there were some Iberian immigrants who also arrived in England with little, the Sephardi poor were, according to Todd Endelman, "in absolute terms, insignificant in comparison to the Ashkenazi poor."[32] The opening pages of *Harrington* represent the Ashkenazim through the figure of the peddler Simon, who inadvertently plants the seeds of Harrington's phobia. Catherine Gallagher has suggested that the novel's Jews "are inverted renderings of the Anglo-Irish" and that the narrative makes every effort to transform "the ragpickers" into "cosmopolitan financiers" in order "to brighten the image of the 'middle nation' to which Edgeworth belonged."[33] I suggest that the Ashkenazim serve less as a starting point from which the novel moves forward than as the second strand of Jewish DNA in the novel, woven together with the Sephardim. The suffering that Simon and his son Jacob endure is of a different order than that of the Monteneros, and it leads us to Moses Mendelssohn, the Jewish Enlightenment's most important philosopher. The story of Mendelssohn, I suggest, provides an alternative model of storytelling and sociability, one that extends the affective and aesthetic reach of the Monteneros' cosmopolitan ideals.[34]

From the opening pages of the novel, Edgeworth associates *The Merchant of Venice* with violence, starting with the (Christian) beggars who masquerade as Simon the rag collector to profit from Harrington's childhood phobia, playing "a malicious, revengeful, ominous-looking Shylock as ever whetted his knife" (79). Shakespeare's "genius" is here dragged into the gutter, rendered "vulgar" by the criminals' performances—but the cruelty of Shylock is no different from that which Harrington later witnesses on the stage when the role is played by the accomplished actor Charles Macklin. The antidote to the vengeful Jewish figure appears in the character of Simon's son, Jacob. Jacob is introduced to the story as a boy selling goods at the school Harrington attends. Jacob responds to the torment he suffers at the hands of Harrington and his friends by enduring it, rather than retaliating: "He was a Jew as unlike to Shylock as it is possible to conceive . . . ; he stood patient and longsuffering, and even of this patience and resignation we made a jest and subject of fresh reproach and taunt" (90). Jacob's stoicism turns outward when he is asked to reveal the name of his father. He refuses to do so, because to disclose his name will bring Simon into view, if only as a memory, for Harrington. In the schoolyard, Jacob's suffering not only protects Harrington, but also furthers his journey away from the early childhood phobia toward the sympathetic identification he feels when Jacob suffers. When Mowbray submits Jacob to torture at the fireplace, Harrington involuntarily responds: "Jacob was resolutely silent; he would not tell his father's name. He stood it, till I could stand it no longer, and I insisted upon Mowbray's letting him off" (97). Here, Jacob's ability to endure pain allows the pain to take hold in Harrington's imagination, as it does when Harrington watches Berenice at the performance of Shakespeare's play, a few years later.

Harrington next meets Jacob as a young man on the road to Cambridge. Jacob is on his last tour as a peddler: "His friend, the London jeweller, had recommended him to his brother, a rich Jew who had a valuable store in Gibraltar" (101). Jacob's distance from the underworld that his father inhabited is marked by his proximity to print culture. Harrington encounters him "by the road-side, reading very intently" (100). Jacob gives Harrington the magazine he is reading, which contains a biography of Moses Mendelssohn: "I soon perceived why the life of Mendelssohn had so deeply interested poor Jacob. Mendelssohn was a Jew born like himself in abject poverty, who by vigorous perseverance made his way through incredible difficulties to the highest literary reputation among the most eminent men of his country and of his age." The life of Mendelssohn recasts the life of the poor Jew as one of virtue and religious principle. We learn of the friendship that guided Mendelssohn through his early life as a reader. On the streets of Berlin, Harrington reads, Mendelssohn met "a young Jew as poor, as ardently fond of literature, and better informed than himself, who undertook to instruct him; and the two friends, sitting in a corner of a retired street in Berlin, used to study together a Hebrew Euclid" (103). Sociable philosophy, rather than crime, is the legacy of Mendelssohn's Ashkenazi poverty.

The visible sign of Mendelssohn's thinking is his suffering body: "With this unpropitious place for study and this low beginning, still he worked on, and in time he compassed learning Latin. With infinite labour, spending sometimes hours over one page, he read Locke in a Latin version. And under and through all these obstacles, he thought and suffered, and suffered and thought, and persevered, till at last he made himself one of the first philosophical writers of his country" (103). Locke's only Latin publication was the *Letter*

Concerning Toleration, a detail that resonates as Mendelssohn develops his own theory of religious tolerance. Pain, in this instance, is generative, expanding the body's capacity to think difference. Thinking and suffering, suffering and thinking—these energies provide an alternative theory of religious identity to that of the detached cosmopolitan Enlightenment subject.[35]

Reading Mendelssohn's biography provides Harrington with a Jewish Enlightenment philosophy. But it is Jacob who serves as his guide to the intricacies of British anti-Semitism. His story of persecution continues beyond the schoolyard and into his adult life, when he is victimized again by Mowbray, in Gibraltar. Jacob tells Harrington, "His first words at meeting me in the public streets were, 'So, are you here? Young Shylock! what brings you to Gibraltar? you are of the tribe of Gad, I think, you *Wandering Jew!*'" (155). For Mowbray, all Jews are nationless Shylocks. A riot in Gibraltar leads to the destruction of the family business that employs Jacob. His reflections on the event reveal the complicity of the British judiciary and British anti-Semitism. Harrington views the Gibraltar incident as an unfortunate aberration whose violence would have been punished by the law had Jacob come forward. He tells Jacob, "If Lord Mowbray had been complained of by Mr Manessa, a court martial would have been held; . . . Jacob said his poor master, who was ruined and in despair, thought not of court-martials— . . . perhaps he . . . dared not, being a Jew, appear against a Christian officer" (157–58). Unlike Harrington, Jacob understands how high up the social ladder English anti-Semitism goes. By contrast, Harrington appears naive, unable to fully comprehend what Jacob is trying to communicate about English xenophobia.[36] Jacob's understanding of the law's bias enables him to develop alternative methods of coping with systemic social and economic injustice.

The ugliness of English anti-Semitism surfaces again in the representation of the Gordon Riots.[37] The narrative describes the riots as a temporary madness fomented by "the most ridiculous reports" of Catholic conspiracies and "the most absurd terrors" of a French invasion. The madness grows even more "ludicrous" (234) when the anti-Catholic mob turns against London's Jews. "Without any conceivable reason, suddenly a cry was raised against the Jews"—a result of an unfortunate rhyme: "'Jews' rhymed to 'shoes' . . . and the cry was '*No Jews, no wooden shoes!*' Thus, without any natural, civil, religious, moral, or political connection, the poor Jews came into remainder to the ancient anti-gallican antipathy felt by English feet and English fancies against the French wooden shoes" (235–36). Sarah Winter argues that Edgeworth, by representing the mob's anti-Semitism as the offshoot of an already arbitrary and random mental aberration, "seems to render mob violence a merely accidental outgrowth of such irrationality—almost a coincidence—and thus seemingly diminishes the social and political dimensions of the rioters' anti-Semitism."[38] But I suggest that Edgeworth highlights the fact that the English don't need a reason to attack Jews, so deep seated is their antipathy. As in the Gibraltar scene, the Gordon Riots draw attention to the alacrity with which Christians set upon their Jewish neighbors.

The antidote to the chants and violence of the rioters lies in the imaginative capacity of their opponents. During the riots, the Montenero family is protected by the oddly named "Widow Levy," an Irish Catholic Orangewoman who is the beneficiary of "Mr Montenero's bounty and . . . Jacob's punctual care" (236).[39] Jacob's alliance with her draws on their shared facility in navigating the street. "The orange-woman delivered your letter and the military are coming," Jacob tells Montenero. "She told me how to get in here" (247). The Widow Levy diverts the rioters who approach the Montenero home with "blunder and bravado, and flattery and *fabling*" (237), redirecting imaginations seduced by anti-Semitic stories such as those told by Nurse Fowler in the novel's opening pages.[40]

In contrast to Jacob and the Widow Levy, Montenero remains vulnerable to the mob's vicissitudes even after it has dispersed. The day after the riots, he is accused of having killed a member of the crowd: "Now, the fact was that no shot had ever been fired by Mr Montenero, but such was the rage of the people at the idea that the Jew had killed a Christian, . . . that the voice of truth could not be heard" (249–50). Harrington proves the gun was never fired, and Montenero is released, both from the court and from the mob. Harrington concludes that justice prevails: "The mob is always in favour of truth and innocence wherever these are made evident to their senses" (252). But the riots proved the opposite. The Jews have nothing to do with the occasion of the Gordon Riots, but the British sensibility tells them that they are appropriate objects of violence, nonetheless. Harrington's confidence in the rule of law rings hollow. What we take, instead, from this scene is the precarity of even wealthy men like Montenero.

After the riots, when the de Brantefield family emerges yet again to menace Jacob, accusing him and his associates of theft, it is Jacob's imagination that foils them. Like the Widow Levy, Jacob proves adept at fabling. He and Harrington plan a visit to the pawnshop where they believe Lady de Brantefield's lost ring may be hiding. Jacob dresses Harrington for the part of a pawnshop regular. "'Now you shall see how well at one stroke I will disguise the gentleman,'"

Jacob tells him. "Jacob then twisted a dirty silk handkerchief round my throat, and this did the business so completely that I defied the pawnbroker and all his penetration" (276). Jacob's creative powers draw on his experiences as a child of the streets. As in the opening pages of the narrative, street art seems particularly potent in its transformative powers. In this instance, they serve as a corrective to, rather than an extension of, the banality of anti-Semitic performances.

Jacob is both of the crowd and distinct from it. Peter Logan suggests that in its efforts to teach its readers a lesson in tolerance, "this narrative addresses a reader who, like Harrington, has already found a way to escape the crowd and become like Montenero."[41] But Harrington has more to learn from Jacob than he does from Montenero precisely because, as Logan's reading of *Harrington* shows, the model of critical detachment that Montenero represents has its limits: "Without Harrington's clearly defined hysteria, Montenero's objectivity is vulnerable to collapse, which is exactly what the narrator describes."[42] Despite his suffering at the hands of the Spanish Inquisition, Montenero cannot quite grasp English bigotry because it does not map onto individualized minds. His attachment to American individualism, where religious differences are viewed as "things which do not affect the moral character," prevents him from recognizing how a collective unconscious houses itself in the British body politic (145). Proximity, in America, breeds familiarity and respect because the nation imagines itself as a collectivity of autonomous subjects, according to Montenero. In England, however, this model is belied by the fact that proximity has done nothing to improve Jewish-Christian relations. Neighborliness, in Europe, requires more than what an ethics of politeness and a respect for privacy can provide.

Jacob, I am suggesting, better grasps the facts of coexistence. Unsurprisingly, it is his discovery of Lady de Brantefield's ring that leads to a Pandora's box of revelations, recounted as a series of storytellings. Mrs. Fowler's secret concerning Mowbray's plot to destroy Harrington is revealed first to Harrington's mother: "My mother was so eager to learn the secret concerning me that she promised to obtain a pardon from Lady de Brantefield for the delinquent" (279). Significantly, it is Mrs. Harrington, earlier discredited as a hysteric, who carries the plot forward from here: "We agreed that my mother was the fittest person to break the matter to poor Lady de Brantefield. If my mother should not feel herself equal to the task, my father said he would undertake it himself, though he had rather have a tooth pulled out than go through it" (281). The reference to tooth pulling reminds us, once again, of the proximity of narrative to pain housed in the mouth. But Mrs. Harrington can manage that pain better than her husband: "My mother rose and said that she would tell the plain fact" (283). Even more importantly, she gathers Montenero into her home so that he, too, can hear the story that involves him so intimately: "My mother's carriage was at the door, it was by this time the hour for visiting. 'I will bring Mr Montenero back with me,' said my mother, 'for I am going to pay a visit I should have paid long ago—to Miss Montenero!'" (287). The scene of narration restores the principles of neighborliness compromised by the riots. With Montenero before them, the revelation of Mowbray's deception produces, initially, "an embarrassing moment of silence," as Harrington's parents contemplate their treatment of the family in the light cast by Mowbray's depravity. Again, Mrs. Harrington moves the conversation forward: "My mother broke [the silence] by saying something about Miss Montenero" (289). Harrington Sr., in turn, renounces his past bigotry: "My prejudices against the Jews I give up—you have conquered them—all, all" (290).

I will revisit the significance of women's storytelling below. But first let's return to the figure of Jacob, who appears at the moment Harrington is ready to leave the house to propose to Berenice. As he has from the early pages of the narrative, Jacob facilitates the crossing of boundaries. In this instance, new social bonds are forged by the gift of a ring: "He begged me, with some hesitation, to accept of a ring which Mr Manessa his partner and he took the liberty of offering me as a token of their gratitude. It was not of any great value, but it was finished by an artist who was supposed to be one of the best in the world" (292). This gift stands at the opposite end of the spectrum from Mr. Montenero's Cano painting. It has no value as an object of exchange other than that conferred by the tradesmen who recognize the skill of the artist who contributed to its making. That is, the beauty of the ring is context specific. Where the beauty of Cano's painting must overcome the hatred of its maker by becoming a disinterested representative of aesthetic genius, here the gratitude of the gift giver contributes to the beauty of the object. As a gift for Berenice, it becomes not only a love token but a sign of a larger moment of communal bonding: "Berenice accepted of the ring in the most gracious, the most graceful manner. 'I accept this with pleasure,' said she, 'I shall prize it more than ever Lady de Brantefield valued her ring: as a token of goodness and gratitude, it will be more precious to me than any jewel could be—and it will ever be dear to me,' added she, with a softened voice, turning to her father; 'very dear, as a memorial to the circumstances which have removed the only obstacle to our happiness'" (293). Berenice's ring marks her belonging not only to Harrington as his betrothed but her belonging to the Jewish community that includes Jacob and her father. Berenice's gift is not Lady de Brantefield's "inestimable ring" (277), fetishized as symbol of family purity and exclusivity, of the ability of the powerful to inflict pain on others. Berenice's ring, by contrast, stands both as a symbol of freedom from that persecution and as a corrective to the forms of possessiveness that foster it.[43]

Jacob's gift returns us to *The Merchant of Venice* and the ring narrative that advances Shakespeare's comic plot. Where in the play the ring allows the Christian women to practice an elaborate joke on their men, here the ring stands not for skepticism but for sincerity, an antidote to the kinds of fictions woven by anti-Semites like Mowbray. The juxtaposition of this ring story to Shakespeare's speaks to the scrutiny of *Merchant* that *Harrington* undertakes. In particular, by refusing the terms that govern Jessica's conversion narrative, Edgeworth makes room for an alternative model of marriage and, more broadly, familial and religious identity.

The revelation that Berenice is, after all, not Jewish but Christian, daughter of a Protestant Englishwoman, is embedded in a story about sincerity and the marriage plot. Montenero describes the secret of Berenice's true identity as a religious test for potential suitors: "My daughter was determined never to marry any man who could be induced to sacrifice religion and principle to interest or to passion. She was equally determined never to marry any man whose want of the spirit of toleration, whose prejudices against the Jews, might interfere with the filial affection she feels for her father—though he be a Jew" (291). Since the narrative never reveals the content of Berenice's mind, it's difficult to see how Harrington has passed the first test: we don't discover what convinces Berenice that Harrington is a true Christian who will not disavow his faith to marry a Jew. Presumably, he *was* willing to test the limits of his confessional allegiance by allowing himself to fall in love with a Jewish woman. While the reader knows that Harrington hoped for Berenice's conversion as a way around this problem, she cannot know this. In the face of this lacuna, the pressure of the test falls more heavily on its second half, regarding Berenice's allegiance to her father. Here Berenice can read the results more readily by measuring the presence or absence of antipathy toward Montenero. This affiliation, I suggest, becomes her test of religious sincerity.

The question of daughterly attachment—or lack thereof—frames the first conversion recounted in *The Merchant of Venice*. Critics of Shakespeare's play have identified how Jessica's opposition to Shylock shores up *Merchant*'s anti-Semitism, setting the daughter's "willing" conversion against her father's forced one.⁴⁴ They have also noted the problems that attend Jessica's conversion. Janet Adelman suggests that Jessica's representation casts light on the Spanish blood laws initiated to deal with concerns about the "purity" of New Christians: "The play's repeated insistence that Jessica cannot escape her father's blood puts Jessica in the company of the *conversos*, Jewish whether or not they convert."⁴⁵ Shakespeare attempts to mitigate against this association, Adelman suggests, by whitening Jessica, an effort that goes only so far to ameliorate anxieties about passing. As Brett Hirsch observes, "Jessica may be 'fair' and 'gentle,' but she is—at least in the eyes of the Christians in the play—still her father's daughter, and as such she will never *be* gentile."⁴⁶ Shakespeare's play hovers anxiously over the conversion, hoping it will stick but unsure that it can.

Catherine Gallagher notes that in *Harrington*, "Berenice is early presented as an anti-Jessica, a daughter who refuses to betray and abandon her Jewish father."⁴⁷ Where Shakespeare goes white, Edgeworth goes dark. Berenice is read as "East Indian" when she first appears in London, as is Montenero, whom Mrs. Harrington first addresses as "Mr. Clive, from India" (135, 147). Where Jessica protests her conversion, Berenice remains silent on the subject of her religious identity.⁴⁸ Our only knowledge of it comes from Montenero's disclosure. This silence, I suggest, takes on particular significance in light of the fact that we've read Berenice as the Jewish daughter of a Jewish father for the entirety of the novel. As Michael Scrivener points out, "Berenice contains the two religions, the experience of being both an insider and an outsider."⁴⁹ As Harrington's wife, her affiliation will remain Jewish insofar as she includes her father in the terms of her marriage. The novel's earlier accounts of interfaith marriages, I have been arguing, support Susan Manly's claim that "the hybridity represented by Berenice remains in the foreground, so that Jewishness is not, as some have suggested, erased."⁵⁰ A hybrid identity, Regina Hewitt notes, "suggests less linear and bifurcated notions of what people can be and what relationships they can form."⁵¹ Interfaith marriage sustains this vision of hybridity by foregrounding the affiliations born of attachment and identification.

As an Anglo-Irish woman, Maria Edgeworth was well versed in the politics of blended identities. She was also alert as to how they might sustain her literary ambitions. In *Harrington*, Edgeworth maps the trajectory of tolerance onto the rise of the woman author in the eighteenth century. When discussing the vapidity of Lady Anne Mowbray, for example, the narrative tells us that "female conversation in general was at this time very different from what it is in our happier days. . . . [F]emale literature . . . had not, as it has now, become general in almost every rank of life" (123–24). The quality of female literature mirrors that of Jacob's ring. In the place of the high art of Shakespeare, Cano, and Murillo, Edgeworth advocates for a ring of great artistry but no "value." The ring finds its textual equivalent in the revised *Merchant* that *Harrington* as a whole represents, a revision made explicit in the novel's final lines. Here, it is the Christians who echo the vengeance of Shylock in the earlier play. When, in response, Montenero counsels patience, Harrington exclaims, "None but a good Christian could do this!" Berenice provides the corrective: "And why not a good Jew?" (295). In this moment, Berenice stands in for Edgeworth, revising Shakespeare and his cultural legacy.

The novel's conclusion, in other words, celebrates the modernization of Shakespeare by a woman author.[52] Edgeworth is an interloper in a male tradition, an editor whose revisions bring to light an alternative narrative, one directed toward the emancipation of both "Shylock" and "Jessica" from the prison of English anti-Semitism. This emancipation, I have suggested here, begins with one mixed marriage and then incorporates another. These marriages retain, rather than disavow, the attachments of the family of origin. The Sephardic Jew who marries into Spanish nobility makes sure Spanish wealth, in the form of an art collection, flows back into the Jewish birth family. The Englishwoman who marries the Sephardic Jew and moves to America maintains her faith rather than converting to her husband's. The novel's conclusion withholds a third mixed marriage but sustains the model of hybridity that the earlier unions bring into view. Toleration requires the intimacy of family relations, including the pain of religious difference, to generate feelings powerful enough to counter those that attend bigotry bred in the bone. It requires the recalibration of the codes of affiliation that attend the companionate marriage and institutional religion. Networks of sociability align the couple and the family, high culture and low, Jewish and Christian Enlightenments, to form a larger kinship structure, one fostered by an embodied practice of neighborly relations.

CONCLUSION

Mansfield Park Closes Its Gates

> "You could not tolerate what you were not used to."
> —Jane Austen, Mansfield Park *(1814)*

British Parliament extended religious toleration to Catholics twelve years after Maria Edgeworth published *Harrington*, in 1829. For England's Jewish community, emancipation came a generation later, in 1858. I have argued that the political history of religious toleration reveals only a partial picture of how tolerance came to be imagined in modern Britain. The eighteenth-century novel tells another, more complicated story about the challenges of peaceful coexistence. Its representations of interfaith marriage, I suggest, expose the limits of political philosophy and show how the public/private divide it maintains shapes both religious and gender identity in the British Enlightenment. By foregrounding women's right to liberty of conscience, the interfaith marriage counters the privatization of religious affect and the naturalization of women's subordination in marriage. Further, interfaith marriage challenges the idea of family religious conformity as the foundation upon which toleration in the public sphere can rest. Instead, we see how a deeper species of tolerance must emerge from a recognition of women and religious minorities as political subjects. The pain of interfaith marriage reminds us that only through an embodied practice that brings us into intimate proximity with religious alterity can we learn what tolerance feels like. We have seen, in the novels studied here, how religious alterity refuses the comforts afforded by terms like "soul mate," requiring instead an acknowledgment of the lover's unfamiliarity. To build a home with a "stranger" is to learn, not once, but over and over again, the hard art of acknowledging difference. The failures of this plot signal the difficulty of maintaining the practice of tolerance, but they also reveal, in the counterfactual stories they entertain, the conditions for an alternative resolution to the challenges it poses. The interfaith marriage plot thus invites us to review the terms governing our narratives of marriage and community, and the ethics of sociability that sustain them.

I identify Maria Edgeworth's *Harrington* as the endpoint of a history whose cultural roots reach into the 1640s. Richardson's *Sir Charles Grandison* serves as the fulcrum between Milton's *Discipline and Doctrine of Divorce*, with which I began, and *Harrington*, where I end my investigation of the interfaith marriage plot. By way of conclusion, I turn to another woman author for whom Richardson's *Grandison* served as a foundational text: Jane Austen. The chasm that separates *Mansfield Park*, written just three years before *Harrington*, and Edgeworth's novel speaks to the religious stakes of the companionate marriage plot with which Austen has come to be synonymous. In *Mansfield Park*, Austen characterizes the possibility of a marriage between Edmund Bertram and Mary Crawford as a marriage of minds whose religious principles differ in a fundamental and, ultimately, irreconcilable ways. What has proven puzzling to many critics is the vilification of Mary Crawford, a character whose vivacity and wit resembles that of so many of Austen's heroines, including Emma. Austen sacrifices the independence of such a mind, I believe, for the sake of communal standards organized around Anglican hegemony, closing the gates on the demands for religious emancipation that threatened the traditional alliance of church and state in the early nineteenth century.

Mansfield Park shows us starkly how religious and sexual orthodoxies shape each other in relation to questions of tolerance—and how the maintenance of community requires, in this instance, the suppression of any skepticism regarding Anglicanism's ability to foster strong communal bonds. Mary Crawford is the voice of dissent, which Austen rewrites as a species of illicit female speech. In a recent essay, Hannah Lee Rogers describes a shift, in late Austen, from tolerance to intolerance. *Emma*, she observes, secures its community in a country house culture that fosters hospitality toward strangers through tasteful marriage regulation. *Persuasion* loosens the tie between community and property, using disgust to secure the boundaries of national culture as it moves out into the world. Rogers's insightful readings identify the paradox of this trajectory. Even as Austen moves away from provincialism toward cosmopolitanism, she builds a higher wall around the garden of English culture by relocating its bricks and mortar in the mind, installing there a "psycho-social filter" to incursions of alterity. Austen's last novel, Rogers concludes, "takes a decisive step toward the Victorian age of empire by relocating this culture onto a British man-of-war."[1] In her summary of the Kantian ideas that *Emma* brings to life, Rogers notes that Kant "devised a notion of hospitality that required tolerance but blocked intermarriage."[2] In *Emma*, Rogers argues, Austen "liberaliz[es] the country house community to include peripheral people only provided they abandon plans to marry into that community."³ *Mansfield Park* brings the religious aspect of the country house community into sharp focus and, in doing so, refuses the version of intermarriage that unites individuals whose religious opinions differ.

In support of a larger thesis regarding the novel's contribution to the secularization of British culture, Colin Jager positions Fanny Price and Mary Crawford as antipodes of religion's privatization, with Fanny's zealotry, reminiscent of romance, serving as a foil to Mary's modern skepticism. I understand them as two sides of a triangle, with Edmund Bertram as the third. Edmund's public religious authority—and by extension, that of the Anglican Church—is rejuvenated by Fanny's service as the moral custodian of the home. She becomes, over the course of the novel, a placeholder for a family religion that will morally restore the Bertram family and, by extension, their estate. The threat of conjugal discord is obviated by the fact that Fanny is educated by her future husband: "Having formed her mind and gained her affections, [Edmund] had a good chance of her thinking like him."⁴ As Edmund moves toward ordination and a career as a clergyman, Fanny shores up Anglicanism's credentials by serving as its moral compass.

Both Edmund and Fanny are preoccupied with women's speech and conduct. Upon arriving at Mansfield Park, Mary Crawford shocks them both by criticizing her uncle. "Was there nothing in her conversation that struck you, Fanny, as not quite right?" Edmund asks. When Fanny concurs—"I was quite astonished!"—Edmund approves: "I am glad you saw it all as I did" (50–51). Edmund, of course, goes on to fall in love with Mary Crawford, whose attractions cloud his moral vision: "[Fanny] was a little surprised that he could spend so many hours with Miss Crawford, and not see more of the sort of faults which he had already observed, and of which she was almost always reminded by a something of the same nature whenever she was in her company" (53). Fanny must tolerate Mary but only until Edmund's judgment catches up to hers and translates her interior reflections into authorized speech and discipline.⁵

Written at a moment when evangelical Protestantism was rapidly gaining ground, *Mansfield Park* insists that a woman's religious authority moves in one direction only: inward.⁶ Fanny's desire to do good never directs its attention beyond the insular community of Mansfield Park. Nor do her moral standards, until Edmund can enforce them, carry any import. As Mary Waldron points out, "Her moral standards are ineffective even to herself, because they are too simple to deal with real-life crisis."⁷ The only occasion where Fanny's dissent has an effect on the household is in her refusal of Henry Crawford, a refusal organized around her attachment to Edmund. But if Fanny's moral standards fail to translate into action, her capacity to gather the household into an affective embrace grows with every new crisis. In the space of the East Room, "everything was a friend, or bore her thoughts to a friend; . . . The room was most dear to her, and she would not have changed its furniture for the handsomest in the house" (119–20). The "home, restraint, and tranquility" of Mansfield Park awaits a morally revitalized parsonage to fulfill its communal mandate (150).

Mary Crawford, by contrast, views Mansfield Park as not quite perfect, "wanting to be completely new furnished" (38). Her critical regard directs its attention to various objects, including, most notably, Anglican orthodoxy, for which she shows no respect. Refusing the requirements of family worship, for instance, Mary remarks that "it is safer to leave people to their own devices on such subjects" (69). More broadly, Mary notes the corruption of the church as an institution and the self-interest and moral lassitude of its clergy. These criticisms are not unusual (having been rehearsed by evangelical Anglicans and Dissenters for fifty years), but Austen casts a cloud of suspicion over Mary's judgments. Edmund repeatedly describes her observations as the effect of having spent too much time in London, against which he pits all of England: "*You* are speaking of London, *I* am speaking of the nation at large" (73). She manifests the particular and degraded; he upholds the universal ideal.

The word "evil" is attached, in jest, to Mary early on by her sister, Mrs. Grant, who regards Mary's criticism of marriage as the reflections of an "evil-minded observer[]" educated in the "bad school for matrimony, in Hill Street," London (37). In a serious vein, Edmund identifies Mary's errors in thought as the product of a female confederacy fostered by urban living. Her London friends, Lady Stornaway and Mrs. Fraser, he writes to Fanny, "have been leading her astray for years" (330). He fears writing to Mary in London, lest she show his correspondence to her women friends: "A letter exposes to all the evil of consultation" (332). Reflecting on Mary's corrupting influence, should she marry Edmund, Fanny's worst fear is "[a] house in town! . . . [T]here was no saying what Miss Crawford might not ask" (327). When the lightning bolt of Maria's elopement with Henry Crawford strikes—a shock that Fanny experiences as a "horrible evil" (346)—it is Mary's response that engages Fanny's and Edmund's full attention. Fanny wonders that there exists a woman "who could treat as a trifle this sin of the first magnitude" (347). Edmund attributes Mary

Crawford's pragmatic response as the effects of prolonged exposure to the town: "This is what the world does!" (357).

Mary's failure to register Maria and Henry's sexual misconduct as a moral catastrophe reveals, to Edmund and Fanny alike, a depth of depravity they can hardly grasp:

> "Cruel!" said Fanny—"quite cruel! At such a moment to give way to gaiety and to speak with lightness, and to you! Absolute cruelty."
>
> "Cruelty, do you call it? ... No ... [t]he evil lies yet deeper; in her total ignorance, unsuspiciousness of there being such feelings, in a perversion of mind which made it natural to her to treat the subject as she did." (358)

Mary notes that divorce and remarriage is possible, that society might accommodate Maria eventually: "There is, undoubtedly, more liberality and candour on these points than formerly" (359). Her suggestion of such a possibility places Mary beyond the pale for Edmund: "All of this together most grievously convinced me that I had never understood her before, and that, as far as related to mind, that it had been the creature of my own imagination, not Miss Crawford, that I had been too apt to dwell on for many months past" (360). The differences of opinion Edmund once contemplated accommodating—"there were points on which they did not quite agree" (200)—now sever them irrevocably. A marriage between them could have unfolded only as a moral disaster.

The narrative corroborates Edmund's view by banishing Mary Crawford not only from his heart but from the companionate marriage plot entirely: "Mary ... was long in finding among the dashing representatives, or idle heirs apparents, ... any one who could satisfy the better taste she had acquired at Mansfield" (369).[8] Fanny, by contrast, is finally able to formalize her moral and affective value by marrying a clergyman. When Fanny and Edmund take up residence at the Mansfield Park parsonage, the circle closes: "The parsonage there ... soon grew as dear to her heart, and as thoroughly perfect in her eyes, as every thing else, within the view and patronage of Mansfield Park, had long been" (372). Fanny's love transforms Edmund's parish community into an extended family housed in a morally renewed church home.

In excising Mary from the world of *Mansfield Park*, Austen relies on an economy of style she herself invented. We know that *Sir Charles Grandison* was a novel Austen greatly admired: "Richardson's power of creating, and preserving the consistency of his characters, as particularly exemplified in *Sir Charles*

Grandison, gratified the natural discrimination of her mind, whilst her taste secured her from the errors of his prolix style and tedious narrative."⁹ *Mansfield Park* circumvents the long and tedious arguments about morality, religious freedom, and women's independence that *Grandison* undertakes by conflating the logic of Anglican orthodoxy—including its prohibitions on women's public speech—with the pleasures of the novel's formal achievements. Claudia Johnson remarks that "Mansfield Park runs smoothly as long as female dissent can be presumed not to exist," and I would add that *Mansfield Park* runs smoothly as long as the unruly plots authored by Clementina and others like her vanish from view.¹⁰

Critics have argued that Austen ironizes the conclusion of *Mansfield Park*, that the novel lays bare the corruptions of patriarchal authority and the various institutions it upholds by refusing to naturalize the incestuous contrivance of cousin marriage.¹¹ But *Mansfield Park*, I believe, makes explicit what is implicit in all of Austen's novels: that religious conformity is a given and that religious sameness between spouses serves as a foundational principle for the companionate marriage. In *Mansfield Park*, Austen had to argue for a norm that *Pride and Prejudice* and *Sense and Sensibility*, first drafted in an earlier moment, took for granted. "There is now a spirit of improvement abroad," Edmund exclaims, aligning evangelical Christianity with Anglicanism (266). But that "spirit of improvement" emerged from a variety of sources in the first two decades of the nineteenth century. Austen casts as moral strangers those who challenge the church's terms of governance.

After Austen, the story of intermarriage shifted its attention away from the management of religious difference to address more directly questions of race and empire and, in the instance of British Jews, assimilation, as well as the mass migrations that began to shape global culture. "The global movement of people," Josephine McDonagh observes, "created new readerships—including subaltern readers—located in different regions of the world."¹² In the aftermath of the Catholic Emancipation Act (1829), those writing about interfaith marriages were less interested in how sexual difference unsettles the public discourse of toleration than in tackling questions of culture and nation. The religious violence of the seventeenth and eighteenth centuries was lodged safely in a past made remote by the conventions of gothic and historical fiction. Talia Schaffer's recent study of the Victorian novel shows how neighbor and cousin unions anchor the plot of "familiar" marriage, a marriage plot that allows women to confirm their values and their communal bonds by marrying a known quantity.[13] Interfaith marriage becomes the "elsewhere" of the novel.

But the questions raised by the eighteenth-century novel's engagement with religious alterity in the private sphere remain unanswered, and now seems a good time to recognize that the challenges of interfaith marriage press on us still. In her 2014 study, *'Til Faith Do Us Part: How Interfaith Marriage Is Transforming America*, Naomi Schaefer Riley reports the findings of the General Social Survey in the United States, which documented an interfaith marriage rate increase from 15 percent in 1988 to 25 percent in 2006. Based on her own 2010 survey, Riley reports a rate of 42 percent in contemporary America.[14] Riley tells stories of couples and the problems that arise in their marriages, arguing that that those entering into mixed unions are unaware of the challenges that lie ahead, relying on weak theories of tolerance and strong theories of love to frame their terms of engagement. Riley concludes by reflecting that "perhaps only a different vision of pluralism" could mitigate the conflicts that her study documents. What might this different vision look like? And how might narrative contribute to its realization?

My readings of the eighteenth-century novel emphasize how narrative exchange can serve as the grounds for religious sociability, ameliorating tensions and sustaining a community of social networks that can support religious pluralism in the home. The pain of tolerance must be shared by a collective body, which develops its resilience by redistributing that pain through the stories it tells about itself. The vulnerable bodies of women and religious minorities support these linguistic experiments and narrative acts. The conflicts of interfaith marriage require not the elision of difference but rather a narrative space in which differences can find meaningful expression. The creation of this space is our shared responsibility.

NOTES

Introduction

1. Defoe, *Religious Courtship*, 32. All italics original unless otherwise. Punctuation or spelling may be lightly modernized for clarity.
2. Defoe, *Religious Courtship*, 51.
3. For my full reading of Defoe's *Religious Courtship*, see Conway, "'Unequally Yoked,'" 11–28.
4. In attending to the novel's sociability, I follow Tita Chico's lead in shifting critical focus away from a "progressive individualism [that has] blinded us to the ideologies of community formation promulgated by the mid-century novel." "Details and Frankness," 63.
5. Collyer, *Letters from Felicia to Charlotte*, 2:257.
6. Staves, *A Literary History of Women's Writing in Britain*, 237.
7. Field, "Counting Religion in England and Wales," 710. Field identifies the difficulty of determining accurate portraits of religious communities in the eighteenth century, noting that "the eighteenth century is commonly seen as 'a pre-statistical age' in religious terms" (694).
8. Field, "Counting Religion in England and Wales," 710–11.
9. "In every part of Europe that was religiously mixed, the taboos [against conversion and mixed marriage] were broken." Kaplan, *Divided by Faith*, 268.
10. Galgano, "Out of the Mainstream," 120. See also Aveling, "The Marriages of Catholic Recusants," 69–71.
11. Gooch, "'Chiefly of Low Rank,'" 251. See also Wanklyn, "Catholics in the Village Community," 210–36. Rebecca Probert and Liam D'Arcy Brown have studied the Catholic community of Coughton Court, in Warwickshire, and its marriages between 1758 and 1795, and they estimate that at least 30 percent of those marriages were Catholic-Protestant. "Catholics and the Clandestine Marriages Act of 1753," 78–82.
12. Kaplan notes the that increases in rates of mixed marriage "hit the Quakers especially hard." *Divided by Faith*, 285. Richard S. Harrison observes the same trend among Irish Quakers in the eighteenth century: "In the first half of the eighteenth century between a quarter and a third of Quaker marriages in Dublin were 'marriages out.'" "'As a Garden Enclosed,'" 94.
13. Hall, *An Historical Study of the Discipline of the Society of Friends*, 25.
14. "The First Church Book," 31.
15. "The First Church Book," 229–30.
16. Milligan, *Quaker Marriage*, 21.
17. See Gordon, *Intermarriage*.
18. Interestingly, in his introduction to *Intermarriage*, Gordon uses term "mixed marriage" to describe "those marriages in which separate religious ideologies are maintained by the parties subsequent to their marriage" (1).

19. Probert, *Marriage Law and Practice in the Long Eighteenth Century*, 341.
20. On the early modern origins of English racism, see Adelman, "Her Father's Blood," 4–30.
21. Meer, "Racialization and Religion," 385–98. Meer's work is informed by J. M. Thomas's analysis of medieval anti-Semitism. See "The Racial Formation of Medieval Jews," 1737–55. Meer suggests that "antisemitism" is preferable to "anti-Semitism," claiming that "the prevailing convention is not to use a hyphen in antisemitism as no phenomenon such as Semitism has ever existed" (395). But since we can talk about "philo-Semitism" in the seventeenth and eighteenth centuries, I will use the term "anti-Semitism" in this study.
22. I am thinking, here, of the striking example provided by Restoration accounts of Hortense Mancini, Duchess of Mazarin and mistress of Charles II. See my account of Mazarin in *The Protestant Whore*, 52–54, 57–61, 123–24.
23. A useful commentary on the religion/spirituality distinction appears in Bouma, *Australian Soul*, 15–16.
24. See, for instance, *The true and affecting history of Henrietta of Bellgrave* (1799) and *The True History of Zoa, the Beautiful Indian, Daughter of Henrietta de Bellgrave* (1799). On the colonial conversion narrative in nineteenth-century fiction, see Viswanathan, *Outside the Fold*. On interracial marriage plots, see Dominique, *Imoinda's Shade*.
25. Probert, *Marriage Law and Practice in the Long Eighteenth Century*, 131n4.
26. On the international interfaith marriages represented in the novels of Charlotte Smith, see Mellor, "Embodied Cosmopolitanism and the British Romantic Writer," 289–300. On the allegories of English-Irish unions sustained by marriage plots in the works of Irish authors, see Lloyd, *Anomalous States*.
27. The uncanny is more often used in association with the gothic, but my subject here is the realist novel. For a reading of toleration and the gothic novel, see Canuel, "'Holy Hypocrisy' and the Rule of Belief," chapter 2 of *Religion, Toleration, and British Writing*, 55–85.
28. Mellor, "Embodied Cosmopolitanism and the British Romantic Writer," 297.
29. Shore, "Was Milton White?," 254.
30. Mills, *Black Rights/White Wrongs*, 29.
31. Bejan, *Mere Civility*, 142.
32. Asad, *Formations of the Secular*, 5.
33. Joan Wallach Scott, "Secularism and Gender Equality," 27. Scott draws on Carol Pateman's account of liberalism's naturalization of male sex privilege, advanced in *The Sexual Contract*. It is not my intention to argue that the companionate marriage plot always already instantiates male sex privilege—only that its plot more often than not resolves ideological contradictions by naturalizing sexual difference. For an insightful account of how some novels resist its imperatives, see Thompson, *Ingenuous Subjection*.
34. Joan Wallach Scott, "Secularism and Gender Equality," 28.
35. Here I follow Talal Asad, who notes that "the terms 'secularism' and 'secularist' were introduced into English by freethinkers in the middle of the nineteenth century," at a moment when "a critical rearticulation was being negotiated between state law and personal morality" (*Formations of the Secular*, 23–24). Charles Taylor traces the *long durée* of secularism to the religious wars of the early modern period in *A Secular Age*.
36. The story of the companionate marriage has been told, brilliantly, many times by literary critics. To name just a few of the most influential studies that have shaped the field of eighteenth-century novel studies: Watt, *Rise of the Novel*; Armstrong, *Desire and Domestic Fiction*; Yeazell, *Fictions of Modesty*; Bannet, *The Domestic Revolution*; Ruth Perry, *Novel Relations*; Thompson, *Ingenuous Subjection*.
37. See Helen Thompson's introduction to *Ingenuous Subjection* for a concise account of this argument.

38. Saba Mahmood provides the most trenchant critique of this feminist tendency in contemporary debates. See *Politics of Piety*. In "Women, Gender, Religion," Elizabeth A. Castelli notes the connection between this tendency and the legacy of the Enlightenment: "Feminists... have tended to read 'religion' as an abstraction solely in negative terms.... This negative rendering of 'religion' is in many respects an ironic holdover from feminism's own Enlightenment inheritance" (5).

39. Susan Stanford Friedman, "Religion, Intersectionality, and Queer/Feminist Narrative Theory," 101.

40. See, for instance, Phyllis Mack's landmark study, *Heart Religion in the British Enlightenment*. See also the essays contained in Section 7 of *Women, Gender, and Enlightenment*, edited by Sarah Knott and Barbara Taylor, and Paula McDowell; chapter 3, "Oral Religio-political Activism and Textual Production," in McDowell, *The Women of Grubstreet*, 128–79; and McDowell, introductory note to *Elinor James*, xvii–xxviii.

41. O'Connell, *The Origins of the English Marriage Plot*, 230. On the dominance of the secularization thesis in eighteenth-century studies, see Snead, "Religion and Eighteenth-Century Literature"; and also Conway and Harol, "Toward a Postsecular Eighteenth Century."

42. Neuman, *Fiction Beyond Secularism*, 186.

43. On the various meanings of "postsecularism," see Conway and Harol, "Toward a Postsecular Eighteenth Century." See also Colin Jager's commentary on the term in his introduction to *Unquiet Things*, especially 19–22.

44. For an account of how Martha Nussbaum and others associate tolerance more generally with the literary imagination, see my introduction to *Imagining Religious Toleration*, 6–8.

45. "Le trajet parcouru par le roman anglais du dix-huitième siècle [est] à la fois *logos* et *praxis* de la tolérance." Morvan, *La tolérance dans le roman anglais*, 439.

46. Bakhtin, *The Dialogic Imagination*, 273–75; Hunter, *Before Novels*, 16.

47. Bender, *Imagining the Penitentiary*, 228.

48. Suzanne Keen's important study, *Empathy and the Novel*, uses cognitive theory and empirical studies of reader responses to advance her thesis. She notes, "Books can't make change by themselves" (xiv). The book has a very useful appendix, "A Collection of Hypotheses about Narrative Empathy" (169–71).

49. Hollander, introduction to *Narrative Hospitality in Late Victorian Fiction*, 1–21.

50. Hale, "Aesthetics and the New Ethics," 322.

51. Hale, "Aesthetics and the New Ethics," 318.

52. Hale, "Aesthetics and the New Ethics," 323.

53. Tønder, *Tolerance*, 3, 4. For an excellent summary of the toleration debate and its critical heritage in political philosophy, see the opening pages of Elaine Glaser's introduction to *Religious Tolerance in the Atlantic World* (1–13).

54. Tønder, *Tolerance*, 13.

55. Tønder, *Tolerance*, 10.

56. I explore Lars Tønder work on tolerance and pain in an essay on plague aesthetics in Daniel Defoe's *A Journal of the Plague Year*. See Conway, "'As So Many Dead Corpses.'"

57. Tønder, *Tolerance*, 120.

58. See, for example, Butler, Gambetti, and Sabsay, introduction to *Vulnerability in Resistance*, 1–11; and Pinto, "The Romance of Consent: Sally Hemings, Black Women's Sexuality, and the Fundamental Vulnerability of Rights," in *Infamous Bodies*, 66–103.

59. Hollander, *Narrative Hospitality in Late Victorian Fiction*, 21.

60. A range of minor realist novels that include interfaith marriage plots include Mary Collyer, *Letters from Felicia to Charlotte* (1744); Elizabeth Griffith, *The Delicate Distress* (1769); and *The Story of Juliana Harley* (1776). *Female Sensibility; Or, the History of Emma Pomfret, a*

Novel: Founded on Facts (1783) introduces the tenets governing *Grandison*'s plot only to vigorously refuse them.

61. On the historical imbrication of tolerance and intolerance, see Walsham, *Charitable Hatred.*

62. Bejan, *Mere Civility*, 141.

63. Bowers, *Force or fraud*, 287.

64. Armstrong and Tennenhouse, "The American Origins of the English Novel," 386–410.

65. Lanser, "Second-Sex Economies," 228.

66. On Dissent and toleration in the 1790s, see Mark Canuel's 2019 essay, "Joseph Priestley's Romantic Progressivism."

67. Mandell, "Bad Marriages, Bad Novels," 51.

68. Benjamin Kaplan claims that "only in recent years have historians turned their attention to what I would call the practice of toleration: the arrangements and accommodations that enable people of different faiths to live with one another peacefully." *Cunegonde's Kidnapping,* 2.

69. Here and in the chapters that follow, all Bible citations are from the King James Version.

70. Levy, "Fitzherbert"; Kebbel, "Fitzherbert."

71. See Mahmood, *Politics of Piety*; Bilge, "Beyond Subordination vs. Resistance"; and Joan Wallach Scott, *The Politics of the Veil.*

72. See "Anti-Semitism Accusations Roil Women's March," *New York Times,* December 24, 2018, A1. Tamika Mallory's remarks were made during her appearance on *The View,* Monday, January 14, 2019.

73. Bejan, *Mere Civility,* 166.

Chapter 1 · Religious Toleration and Interfaith Marriage, 1640–1720

1. The story of how marriage and politics became intertwined over the course of the seventeenth and eighteenth centuries is long and complex, as is the story of religious toleration's evolution as a lynchpin of modern liberalism. On the imbrication of gender and political discourse in the early modern period, see Achinstein, "Early Modern Marriage in a Secular Age"; Kahn, *Wayward Contracts*; Dolan, *Whores of Babylon* and *Marriage and Violence.* Cultural historians who study the family in the long eighteenth century include Weil, *Political Passions,* and chapter 4 of *A Plague of Informers*; Ng, *Literature and the Politics of the Family*; and Bowers, *The Politics of Motherhood,* and *Force or Fraud.*

The commentary on the evolution of religious toleration over the seventeenth and eighteenth centuries is vast. A sample of work on this subject, from the early twentieth to early twenty-first century, includes Seeton, *The Theory of Toleration under the Late Stuarts*; Barlow, *Citizenship and Conscience*; Jordan, *The Development of Religious Toleration in England*; Grell, Israel, and Tyacke, *From Persecution to Toleration*; Webb, "From Toleration to Religious Liberty"; Marshall, *John Locke, Toleration and Early Enlightenment Culture*; Zagorin, *How the Idea of Religious Toleration Came to the West.*

2. Gouge, *Of Domesticall Duties, Eight Treatises,* 193. For an overview of the historiography of the companionate marriage, see Dolan, *Marriage and Violence,* 27–28.

3. Prynne, *The Popish Royall Favorite,* 64.

4. Milton, *Eikonoklastes,* 324. Complaints about the Stuart kings' marriages to Catholic wives were constant throughout the seventeenth century. Forty years after Milton, the *Athenian Mercury* rehearsed his thesis concerning the corruption of interfaith unions between monarchs: "Some of the greatest Men in the Kingdom have publickly asserted, that England owes most, if not all her miseries for these 50 years past, to her being thus unequally yoked with Unbelievers." *Athenian Mercury,* May 31, 1692.

5. See Bill Stevenson, "The Social Integration of Post-Restoration Dissenters."

6. Underhill, *Records*, 147.

7. Underhill, *Records*, 173. The same church book goes on to record instance after instance of marriage between Independents and "carnall" men and women.

8. Underhill, *Records*, 24.

9. Frances Dolan approaches the problem of difference within marriage in early modern writing through the lens of heterosexuality. See *Marriage and Violence*, 40–49.

10. Brinsley, *A Looking-Glass for Good Women*, 41.

11. Greenham, "A Treatise of a Contract Before Mariage," 124–25. Patricia Crawford notes that after the Reformation, "most divines agreed that a wife should place obedience to God and the true church above her duty to her husband. . . . The extent of obedience to authority was of central concern in England up to the Civil Wars [and after], and religion gave scope for defiance." *Women and Religion in England*, 52.

12. Annabel Patterson notes the irony here: "Milton *discovered* for himself the principle of companionate marriage as Protestantism was still inventing it, and the engine of his discovery was disappointment and humiliation." "Milton, Marriage, and Divorce," 282. I agree with those critics, including Patterson and James Grantham Turner, who highlight the divorce tracts' misogynous tendencies, but my reading attends to those moments when Milton seems to balance the scales evenly. Milton's understanding of marriage and divorce has received close critical attention. For an overview, see Suzuki, "Marriage and Divorce"; and Van den Berg and Howard's introduction to *The Divorce Tracts of John Milton*. See also Song, "Love against Substitution."

13. Milton, *Complete Prose Works*, 2:261. Future references will be cited parenthetically. James Turner notes that "questions of sexuality . . . haunt Milton's discourse of toleration." Here I reverse the terms to trace how the question of toleration haunts discourses of sexuality. "Libertinism and Toleration," 107.

14. Milton repeats this point in *Tetrachordon* two years later: "If there be found between the pair a notorious disparity either or wickedness or heresie, the husband by all manner of right is disingag'd from a creature, not made and inflicted on him to the vexation of his righteousness; the wife also, as her subjection is terminated by the Lord, being her self the redeem'd of Christ, is still not bound to be the vassall of him, who is the bond slave of Satan" (2:591). In "Of Christian Doctrine" (c. 1660) Milton softens his stance: "If the marriage is already contracted it should not be dissolved while there is still any hope of winning over the unbeliever." *De Doctrina Christiana*, 369.

15. As James Turner has pointed out, Milton succeeds, here and elsewhere in his writing on divorce, "in making centuries of Pauline orthodoxy sound like 'peevish personalities.'" "The Aesthetics of Divorce," 38.

16. For a consideration of Milton's complex understanding of and advocacy for toleration, see the essays in Achinstein and Sauer's edited collection, *Milton and Toleration*.

17. Cable, "Secularizing Conscience in Milton's Republican Community," 268. Milton's attachment to liberty of conscience over toleration has been well documented. See, for example, Maltzahn, "Milton, Marvell, and Toleration," 86–106; Smith, "Milton and the European Contexts of Toleration"; and Turner, "Libertinism and Toleration."

18. Ames, *Conscience with the Power and Cases Thereof*, 55.

19. *An Expedient to Preserve Peace and Amity Among Dissenting Brethren*, 15.

20. Goodwin, *Independencies Gods Veritie*, 8.

21. These terms are taken from Locke's early writings on toleration, *Two Tracts on Government*, 238.

22. Blair Worden notes that "more often than not in puritan England, toleration was a dirty word." "Toleration and the Cromwellian Protectorate," 200.

23. Schochet, "From Persecution to 'Toleration,'" 127.

24. *Letter of the Presbyterian Ministers in the City of London . . . Against Toleration*, 8, 10.

25. Featley, dedicatory epistle to *The Dippers Dipt*.
26. *An Answer to a Book, intituled, The Doctrine and Discipline of Divorce*, 8–9.
27. *An Answer to a Book, intituled, The Doctrine and Discipline of Divorce*, 36.
28. Edwards, *The Second Part of Gangraena*, 10–11. On the Attaway incident, and sectarian women's bids for independence more generally, see Keith V. Thomas, "Women and the Civil War Sects." What little we know about Attaway is summarized in Ariel Hessayon's *DNB* entry: "Attaway, Mrs. (fl. 1645–46), Baptist Preacher."
29. Bernard, *The Independents Catechisme*, 25–27.
30. Seaman, *Solomons Choice*, 44.
31. Thorowgood, *Moderation Justified*, 11–12.
32. Rous, *The Ancient Bounds*, 15.
33. Goodwin, *Independencies Gods Veritie*, 8.
34. Burton, *Conformities Deformity*, 21, 23.
35. *A Letter of the Presbyterian Ministers in the City of London*, 6.
36. Walwyn, *Toleration Justified, and Persecution Condemned*, 11
37. Williams, *The Bloudy Tenent of Persecution*, 242.
38. Locke's theory of toleration has been exhaustively examined and debated since the first English translation appeared in 1689. For an overview of the criticism, see Richard Vernon's "Further Reading."
39. Windstrup, "Freedom and Authority," 249.
40. For an excellent account of Locke's shift in thinking between 1660 and 1689, see McClure, "Difference, Diversity, and the Limits of Toleration"; and chapter 4 of Teresa M. Bejan's *Mere Civility*.
41. Locke, "A Letter Concerning Toleration," in *Two Treatises of Government and A Letter Concerning Toleration*, 215. Future references will be cited parenthetically.
42. Locke makes "the individual, not the family, the basic unit of political society," Ruth Grant observes. "John Locke on Women and the Family," 299.
43. Vernon, introduction to *Locke on Toleration*, xiv.
44. Kessler, "John Locke's Legacy of Religious Freedom," 491.
45. Not surprisingly, Locke supported the moral reform movement that emerged in the 1690s. I have written about Locke's connection to that movement elsewhere; see *The Protestant Whore*, 83–84.
46. Popkin and Goldie, "Scepticism, Priestcraft, and Toleration," 100. Popkin and Goldie's essay serves as a useful corrective to the contemporary vision of toleration as a secular (in the skeptical sense) imperative. Throughout the Enlightenment, they observe, "arguments for toleration were broadly evangelical in nature. They were confessional, not secular, and they debated toleration and the relationship of the church to the state within the context of the Christian duty to evangelise" (99).
47. On Locke's reservations regarding liberty of conscience, see Kraynak, "John Locke"; P. J. Kelly, "Authority, Conscience, and Religious Toleration"; and McClure, "Difference, Diversity, and the Limits of Toleration," 369. On toleration discourse that advanced a more comprehensive liberty of conscience, see Sowerby, *Making Toleration*, 57–78.
48. For a survey of the debate about the nature of Locke's sexual contract and liberal defenses of Locke against the Pateman critique, see the essays included in the appendix to Locke, *Two Treatises of Government*; and the essays included in *Feminist Interpretations of John Locke*, edited by Nancy J. Hirshmann and Kirstie M. McClure.
49. *Two Treatises of Government*, 133, 135. Future references will be cited parenthetically.
50. Pritchard, *Religion in Public*, 116.
51. Leslie, preface to *Concerning marriages in different communions*, A.4.
52. Payne, *Family Religion*, 94.

53. Both Elizabeth Pritchard and Teresa Bejan provide illuminating readings of *Some Thoughts Concerning Education*. See Bejan, *Mere Civility*, 132–35; and Pritchard, chapter 5, "Secular Family Values," *Religion in Public*.

54. Hunter, *Before Novels*, 266.

55. For a concise and insightful account of the Act of Toleration's immediate reception history, see Sowerby, *Making Toleration*, 250–55. See also, Stevens, *Protestant Pluralism*.

56. Tillotson, "Sermon II: Concerning Family-Religion," in *Six Sermons*, 72.

57. Tillotson, "Sermon II," 82.

58. Payne, "The Epistle Dedicatory," in *Family Religion*, n.p.

59. Cambers and Wolfe, "Reading, Family Religion, and Evangelical Identity in Late Stuart England," 877.

60. Shower, *Family Religion*, 6.

61. Shower, *Family Religion*, 36.

62. Slater, *An Earnest Call*, 8.

63. Slater, *An Earnest Call*, 311–12.

64. Slater, *An Earnest Call*, 53.

65. Henry, *A Sermon Concerning Family-Religion*, 58.

66. Kirkwood, *A New Family-Book*, 166.

67. *Athenian Mercury*, December 29, 1691.

68. *Athenian Mercury*, December 29, 1691.

69. Leslie, *Concerning marriages in different communions*, 41.

70. West, *A Treatise Concerning Marriage*, 8. Meticulous record keepers, the Quaker meeting minutes of the eighteenth century repeat, over and over again, the necessity of endogamy. A typical entry is this 1734 admonition: "We do exhort Friends every where, that in the Great concern of Marriage, whereon much of the Comfort and Happiness of Life depends, they be mindful to proceed in the Fear of the Lord, and have an Eye to Him for Counsel and Instruction in their Choice; the Neglect of which has been the Ruin of many Families, and tended much to the Reproach and Dishonour of our Holy Profession." *The Epistle from the Yearly-Meeting*, 3.

71. West, *A Treatise Concerning Marriage*, 26–7.

72. Henry Howard was raised a Catholic, but he converted to Protestantism under Charles II. For a cogent account of his career in the courts of Charles and James, as well as William and Mary, see Rachel Weil's entry on Howard in the *Oxford Dictionary of National Biography Online*. Weil reads the Norfolk divorce in relation to two other divorces of the period in *Political Passions*, 121–41.

73. *A True Account of the Proceedings Before the Lords; between the Duke and Dutchess of Norfolk*, 41, 43.

74. *The Case of a Divorce by Act of Parliament*. Add. MS 32523, fol. 43.

75. *The Case of a Divorce by Act of Parliament*, fol. 45.

76. *The Case of a Divorce by Act of Parliament*, fol. 46.

77. *A True Account of the Proceedings Before the Lords; between the Duke and Dutchess of Norfolk*, 13.

78. Sowerby notes the strange mixture of political discourses in the defenses of James's tolerationist policy: "Repealers [those who advocated the repeal of Test and Corporate Acts] mixed a rhetoric of liberty that seems profoundly whiggish with a rhetoric of obedience to monarchical authority that seems profoundly tory." *Making Toleration*, 68.

79. Evelyn, *Diary*, 394.

80. Susanna Wesley, *Complete Writings*, 71. Future references will be cited parenthetically.

81. *The Genuine Remains of the late Pious and Learned George Hickes*, 238. I have modernized the script: yr to "your," etc. Future references will be cited parenthetically.

82. Samuel Wesley, *Life of Our Blessed Lord & Savior Jesus Christ*, 40. In *Memorials of the Wesley Family*, George J. Stevenson claims that these lines represent Samuel Wesley's "poetic portrait of his wife" (62), but Wesley himself opposes such a claim in one of his notes to the poem: "Undoubtedly the *Blessed Virgin* was endu'd with all *Conjugal* as well as *Solitary Graces* and *Virtues*, and accordingly from her I here draw the Picture of a *good Wife*; more defensibly I'm sure than the contrary is often done by the *Italian* Painters, who from their *Wives*, and sometimes *Mistresses*, usually draw their *Madonna's*, or Pictures of the Blessed Virgin" (67–68).

83. On the relation of nonjurors to Queen Anne, see Apetrei, "'Call No Man Master upon Earth.'" Apetrei's essay provides an astute account of Astell's defense of women's right to the liberty of conscience.

84. Charles Wallace notes "the importance to her of 'a Conscience void of offense,' already visible in her letters, . . . appear[s] again and again in the private confessional of her devotional journals." Susanna Wesley, *Complete Writings*, 202.

85. John Rylands MS DDWF 23/3. Marriot's article on Samuel Wesley's criticism of Socinian principles appears in the *Wesleyan-Methodist Magazine* 20, 3rd ser. (1841): 1019–20. Bishop Bull, a leading Restoration Anglican theologian, had had to defend himself against charges of Socinianism in 1685.

86. Here I echo George Starr's claim regarding the role of conversation in conduct books. The process of debate among family members in conduct manuals, he suggests, "encourages a belief that when all relevant circumstances and motives are taken into account, morally sound judgments about a given course of action can be reached." Introduction to *Religious Courtship*, 22.

87. Hickes recommended the Wesleys consult the archbishop of York about their marital problems. Susanna notes, "When he [Samuel] return'd he absolutely refus'd a reference, & so I thought it unnecessary to write to the Archbishop." *The Genuine Remains of the late Pious and Learned George Hickes*, 240.

88. Misty G. Anderson, *Imagining Methodism in Eighteenth-Century Britain*, 52.

89. Webb, "From Toleration to Religious Liberty," 176.

90. Webb, "From Toleration to Religious Liberty," 193.

Chapter 2 · Sir Charles Grandison's *Religious Disturbances*

1. Misty Anderson analyzes this moment in *Sir Charles Grandison* in the opening pages of *Imagining Methodism in Eighteenth-Century Britain* (1–2).

2. For a full account of Lennox's treatment of the Richardsonian novel, see my "'Uncommon Sentiments.'" Lennox's hostility to *Sir Charles Grandison*'s stance on religious toleration was shared by other women readers of the novel.

3. Lennox, *Henrietta*, 78.

4. Lennox, *Henrietta*, 78

5. Lennox, *Henrietta*, 77.

6. Richardson, *Correspondence*, ed. Schellenberg, 171.

7. Bonnie Latimer has written a detailed account of Richardson's interest in, and response to, the Jewish Naturalization Act. See "Samuel Richardson and the 'Jew Bill' of 1753," 539.

8. Chico, "Details and Frankness," 45.

9. See Teri Doerksen, "*Sir Charles Grandison*"; Temple, "Printing like a Post-colonialist"; Wolfgang Franke, "Richardson's *Grandison* as a Novel for Debate"; Dussinger, "The Negotiations of *Sir Charles Grandison*"; Mello, "'Piety and Popishness'"; Carnes, chapter 4 of *The Papist Represented*.

10. The political moment of *Clarissa*'s publication was steeped in violence, with the Jacobite Rebellion and its bloody judicial aftermath raising specters of the seventeenth century's religious conflicts. On *Sir Charles Grandison*'s interest in Jacobitism, see Brückmann, "'Men, Women and Poles'"; Doody, "Richardson's Politics"; Golden, "Public Context and Imagining

Self in *Sir Charles Grandison*"; Bowers, *Force or Fraud* (300–303). *Grandison*, as Bowers points out, was written in a moment when Jacobitism no longer appeared an active threat: "Richardson reveals, when it is finally safe, an equivocal sympathy for the Stuart cause" (300).

11. Richardson, *Sir Charles Grandison*, 1743. All references are to the Cambridge University Press edition, whose four *Grandison* volumes are page numbered consecutively.

12. For a detailed reading of Hogarth's representation of Jewishness in this print, see Solkin, "The Excessive Jew in *A Harlot's Progress*."

13. Newman, "Anglo-Jewry in the 18th Century," 1–10. One example is Joseph Salvador (an active supporter of the Jewish Naturalization Act of 1753), who had relationships with courtesans Margaret Caroline Rudd and Kitty Fisher, and the Countess de Moriencourt. On Salvador's sexual affairs, see Vanneste, *Global Trade and Commercial Networks*, 126–39; and also Katz, *Jews in the History of England*, 271. Interestingly, the biographical account of Salvador that appears in the *Jewish Historical Society of England: Transactions* account does not mention his libertinism and contrasts his example to that of another leading financier of the period, Samson Gideon: "While Gideon wriggled impatiently under the disabilities affecting Jewry and, in the end, sought to throw them off by quitting the synagogue, Salvador, equally inhibited and indeed more eligible socially for any honours, chose to remain a Jew and carry on the fight from within the community." Woolf, "Joseph Salvador, 1716–1786," 112. The volume does include, however, a copy of Reynolds's portrait of courtesan Kitty Fisher as Cleopatra, with an insert portrait of Salvador that has been taken from *The Jewish Infirmary*: both images suggest sexual misconduct.

14. Solkin, "The Excessive Jew in *A Harlot's Progress*," 223.

15. In 1746, Meyer Schomberg attacked the sexual practices of the Sephardim, no doubt thinking of Sarmento:

> In this generation there has procreated, swarmed and multiplied exceedingly, a generation that is pure in its own eyes. . . . They prate that they are men of worth and modesty but from their deeds every man of good heart sees that they love whoredom and adultery. Not only do they lie with women, daughters of the gentiles, . . . but they also live and dwell and lodge with them in intimate embrace and reject the kasher daughters of Israel who are our own flesh and blood. . . . They do not know or understand God's decree given by his Prophet Malachi. . . . If a man marries the daughter of a strange god then God will cut off him who does that.

"Emunat Omen" (The true faith) 101, 103. Although Schomberg's manuscript was never published in his lifetime, it rehearses the common refrains of both mid-century moralists and those opposed to mixed marriage.

16. He appears on the subscription list to Henry Pemberton's *A View of Sir Isaac Newton's Philosophy* in 1728, and a proposal for subscription to his own Portuguese-English dictionary appears in 1734.

17. Samuel, "Sarmento, Jacob de Castro."

18. *The Jerusalem Infirmary, A Farce*, 104–9.

19. My reading of *Grandison* focuses on Jewish difference as an instance of religious difference, most specifically. It is not my intention to collapse questions of faith and ethnicity but rather to think through the religious question of sincerity in relation to mixed marriage/conversion taboos.

20. Crome, "The 1753 'Jew Bill' Controversy," 1452. "As the eighteenth century advanced, the number of marriages between Jewish men and non-Jewish women increased. The progressive removal of social barriers between Jew and non-Jew made this inevitable," observes Albert M. Hyamson, *The Sephardim of England*, 176. "Between 1740 and 1800," Jane S. Gerber notes, "the number of marriages celebrated at Bevis Marks fell by 43 percent, as radical assimilation undercut the strength of the organized Sephardic community." *The Jews of Spain*, 205.

21. Vanneste, *Global Trade and Commercial Networks*, 125–26. Promoters of Jewish naturalization argued that this cultural blending contributed to a process of assimilation that had been underway for hundreds of years. A generation earlier, John Toland had reminded his readers that many English Jews converted when faced with expulsion by King John in the thirteenth century and that Jewish children had been kidnapped from their families and adopted out to the Christian community during this period: "By your Learning you . . . know how considerable a part of the British inhabitants are the undoubted offspring of the Jews . . . and how many worthy Prelates of this same stock, not to speak of Lords or Commoners, may at this time make an illustrious figure among us." Dedication to *Reasons for Naturalizing the Jews in Great Britain and Ireland*.

22. Endelman, *Jews of Georgian England*, 269.

23. *Annual Register* 1 (1759): 113.

24. For a succinct account of this history, see "The Extinction of Spain's Jews and the Birth of the Inquisition," in Nirenberg's *Anti-Judaism*, 217–45. See also, Gerber, *The Jews of Spain*.

25. Gerber, *The Jews of Spain*, 143.

26. Gerber, *The Jews of Spain*, 202.

27. Shapiro, *Shakespeare and the Jews*, 18.

28. Richard Barnett writes that in 1730 Sarmento entered into "a courteous correspondence with the Secretary of the Royal Academy of Lisbon" and a year later was writing to Dom Joao V of Portugal about the reform of medicine in Portugal. "Dr. Jacob de Castro Sarmento," 87.

29. "One characteristic of the eighteenth-century godly man," Jeremy Gregory has observed, "was that he was urged to avoid as much as possible religious disputes." "Homo Religious," 104.

30. James Grantham Turner, "Sexuality," 259.

31. Samuel, "Gideon, Samson (1699–1762), financier."

32. The editor of the *BM Satires/Catalogue of Political and Personal Satires* puts question marks after the names of Pelham and Thomas Pelham-Holmes, but they seem the likeliest targets here.

33. See Stow, *Jewish Dogs*, xiv–xv.

34. In an unpublished essay, Elizabeth Kraft suggests that "Merceda is allowed the last word and given the upper hand" in his exchange with Bagenhall. "Forced Conversion in the 1750s: *Grandison* Hits a Nerve" (paper presented at the ASECS annual meeting, Portland, OR, 2008). Quoted with permission.

35. Burnet, *Some Passages of the Life and Death of the Right Honourable John Earl of Rochester*, 160.

36. *Vox Populi Vox Dei or the Jew Act Repealed* (November 1753); the success of the repeal is symbolized by the broken circumcision knife in the centre foreground.

37. Of the fear of castration by Jews so common to the period, Dana Rabin remarks, "The threat seems to have been based on an anxiety about difference: a fear of being taken unawares, fear of an infiltration by the Jews as well as a fear that universal circumcision would erase the distinction between different groups and erode their particularity as Christians, as Anglicans, and as Britons" (160). Rabin, "The Jew Bill of 1753." See also Wolper, "Circumcision as Polemic in the Jew Bill of 1753."

38. Latimer, "Samuel Richardson and the 'Jew Bill' of 1753," 530.

39. In linking Clementina to Clarissa, I follow John Sitter's lead: "It is the noble Italian who has inherited many of Clarissa's most interesting qualities: her spirited resistance to her family, her 'wounded mind,' her passionate yet slightly marmoreal grandeur, even the detail at one point of disordered typography which signals her turmoil 'by the disposition of the lines.'" *Literary Loneliness in Mid-Eighteenth-Century England*, 205. Similarly, Lois A. Chaber claims that "tragedy hovers over the seemingly comic world of *Grandison*." "'Sufficient to the Day,'" 283. More recently, Patrick Mello has argued that "the potential for tragedy in Clementina's story

confronted readers still grappling with the implications of Clarissa's rape and death with a new object for their sympathy" "'Piety and Popishness,'" 530.

40. David L. Anderson remarks on the pervasiveness of this motif in the eighteenth-century French novel: "The continuing presence of Abélard and Héloïse in French literature is worthy of note in itself, and is all the more so in view of the fact that the symbolic pattern of the archetypal story emerges as the basis for developing novelistic techniques." "Abélard and Héloïse," 44.

41. Of course, Clementina is not the first to fall in love with a philosopher. As the first round of marriage negotiations break down, the story of Abelard and Heloise comes into focus.

42. Earlier in the century, Defoe's Roxana remarks the impossibility of acting outside of social convention when the Dutch merchant offers to secure her estate independently of his in marriage: "As to having him, and make over all my Estate out of his Hands, so as not to give him the Management of what I had, I thought it would be not only a little Gothick and Inhumane, but would be always a Foundation of Unkindness between us." *Roxana, the Fortunate Mistress*, 186–87.

43. Chico, "Details and Frankness," 63. For an alternative reading of how pain works in *Sir Charles Grandison*, see Barr, "Richardson's *Sir Charles Grandison* and the Symptoms of Subjectivity."

44. "Mais pourquoi cette Clementine est-elle si intéressante dans sa folie? C'est que n'étant plus maîtresse des pensées de son esprit ni des mouvements de son cœur, s'il se passait en elle quelque chose honteuse, elle lui échapperait. Mais elle ne dit pas un mot qui ne montre de la candeur et de l'innocence, et son état ne permet pas de douter de ce qu'elle dit." Diderot, "Éloge de Richardson," 910.

45. I allude here to Ann Banfield's thesis regarding the ability of literary language to free linguistic performance "from the tyranny of the communicative function." *Unspeakable Sentences*, 227. The "universal grammar" to which Banfield draws our attention is rooted in the practices of "represented speech and thought" (free indirect discourse) whose appearance coincides with the rise of the novel and whose first examples are to be found in France. Anne Waldron Neumann makes a strong case for *Sir Charles Grandison* as a significant contributor to the tradition Banfield describes. See "Free Indirect Discourse in the Eighteenth-Century Novel."

46. Clementina, in other words, appears poised to write the conclusion of a French novel. The connections between Richardson's novel and the novel of *refus* takes us too far from our subject, here, but they warrant further investigation, especially in light of Clementina's status as a latter-day Heloise. See David L. Anderson, "Abélard and Héloïse."

47. Toni Bowers argues that, for Richardson, "Roman Catholicism . . . epitomised the perversion of patriarchal authority." But in addition to its meddling priests, the novel represents spaces within the Catholic Church that reflect its long-standing interest in women's spiritual authority, writ large in the Marian tradition. "Family," 246.

48. Clementina's fall here registers as a devolution from Style to character, to use D. A. Miller's terms (*Jane Austen, or The Secret of Style*). Katharine Ann Jensen notes how French literary culture used the idea of women's inability to master standard French to limit their claims to authorship. La Bruyere, she notes, "believes some women's letters could exemplify not only better letter writing than men's but the best writing in the French language, except that women make mistakes in writing." *Writing Love*, 20.

49. On the literary traditions that emerged from this understanding of masochistic femininity, see Jensen, *Writing Love*, especially chapters 1 and 2.

50. Richardson to Lady Bradshaigh, January 14, 1754, *Correspondence*, ed. Sabor, 2:348.

51. Richardson to Lady Echlin, May 17, 1754. *Correspondence*, ed. Sabor, 2:438.

52. Barbauld, "Life of Samuel Richardson," cxix; Walter Scott, "Prefatory Memoir to Richardson," xxxvii. Hazlitt, *Complete Works*, 6:20. Ruskin, *Works*, 35:308. Twentieth-century criticism

developed a skeptical voice more attuned to Charlotte Grandison's ironic wit than Clementina's visionary reflections, for the most part.

53. This reading counters Patrick Mello's claim that *Grandison* advocates for "an emergent cosmopolitanism, one grounded on sympathy and a complete acceptance of freedom of conscience as an unquestioned, fundamental human right." "'Piety and Popishness,'" 527.

54. My reading of Harriet's love as the anchor of her identity draws on Katherine Binhammer's claim that "love, not desire, is the 'master key' for female subjectivity in the eighteenth century." *The Seduction Narrative in Britain*, 9.

55. Wendy Jones provides an insightful analysis of the novel's representation of "companionate" and "sentimental" love in *Consensual Fictions*, 70–80.

56. Albert J. Rivero adroitly untangles the romance/realism knot in "Representing Clementina."

57. Jones, *Consensual Fictions*, 76.

58. Amanda Vickery and others have effectively challenged Nancy Armstrong's thesis that domestic ideology increasingly restricted women to the home in eighteenth-century Britain. But *Grandison* sets in stark opposition those women who wander and those who don't. The family and the family seat take on significance in the novel's larger political landscape, which space precludes me from drawing here.

59. As Wendy Brown notes, "A presumption of difference, organized by a heterosexual division of labor, and underpinned by a heterosexual family . . . underscore[s] the difference between formal and substantive equality." *Regulating Aversion*, 74.

60. Wendy Jones provides an astute reading of Charlotte's characterization in *Consensual Fictions*, 93–98.

61. Ruth Perry traces the evolution of Richardson's increasingly conservative views of sexual difference and maternity, focusing her attention on his representation of breastfeeding: "By the time of *Sir Charles Grandison*, a woman's wifely obedience was guaranteed by her reproductive services, her willingness to undertake the lowly task of nursing her own child." "Colonizing the Breast," 230.

62. Chico, "Details and Frankness," 63.

63. Gwilliam, *Samuel Richardson's Fictions of Gender*, 150; Harris, *Samuel Richardson*, 134; Eaves and Kimpel, *Samuel Richardson*, 397. See also Wendy Jones, "The Dialectic of Love in *Sir Charles Grandison*," 32; and Doody, *A Natural Passion*, 274.

64. Taylor, "Porous and Buffered Selves."

65. Doody, *A Natural Passion*, 274. Thackery noted, in his 1868 remarks on Richardson, that Grandison's religion "is, in fact, merely the application of the laws of good society to the loftiest sphere of human duty." "Richardson's Novels," 60.

66. This question preoccupies Harriet when she first entertains the idea that Sir Charles might love her: "Who, my dear, large as his heart is, can be contented with half a heart?" (640). "Perhaps," Eaves and Kimpel speculate, "sensible charitableness is not the kind of goodness which can be imaginatively realized, perhaps it did not lie in the level of the mind from which poetry comes, as the goodness of Clarissa (and the vice of Lovelace) did" (*Samuel Richardson*, 398). That Harriet's affective zealotry proves a narrative spur while Charles's "sensible charitableness" kills representation on the page speaks, I believe, to the tension the novel stages between love and (limited) toleration.

67. Richardson to Alexis Claude Clairaut, July 5, 1753, *Correspondence*, ed. Schellenberg, 95. Richardson goes on to express his hope that he has done credit to the Catholic clergy, noting that "a very eminent Clergyman told me . . . that I should be thought by some, to be more of a Catholic than a Protestant, for that I had made as amiable a Confessor, as a Protestant Divine" (96).

68. Sabor, "'A Safe Bridge over the Narrow Seas,'" 168.

69. Richardson to Lady Bradshaigh, December 8, 1753, *Correspondence*, ed. Sabor, 1:319.
70. John Allen Stevenson, "'A Geometry of His Own,'" 47. Doody, "Samuel Richardson," 114.
71. Bowers, *Force or Fraud*, 303.
72. Richardson to Johannes Stinstra, June 2, 1753, *Selected Letters*, 230.
73. Richardson to Lady Bradshaigh [late September to early October 1755], *Correspondence*, ed. Sabor, 2:575.
74. Richardson to Elizabeth Carter, August 17, 1753, *Correspondence*, ed. Schellenberg, 134.
75. Carnes, *The Papist Represented*, 140.
76. Richardson to Cox Macro, March 22, 1754, *Correspondence*, ed. Schellenberg, 199. Emphasis added.
77. Richardson to Macro, 198.

Chapter 3 · Frances Brooke's Civil Disputes

1. Brooke, preface to *The Excursion*, 2:vii.
2. *Critical Review* 16 (July 1763): 45. Novel criticism since the eighteenth century has continued to draw comparisons between Richardson and Brooke, noting, in particular, how their novel writing organizes itself around the representation of female consciousness. See, for example, Katharine Rogers, "Sensibility and Feminism." Lorraine McMullen and W. H. New provide an overview of the reception histories of Brooke's works in *An Odd Attempt in a Woman*.
3. For a detailed account of John Brooke's career in Canada, see Mary Jane Edwards's introduction to *The History of Emily Montague*, xvii–xxxvi.
4. Fownes, *An Enquiry into the Principles of Toleration*, 21.
5. Ann Edwards Boutelle argues that "Brooke explicitly debunks the man-is-master expectation which the Richardsonian novel had created." "Frances Brooke's *Emily Montague*," 8.
6. What follows draws on Pam Perkins's insightful account of the novel's representation of marriage as political allegory. See "Imagining 18th Century Quebec," 151–61. Criticism that attends to the novel's feminist and colonial engagements tends to follow one of three trajectories: First, that the novel serves as imperial mouthpiece and its gender politics collude with this project. See, for example, Merrett, "The Politics of Romance in *The History of Emily Montague*"; and Devereux, "'One Firm Body.'" Second, critics argue that the novel's progressive and conservative impulses result in narrative incoherence. See Wyett, "'No Place Where Women Are of Such Importance'"; and Vesselova, "'The Strongest Tie to Unity and Obedience.'" Third, critics argue that the novel's epistolary form prevents any one ideological perspective from carrying more weight than another. See, for example, Moss, "Colonialism and Postcolonialism in *The History of Emily Montague*"; Howells, "Dialogism in Canada's First Novel"; and Benedict, "The Margins of Sentiment."
7. Later in the chapter I return to Nancy Armstrong and Leonard Tennenhouse's arguments regarding the relation between captivity narrative and the eighteenth-century novel. See "The American Origins of the English Novel."
8. Boutelle reads the novel's alignment of marriage and liberal feminism more positively than I do. See "Frances Brooke's *Emily Montague*," 7–16.
9. Arch focuses on the epistolary correspondence as the structural principle that reveals the gap in Brooke's imperial logic: "In Brooke's vision of center and periphery, the distances between people cannot be bridged by letters." "Frances Brooke's 'Circle of Friends,'" 467.
10. Lanser, "Second-Sex Economies," 236.
11. Lanser, "Second-Sex Economies," 228.
12. See New, "*The Old Maid*." On Frances Brooke's role as editor, see Kathryn R. King, "Frances Brooke, Editor, and the Making of *The Old Maid*."
13. Brooke, *The Old Maid*, 41. Future references will be cited parenthetically.
14. On the problematical alignment of (white) female subjection with enslavement, see Ferguson, *Subject to Others*, 281.

15. Schellenberg, *The Professionalization of Women Writers in Eighteenth-Century Britain*, 59.

16. Gallagher, "Embracing the Absolute," 24–33.

17. Brooke, *The History of Lady Julia Mandeville*, 26. Future references will be cited parenthetically.

18. Schellenberg, *The Professionalization of Women Writers in Eighteenth-Century Britain*, 48.

19. McMullen and New, *An Odd Attempt in a Woman*, 18.

20. *Critical Review* 16 (July 1763): 45.

21. "On nous parle encore d'une Mylady Anne Wilmot, éspece de folle qu'on a voulu sans doute ressembler à Miss Howe." *Année Litéraire* (1764): 175.

22. Feminist historians have identified Indigenous women who traversed the corridor between Montreal and Albany as key players in a transnational trade network. This history remains, for the most part, unexamined. As Angela Wanhalla observes, "Scholars have yet to explore Indigenous women's participation in imperial networks or elaborate the variety of ways in which they were active mobile subjects." "Indigenous Women, Marriage, and Colonial Mobility," 210. See also Noel, "'Fertile with Fine Talk.'"

23. Benedict, "The Margins of Sentiment," 14.

24. Brooke, *The History of Emily Montague*, 80. Future references will be cited parenthetically.

25. On the economics that complicate this idealization of Canada as a place of prosperity, see Binhammer, "The Failure of Trade's Empire in *The History of Emily Montague*."

26. Binhammer, "The Failure of Trade's Empire in *The History of Emily Montague*," 314.

27. Julie Ellison and Stephen Arch make related claims about the effect the North American setting has on the novel's ideological imperatives. Ellison observes that "for white couples in transatlantic novels, financial stress in British settings and cross-racial tension in North American ones have a curiously analogous relationship." Arch notes, "Brooke wants to imagine cultivated sensibility and the free choice of a marriage partner as the marker and prerogative of a rising middle class that, in the novel, is threatened by the centrifugal forces of the colonial empire." Ellison, "'There and Back,'" 310; Arch, "Frances Brooke's 'Circle of Friends,'" 473.

28. In *The Savage and Modern Self*, Robbie Richardson argues that "by internalising the Indian, the self becomes modern, a cosmopolitan, masculine, and individualistic subject" (166). The relationship between British women's writing and indigeneity has yet to be explored.

29. Audra Simpson notes that "those whom they [colonists] encountered . . . were, in the case of the Haudenosaunee, led by women. But even this mode of "leadership" was shared with men. As to be expected, British and Dutch traders and politicos found these gendered arrangements to be unusual." "The Sovereignty of Critique," 690.

30. Karen O'Brien writes with great perspicacity on gender and the domestic-social-political continuum in the Enlightenment imagination. See her introduction to *Women and Enlightenment in Eighteenth-Century Britain*, 1–34.

31. See Stanbridge, *Toleration and State Institutions*.

32. M. Dorothy George, "Catalogue of Political and Personal Satires in the British Museum," V, 1935, quoted in British Museum Collection Online record: www.britishmuseum.org/collection/object/P_1868-1212-9.

33. Colley, *Britons*, 134.

34. Welland, "Interest Politics and the Shaping of the British Empire," 213. James Axtell notes that a decade later, in the 1770s, "it became a commonplace of the conservative Northite press that Presbyterians were doctrinally and politically more dangerous than Roman Catholics." *The Invasion Within*, 206.

35. For a history of Anglicanism's role in promoting toleration abroad as a form of statecraft, see Bulman, *Anglican Enlightenment*.

36. Canuel, *Religion, Toleration, and British Writing*, 16.

37. Schellenberg, *The Professionalization of Women Writers in Eighteenth-Century Britain*, 52.

38. Here I confirm Mary Helen McMurran's view that "Fermor's letters, written in the voice of an exemplary patriarch and British citizen, articulate a consistent agenda of strong-arm colonial transfer. It is misleading, however, to present Fermor's policy as the political and cultural message of the novel, not least because his views on Quebec were foiled both by historical circumstances and by Brooke's central characters, Edward Rivers and Arabella Fermor, whose letters far outnumber his." *The Spread of Novels*, 149. The historical record confirms that the dream of Anglican hegemony was never likely to be realized. James Axtell writes that "the English had little success in converting Indians to Christian civility and virtually no success in persuading French Catholics to become anglicized Protestants." *The Invasion Within*, 302. John Walsh and Stephen Taylor identify Anglican indifference to the project: "Despite the rapid growth of the empire, the Church of England showed little interest in the conversion of the heathen." Introduction to *The Church of England c.1689–c.1833*, 15.

39. Devereux, "'One Firm Body,'" 468.

40. Given our contemporary tendency to associate "religion" with states and institutions, and in the context of colonial-settler culture, with Christianity, it sounds awkward to refer to French-Indigenous marriages as "interfaith," and so I use "mixed" here, instead. However, the distinction between "spirituality" and "religion" is a false one. As Gary Bouma notes, "Like any other human activity, anything spiritual done more than once and by a group quickly becomes socially organised and hence religious." *Australian Soul*, 15.

41. Little, *The Many Captivities of Esther Wheelwright*, 104. See also McMurran, *The Spread of Novels*, 147.

42. Bumsted, "The Cultural Landscape of Early Canada," 371. See also Kirk, *Many Tender Ties*; Lanser, "Second-Sex Economics"; Gail D. Macleitch, "'Your Women Are of No Small Consequence'"; Peterson, "Women Dreaming"; Sleeper-Smith, "Women Kin and Catholicism."

43. In *The Many Captivities of Esther Wheelwright*, Little quotes a letter written by Wheelwright to her birth mother, in which she describes her decision to consecrate herself "wholly unto the Lord, to whom I belong without reserve," and the "impossibility" for her "to return to you, which you and my dear Father have so often repeated in past times" (182).

44. My argument here moves in a direction opposite that of Cecily Devereux, who claims that French Canada functions in the novel "as a site within which Britain's 'other' could be contained and neutralized through political and cultural assimilation." "'One Firm Body,'" 475.

45. Little, *The Many Captivities of Esther Wheelwright*, 8.

46. Little, *The Many Captivities of Esther Wheelwright*, 81–82.

47. Armstrong and Tennenhouse, "The American Origins of the English Novel," 394, 398.

48. Armstrong and Tennenhouse, "The American Origins of the English Novel," 388.

49. Gayle K. Brown, "'Into the Hands of Papists,'" 11. Pam Perkins sets *Emily Montague* against captivity narratives, which she describes as peculiarly "American": "These captivity episodes, like the sentimental accounts of the sublimely threatening American wilderness, create a sense of a dangerously threatening new world, one which is very obviously different from Brooke's Canada." "Frances Brooke, Emily Montague, and Other Travellers," 427. I am arguing that the difference is not as stark as Perkins suggests and that the inclusion of Esther Wheelwright's narrative signals Brooke's interest in captivity and its aftermath, an interest that carries over into the novel's reflections on Catholic women more generally.

50. Armstrong and Tennenhouse, "The American Origins of the English Novel," 398.

51. Harland-Jacobs, "Incorporating the King's New Subjects," 212. Harland-Jacobs observes the paradox in the policy maintained by both Murray and Carleton: "Accommodation ... became a key strategy in Britain's repertoire of imperial rule at the precise moment when that rule was becoming more authoritarian in nature" (223).

52. McMurran, *The Spread of Novels*, 107.
53. Guest, *Small Change*, 158.
54. Eagles, *Francophilia in English Society*, 59.
55. McMurran, *The Spread of Novels*, 150.
56. Hammill, "'A Daughter of the Muses,'" 437.
57. Messenger, "Arabella Fermor," 170.
58. On the significance of Arabella's bilingualism, see McMurran, *The Spread of Novels*, 153–54.
59. Hammil, "'A Daughter of the Muses,'" 443–44.
60. On Edward's cosmopolitanism, see McMurran, *The Spread of Novels*, 150–52.
61. Arch, "Frances Brooke's 'Circle of Friends,'" 477.
62. McCarthy, "Sisters under the Mink," 340. See also Edwards, "Frances Brooke's Politics and *The History of Emily Montague*"; and, more recently, Vesselova, "'The Strongest Tie to Unity and Obedience.'"
63. Arch, "Frances Brooke's 'Circle of Friends,'" 474.
64. Pollak, "Introduction: Modernity, Incest, and Eighteenth-Century Narrative."
65. Bartolomeo, "The Sentimental Novel in America," 173.
66. Binhammer, "The Failure of Trade's Empire in *The History of Emily Montague*," 318.
67. Here I draw on Heather Welland's study of eighteenth-century British colonial policy: "India and Quebec were twinned in the public imagination throughout much of the 1760s and 1770s; and attempts to draft legislation for Quebec in 1764, 1766–67, and 1773–1774 coincided with the East India Company enquiries." "Interest Politics and the Shaping of the British Empire," 181. See also Sainsbury, *Disaffected Patriots*.
68. Sainsbury, *Disaffected Patriots*, 51.
69. *A Letter to the Minister on the Subject of the East-India Dividend*, 4.
70. Almon, *The Revolution in MDCCLXXXII Impartially Considered*, 14–15.
71. Writing to her publisher, James Dodsley, to apologize for the novel's lack of success, Brooke remarked on the tedium of the plot, heightened by the novel's excessive length: "Its being 4 vols, as it was published all at once, was against it: it's being published by subscription was more so; & it's having too little variety of story for the length of it." Letter, August 29, 1770, British Library, Add MS 29747 f. 68.
72. See Nussbaum, *Torrid Zones*.
73. Macaulay, *An Address to the People of England, Scotland and Ireland*, 10, 15.

Chapter 4 · Elizabeth Inchbald among the Cisalpines

1. For a detailed account of Inchbald's Jacobin affiliations, see Gary Kelly, *The English Jacobin Novel*. Recent monographs on British Catholicism that study Inchbald include Tomko, chapter 2 of *British Romanticism and the Catholic Question*, 14–51; and Carnes, chapter 5 of *The Papist Represented*, 149–84. Essays include Keegan, "'Bred a Jesuit'"; Judson, "The Psychology of Satan"; Young, "Elizabeth Inchbald's 'Catholic Novel' and Its Local Background"; Kramer, "Rethinking Surrender.'"
2. Mandell, "Bad Marriages, Bad Novels," 52, 70.
3. Judson, "The Psychology of Satan," 620.
4. Tomko and Carnes reach very different conclusions about the significance of the Cisalpine movement for Inchbald. Tomko identifies the Cisalpines as too male and aristocratic for Inchbald, whose reform program, he maintains, reflects her "unique political and personal position." Tomko, *British Romanticism and the Catholic Question*, 199. For Carnes, the Cisalpines shaped the early years of Inchbald's political development: "Inchbald may have come to political radicalism in the 1790s *through* the Cisalpinism that agitated her religious community

in the 1780s." *The Papist Represented*, 175–76. Neither reads *A Simple Story* through the lens of Cisalpine philosophy.

5. Berington, *Reflections Addressed to the Rev. John Hawkins*, 22. Joseph Berington was not a member "proper" of the Catholic Committee—but his cousin, Charles Berington, was, after 1788. In 1782, the Catholic Committee's lay members included Lord Stourton, Lord Petre, John Throckmorton, Thomas Stapleton, Thomas Hornyold, and Charles Butler (secretary to the committee). In 1787, three clergymen joined the group: Bishop James Talbot, Charles Berington, and Joseph Wilkes, a Benedictine monk whose disciplining by the Catholic Church in the 1790s caused much controversy. See Connell, *The Roman Catholic Church in England*. I will return to the specific reform program of the Catholic Committee below; here I focus on the work of their key writers, Joseph Berington and Alexander Geddes, whose patron was Lord Petre.

6. For an account of Dissent's increasingly sympathetic stance toward Catholicism in the later eighteenth century, see Fitzpatrick, "From Natural Law to Natural Rights?"

7. Heywood, *The Right of Protestant Dissenters, to a Compleat Toleration*, 24.

8. After 1790, both Dissent and mainstream Anglicanism adopted more sympathetic views of Catholics. Maria Purves documents this shift in her introduction to *The Gothic and Catholicism* (1–24). In his study of late eighteenth-century Protestant ideologies, G. M. Ditchfield observes, "By the 1790s it was no longer plausible to conceive of Dissenters as allies of the Church of England in a common Protestant front against the external and internal threat of Popery." "'The Right of Private Judgement, with the Case of Public Safety,'" 18.

9. Berington, *State and Behaviour*, 137–38, 139–40, 138–39, 141.

10. Berington, *State and Behaviour*, vi. Mark Goldie notes that Alexander Geddes, like Berington, "constantly asserted the Englishness of native Catholics. The 'Catholic' was distinct from the 'papist.'" "Alexander Geddes," 421.

11. Geddes, *Letter to a Member of Parliament*, 29.

12. *Heads of a Bill*, n.p. In a letter, *To the Catholics of England*, the Catholic Committee explained, "As they continue to dissent in certain points of faith from the Church of England, the Act styles them Dissenters;—As they continue members of the Catholic Church,—the Act styles them Catholics;—and as they have protested against certain pernicious doctrines attributed to them,—the Act styles them Protesting Catholic Dissenters" (3).

13. Of English Catholicism in the later eighteenth century, John Bossy notes "a growing convergence of Catholicism and Dissent." *The English Catholic Community*, 13.

14. Berington, preface to *State and Behaviour*, vi.

15. Geddes, *Cursory Remarks on a Late Fanatical Publication*, 50.

16. Goldie, "Alexander Geddes," 418.

17. Berington, *Reflections Addressed to the Rev. John Hawkins*, 26–27.

18. Berington, *Reflections Addressed to the Rev. John Hawkins*, 26–27. O'Leary, *A Review*, 25.

19. O'Leary, *A Review*, 29. Berington, *Reflections*, 29.

20. For an account of the composition of Inchbald's novel, see Anna Lott's introduction to *A Simple Story*, 23–27.

21. Tomko, "'All the World Have Heard of the Devil and the Pope,'" 124. See also Tomko, "Between Revolutionary Jacobins and English Catholic Cisalpines." For an account of Inchbald's engagement with the liberal Catholic community in Britain before 1780, see Carnes, *The Papist Represented*, 155–56.

22. A brief period around 1803 was spent at another Catholic community for women on the outskirts of London, Annandale House at Turnham Green. "Elizabeth Inchbald," in *Orlando*.

23. Francis Young, "Elizabeth Inchbald's 'Catholic Novel' and Its Local Background," 583. Indeed, Young speculates that Inchbald herself was the product of a mixed marriage: "The evidence for Inchbald's mother not being a Catholic is fairly conclusive" (582).

24. This play, along with *The Mogul Tale* (1783), has been read for its contributions to late eighteenth-century understandings of race, empire, and gender. See Choudhury, *Interculturalism and Resistance in the London Theatre*; O'Quinn, *Staging Governance*; Green, "'You Should Be My Master.'" Michael Tomko is alone in setting *The Mogul Tale* against the backdrop of Inchbald's Catholic understanding of toleration. See "All the World Have Heard of the Devil and the Pope."

25. Inchbald, *Such things are*, 4. Future references will be cited parenthetically.

26. Inchbald tells us the play is set in Sumatra in her prefatory remarks, but characters routinely identify India as their location.

27. Misty G. Anderson, *Female Playwrights and Eighteenth-Century Comedy*, 199.

28. Balfour, "Promises, Promises," 239.

29. Balfour, "Promise, Promises," 243.

30. Balfour, "Promises, Promises," 244.

31. In a 2010 essay, Eun Kyung Min provides an insightful account of promises in *A Simple Story*, noting that novel sustains "a rich account of the ethical realm neglected by social contract theory: the ethics of sexual love and difference, marriage, parenthood, and intergenerational bonds." "Giving Promises," 107.

32. Eamon Duffy observes, "The last twenty years of the 18th century saw the English Catholic community torn asunder by the disputes which, to contemporaries, seemed certain to end in schism with Rome, and so destroy the heritage of the martyr church." "Ecclesiastical Democracy Detected," 193. Carnes notes that *A Simple Story* "should be read as a response to this complex moment of Catholic in-fighting, contradiction, and betrayal" but does not attend to the Cisalpine controversies in any detail. *The Papist Represented*, 176.

33. Geddes, *Cursory Remarks on a Late Fanatical Publication*, 42.

34. *Encyclical Letter*, 39.

35. Plowden, *Observations on the Oath Proposed by the English Roman Catholics*, 66.

36. Throckmorton, *A Letter Addressed to the Catholic Clergy*, 22.

37. Milner, *Divine Right of the Episcopacy*, 36

38. Milner, *Divine Right of the Episcopacy*, 117.

39. Berington, *Reflections Addressed to the Rev. John Hawkins*, x.

40. Berington, *Reflections Addressed to the Rev. John Hawkins*, xi.

41. Bridget Keegan explores the Jesuit tradition in detail in "'Bred a Jesuit.'"

42. Inchbald, *A Simple Story*, 3. Future references will be cited parenthetically.

43. Carnes, *The Papist Represented*, 167

44. Osland, "Heart-Picking in *A Simple Story*," 98; Balfour, "Promises, Promises," 240.

45. Emily Hodgson Anderson, "Revising Theatrical Conventions in *A Simple Story*," 12.

46. Osland, "Heart-Picking in *A Simple Story*," 89.

47. Carnes provides a cogent account of Miss Milner's anti-Catholic jokes in *The Papist Represented*, 166–67.

48. Carnes, *The Papist Represented*, 157

49. Min, "Giving Promises," 112.

50. See chapter 2, "Elizabeth Inchbald," in Gary Kelly, *The English Jacobin Novel*, 64–113.

51. Catherine Craft-Fairchild writes, "The final paragraphs of Inchbald's novel implicate the 'PROPER EDUCATION' of woman, the type of education promoted by writers such as Sarah Scott, Jane West, and Hannah More, as one intended to suppress female desire" (*Masquerade and Gender*, 116). Jane Spencer describes this final admonition as "an unintegrated moral tag. . . . [E]ducation in this novel functions negatively, not adding wisdom but adding taboos. The female desire which it is meant to stifle is the novel's more fundamental concern." Introduction to *A Simple Story*, xiv–xv. More recently, Sharon L. Decker has complicated this account by focusing on Matilda's embodied affect and its relation to education. See "The Problem with Binaries."

52. Eamon Duffy observes that "a central part of their [the Catholic Committee's] campaign to present Catholicism as an integral part of English religious pluralism was a campaign for the closure of the European colleges and communities, and their replacement by academies in England itself." *Peter and Jack*, 21.
53. Berington, *State and Behavior*, 171, 180.
54. Geddes, *Letter to a Member of Parliament, on the Case of the Protestant Dissenters*, 171.
55. Duffy, *Peter and Jack*, 20–21.
56. Berington, *An Essay on the Depravity of the Nation*, 25–26, 27.
57. Berington, *An Essay on the Depravity of the Nation*, 27.
58. Berington, *An Essay on the Depravity of the Nation*, 30.
59. Kramer, "Rethinking Surrender," 105.
60. Again, Jane Spencer's view is representative: "Its dramatic situation is representative of the gothic novels so popular in Inchbald's time. It presents us with an extreme of patriarchal tyranny." Introduction to *A Simple Story*, xix. In an early reading of Inchbald, I followed this critical trajectory, organizing my account of *A Simple Story* around the dynamics of desire and transgression. See *Private Interests*, 195–209.
61. Tomko, *British Romanticism and the Catholic Question*, 79.
62. Carnes, *The Papist Represented*, 176.
63. O'Quinn, *Staging Governance*, 156.
64. "Mrs Woodley" was the author name Inchbald used when *The Mogul's Tale* was performed at the Haymarket Theatre in 1784. Manvell, *Elizabeth Inchbald*, 31.
65. Jager, "Translating Love in *Prometheus Unbound*," 253.
66. Hershinow, *Born Yesterday*, 2.
67. Hershinow, *Born Yesterday*, 10.
68. Hershinow, *Born Yesterday*, 11.
69. Hershinow, *Born Yesterday*, 85.
70. Here I read against the critical grain, which reads Matilda as a corrective to her independent mother. Jane Spencer's view is representative: "Lady Matilda, unlike her mother, is a passive maiden waiting to be rescued; she does not challenge authority or assert her desires; and unlike her mother, she ends happily. The second half of the novel, then, can be read as a kind of atonement on Inchbald's part for the boldness of the first." Introduction to *A Simple Story*, xx. A more recent account of the novel's construction of Matilda as "an exemplary and static figure" can be found in Amy Pawl's essay, "Only a Girl?," 129.
71. Hershinow, *Born Yesterday*, 2.
72. Catherine Craft-Fairchild notes that "the mutuality and equality of the second relationship in some ways remedy the oppression and inequality of the first." *Masquerade and Gender*, 119.
73. Wallace, "Wit and Revolution," 111.
74. Min, "Giving Promises, 126.
75. Here my reading counters Miriam Wallace's claim that "potential romance for Matilda with Rushbrook remains insubstantial in comparison with the narrative investment in paternal prohibition and daughterly transgression." "Wit and Revolution," 111.
76. Chinnici, *The English Catholic Enlightenment*, 98.
77. Tomko, *British Romanticism and the Catholic Question*, 85.
78. Wendy C. Nielsen argues that Godwin "undoubtedly influenced this decision." "A Tragic Farce," 279. Thomas C. Crochunis notes that Godwin's desire to see the play suppressed "raised questions about what kinds of political discourses surrounding gender and revolution were possible" in the early 1790s. "Pre- and Post-realist Dramaturgy," 343.
79. Tomko reads the play less darkly in "Remembering Elizabeth Inchbald's *The Massacre*," 1–18. John Robbins casts light on the significance of women's witnessing in "Documenting Terror in Elizabeth Inchbald's *The Massacre*," 605–19.

80. George Grinnell provides an astute account of the politics of neighborliness in "Timely Responses," 645–63.

81. As Jill Heydt-Stevenson and Charlotte Sussman observe, "This was an age when the constitution of the nation was being thoroughly re-imagined—indeed revolutionized—and consequently the kinds of 'imagined community' proffered by Romantic-era fiction vary widely." "'Launched upon the Sea of Moral and Political Inquiry,'" 21.

Chapter 5 · Maria Edgeworth's Jewish Enlightenment

1. "The novel's failure," argues Rachel Schulkins, "can be attributed not only to the revelation that Berenice is in fact a Christian but also to Edgeworth's failure of the imagination, prevalent throughout the novel." "Imagining the *Other*," 478. "Berenice's suddenly disclosed Christianity is a way of converting her," claims Michael Ragussis. *Figures of Conversion*, 77. Neville Hoad is more generous in his suggestion that it represents "the boundaries of tolerance" rather than "a failure of Edgeworth's nerve or commitment to pro-Jewish representations." But he concludes, like Ragussis, that it precludes the possibility of mixed marriage tout court: "The presentation of Berenice as always and already Christian, Protestant, and descended from the daughter of an English gentleman keeps the irrational threat of miscegenation on foreign soil—Spain—and outside the time-span of the novel." "Maria Edgeworth's *Harrington*," 128. Angelina Del Balzo makes a similar claim: "*Harrington* cannot imagine a place for Judaism as a legitimate religious or cultural option, or part of an acceptable form of interreligious marriage." "'The Feelings of Others,'" 690.

Del Balzo's essay provides a recent overview of the critical debates surrounding the novel's toleration politics in its opening pages ("'The Feelings of Others,'" 685–704). For an account of the Mordecai/Edgeworth exchange that prompted the novel's composition, see *The Education of the Heart: The Correspondence of Rachel Mordecai and Maria Edgeworth*, edited by Edgar E. MacDonald; and Catherine Craft-Fairchild, "The 'Jewish Question' on Both Sides of the Atlantic." On Rachel Mordecai's eventual conversion to Christianity, see Jean E. Friedman's biography of Mordecai, *Ways of Wisdom*.

2. Yoon Sun Lee, "Bad Plots and Objectivity in Maria Edgeworth," 35.
3. Edgeworth, *Harrington*, 2:174–75.
4. Tønder, *Tolerance*, 106.
5. Hewitt, "Maria Edgeworth's *Harrington* as a Utopian Novel," 304.
6. My reading builds on the extensive critical commentary on the novel's representation of pain and its cures. Michael Ragussis argues that Edgeworth's narrative represents "an etiology of the disease of racial terror," a phobia that Harrington must overcome by "mastering the primal scene." *Figures of Conversion* (67, 76). Neville Hoad describes the novel as a narrative of "proto-psycho-analytic cure." "Maria Edgeworth's *Harrington*," 122. Judith Page describes Edgeworth as a "good moral doctor" capable of curing what ails the body politic. *Imperfect Sympathies*, 150. Peter Logan attributes the novel's aversion to pain to Edgeworth's "effort to buttress the tale's emphasis on self-mastery—that is, on Harrington's capacity for being cured [from his childhood hysteria]." "Harrington's Last Shudder," 111. In a very different register, Natasha Tessone argues that the novel challenges Burke's association of pain with sympathy and national prejudice: "Edgeworth . . . probes the link between imagining the broken human body and imagining the body politic—the aesthetics of pain so central to the contemporary efforts at theorizing what it is that constitutes community." "Homage to Empty Armor," 445. Other critics have attended to pain's generative aspect in fostering sympathetic identifications. Ragussis explores this line in chapter 5 of *Theatrical Nations*. See also Del Balzo, "'The Feelings of Others.'"

7. On how Edgeworth uses the marriage plot to advance an identity politics organized around sameness, see John Plotz's reading in *The Absentee in the Crowd*, 45–50.

8. Edgeworth, *Harrington*, ed. Susan Manly, 131–32. Future references will be cited parenthetically.

9. Here I follow Manly: "Harrington's 'delight' here is one of confident command as a reader and interpreter" (introduction to *Harrington*, 24), and also Ragussis, whose reading of this scene highlights how Berenice "become[s] an erotic spectacle that rivals and supercedes the spectacle of Jewishness on the stage." Ragussis argues that this moment is "perilously balanced between sympathetic identification and erotic mastery." I would suggest that the two poles are not opposed but exist on a continuum in relation to the companionate marriage. *Theatrical Nation*, 158.

10. Plotz claims that "the key to success throughout Edgeworth's work is the ability to put boundaries to use." *The Absentee in the Crowd*, 57.

11. Natasha Tessone provides an extremely insightful reading of Edgeworth's critique of the museum and its artifacts in "Homage to Empty Armor."

12. Logan, "Harrington's Last Shudder," 130.

13. On print culture's mediating function in relation to the bigotry of the "crowd," see Plotz's introduction to *The Absentee in the Crowd*, 1–14.

14. Kilgour, *From Communion to Cannibalism*, 8.

15. Kilgour, *From Communion to Cannibalism*, 16.

16. M. Dorothy George, *Catalogue of Political and Personal Satires in the British Museum*, vol. 6, 1938, quoted in British Museum Collection Online record: www.britishmuseum.org/collection/object/P_1892-0714-449.

17. *Public Advertiser*, December 14, 1771.

18. *Public Advertiser*, December 14, 1771.

19. Ragussis remarks the scene at the Surgeons Hall as an instance of "the public's growing appetite for the embodied figure of the Jew." The attention paid to the teeth, he goes on, satirizes "the apparently more polite and fashionable world of Georgian England, where the teeth of executed Jews eventually adorn the beaux and belles of London." *Theatrical Nation*, 124–25.

20. Plotz, *The Crowd*, 63. Catherine Gallagher observes how close Montenero's treatment of the painting comes to confirming anti-Semitic fantasies "about the disproportionate power of the Jews over symbolic systems, their omnipresence, and their financial ability to monopolize commodities." *Nobody's Story*, 318. I suggest that the reference to the Gibraltar riot qualifies Montenero's claims to power in this scene.

21. Jerome Friedman, "Jewish Conversion, the Spanish Pure Blood Laws and Reformation," 11. Yirmiyahu Yovel also observes the high number of these marriages before the Inquisition in *The Other Within*, 63.

22. Yovel, *The Other Within*, 60, 61.

23. Jerome Friedman, "Jewish Conversion, the Spanish Pure Blood Laws and Reformation," 11.

24. On the Inquisition's treatment of *conversos*, see Yovel, *The Other Within*, chapter 9, 153–75.

25. Gerber, *The Jews of Spain*, 140.

26. Cumberland, *Observer* 4 (1785): 12.

27. Shapiro, *Shakespeare and the Jews*, 24.

28. Plotz, *The Crowd*, 55.

29. Plotz, *The Crowd*, 59–60.

30. Walsham, *Charitable Hatred*, 319.

31. "The flow of poor Jewish aliens became especially heavy from the 1770s on," Todd M. Endelman notes. *The Jews of Georgian England*, 173.

32. Endelman, *The Jews of Georgian England*, 171.

33. Gallagher, *Nobody's Story*, 307.

34. What follows draws on Susan Manly's excellent essay on Edgeworth's study of Mendelssohn. See "*Harrington* and Anti-Semitism."

35. Manly places the emphasis on Mendelssohn's ability to overcome suffering ("*Harrington* and Anti-Semitism," 241–43). Edgeworth, I believe, is interested in how suffering might be integrated into Enlightenment subjectivity.

36. Notably, Jacob never gives up his distrust of Mowbray and proves, finally, a better reader of him than Mr. Montenero. Peter Logan notes that Montenero's objectivity, in the final instance, does not protect him from being a dupe to Mowbray's schemes. "By failing to see through the artifice of Mowbray's performance and being moved instead to confuse its dramatic power with factual truth, Montenero is finally defined as one of the crowd at Mowbray's final play, the staging of Harrington's insanity." "Harrington's Last Shudder," 138.

37. Of all the authors this study examines, no one had the personal experience of religious violence to which Maria Edgeworth could lay claim. Edgeworth's father was set upon during the peasant revolt of 1798 by Protestants who suspected him of serving as a French spy, a mistake made possible by Edgeworth's insistence that his yeomen militia include Catholics. To avoid Catholic rebels, Edgeworth moved his family to the Protestant town of Longford; it was here that he was accosted by a mob. He packed up his family and returned to the Edgeworth estate the next day. Later, after her father's death, Maria Edgeworth became a champion for Catholic emancipation in Ireland. See Butler, *Maria Edgeworth*, 137–39, 451, for an overview of Edgeworth's life and the sectarian conflicts her family negotiated in Ireland; and also Susan Manly's account of its significance in "Burke, Toland, Toleration," 153.

38. Winter, "The Novel and Prejudice," 92.

39. I am persuaded by Natasha Tessone's claim that "by pairing the wealthy Jewish collector Montenero with the Irish orange-woman, the novel destabilizes Montenero's own Jewish identity, offering, in the spirit of Edgeworth's best Irish fiction, an alternative perception of religious and national identities as fluid, porous entities." "Homage to Empty Armor," 461. But I suggest that the scene gives more weight to Jewish identity, as in the instance of Widow Levy's name, while nodding in the direction of Edgeworth's own Anglo-Irish identity. On Widow Levy as a figure for Edgeworth herself, see Gallagher, *Nobody's Story*, 323–25.

40. Catherine Gallagher observes, "Mrs. Levy's language, like Edgeworth's own, . . . is often fictional." *Nobody's Story*, 323.

41. Logan, *Nerves and Narratives*, 134.

42. Logan, *Nerves and Narratives*, 137.

43. While copyediting this chapter in its manuscript form, Emily Sugerman noted, "Edgeworth's rewriting of Portia's ring trick in *Merchant of Venice* also reminds me of Tubal's report to Shylock that, in addition to running away, Jessica has traded away a family ring with sentimental value (her mother had given it to Shylock) in exchange for a monkey. In Shakespeare, the circulation of the ring indicates a breakdown of Jewish filial piety." My thanks to Emily for sharing this critical insight. Tubal's comment appears in act 3, scene 1, line 111.

44. See Metzger, "'Now by My Hood, a Gentle and No Jew'"; Hirsch, "'A Gentle and No Jew'"; Adelman, "Her Father's Blood."

45. Adelman, "Her Father's Blood," 13.

46. Hirsch, "'A Gentle and No Jew,'" 129.

47. Gallagher, *Nobody's Story*, 311. Gallagher reads this attachment as an allegorical stand-in for Edgeworth's relationship with her own father: "When she undertook *Harrington* . . . in a state of contrition for having accused the Jews of being a usurious nation, might she not also have wanted to expiate her guilt for unwittingly casting her father in the role of an unsatisfiable creditor?" (310).

48. Jessica's insistence is not unambiguous, however: "The Jessica of act 5 *may* be read . . . [as] an emblem of postcoital regret, ruing not her rebellion against patriarchal authority but the terms of her new commitment to it and the meager possibilities for unalienated pleasure they provide." Metzger, "'Now by My Hood, a Gentle and No Jew,'" 59.

49. Scrivener, *Jewish Representation in British Literature*, 117.
50. Manly, "Burke, Toland, Toleration," 163.
51. Hewitt, "Maria Edgeworth's *Harrington*," 309.
52. Ragussis focuses on the Jewish recasting of Shakespeare made possible by Montenero, rather than Berenice: "The Jew is given the chance to dismantle the holy scripture of anti-Semitism." *Figures of Conversion*, 83.

Conclusion

1. Hannah Lee Rogers, "Philosophy in Austen's Pump Room," 325, 338, 340.
2. Rogers, "Philosophy in Austen's Pump Room," 330.
3. Rogers, "Philosophy in Austen's Pump Room," 324.
4. Austen, *Mansfield Park*. Future references will be cited parenthetically.
5. On the novel's investment in correction, see Mark Canuel's insightful essay, "Jane Austen and the Importance of Being Wrong."
6. In *The Romantic Reformation*, Robert Ryan describes a "quickening" of religious fervor among Dissenting Protestants in the 1790s and early nineteenth century, noting that "Anglican clergymen who had tended to ignore or deride the Methodists had to take more seriously a newly invigorated Dissent with its tradition of defiance of the established political and ecclesiastical order" (25).
7. Mary Waldron, "The Frailties of Fanny," 273. For the opposing view, see Benis, "Spatial Consciousness and Spiritual Practices in Austen's *Mansfield Park*."
8. Here I depart from Jager, who reads Fanny's victory over Mary as only partial: "The novel has a vested interest in a more modern world, one in which Mary can go her own way and so make room for Fanny." *The Book of God*, 157. Mary is not free, finally, but banished to her sister's home at the novel's conclusion.
9. James Edward Austen-Leigh, *A Memoir of Jane Austen and Other Family Recollections*, 141.
10. Johnson, *Jane Austen*, 112.
11. Claudia Johnson is representative: "The highly conventionalized moral oppositions touted in the conclusions [of *Mansfield Park*] . . . will not bear the scrutiny Austen's own style is always inviting." *Jane Austen*, 120. More recently, Christina Lupton argues that *Mansfield Park* "makes the artificial closure of the marriage plot the condition of her revealing her book's commitment to an uncertain future." "Contingency, Codex, the Eighteenth-Century Novel," 1182.
12. McDonagh, *Literature in a Time of Migration*, 6–7. Heather McNeff's 2013 dissertation, "Finding Happiness," provides an overview of short fiction, drama, poetry, and novels that represent interfaith marriage in Romantic fiction. (Of the thirteen novels she studies, five are by Walter Scott, and only two are published before 1798.) Although I am not persuaded by McNeff's argument that Romantic fiction uses the occasion of interfaith marriage to investigate "positions relating to happiness," I concur with her sense that religion, in the texts she studies, is not the primary focus of the plot (3). On the imperatives of the conversion narrative in nineteenth-century fiction, see Ragussis, *Figures of Conversion*.
13. Schaffer, *Romance's Rival*.
14. Riley provides rates for other countries in the notes to *'Til Faith Do Us Part*.

BIBLIOGRAPHY

Primary Texts

Manuscripts

BRITISH LIBRARY, LONDON

Add. MS 32,523, fol. 43. *The Case of a Divorce by Act of Parliament.*
Add. MS 29,747, fol. 68. *Letter.*

LAMBETH PALACE LIBRARY

The Genuine Remains of the late Pious and Learned George Hickes D.D. and Suffragen Bishop of Thetford, ed. Thomas Bedford, MS. 3171

JOHN RYLANDS LIBRARY, MANCHESTER

MS DDWF 23/3.

DR. WILLIAM'S LIBRARY, LONDON

First Church Book of Rothwell Congregation Church Northamptonshire, 1655–1708.

Printed Primary Sources

NEWSPAPERS AND PERIODICALS

Année Littéraire
Annual Register
Athenian Mercury
The Cornhill Magazine
Critical Review
Public Advertiser

TRACTS AND BOOKS

Almon, John. *The Revolution in MDCCLXXXII Impartially Considered.* 2nd ed. London, 1782.
Ames, William. *Conscience with the Power and Cases Thereof.* London, 1639.
An Answer to a Book, intituled, The Doctrine and Discipline of Divorce restored to the good of both Sexes from the bondage of the Canon Law. London, 1644.
Assheton, William. *Toleration Disapprov'd and Condemn'd, by a Letter of the Presbyterian Ministers in the City of London, . . . and by Twenty Eminent Divines . . . in Their Sermons before the two Houses of Parliament on Solemn Occasions, between the Years 1641 and 1648* [1670]. London, 1736.

Austen, Jane. *Mansfield Park*. Edited by James Kinsley. Oxford: Oxford University Press, 2008.

Austen-Leigh, James Edward. *A Memoir of Jane Austen and Other Family Recollections*. Edited by Kathryn Sutherland. Oxford: Oxford University Press, 2002.

Austin, William. *Letters from London: Written during the years 1802 & 1803*. Boston: W. Pelham, 1804.

Berington, Joseph. *An Essay on the Depravity of the Nation, with a view to the Promotion of Sunday Schools,&c*. London, 1788.

Berington, Joseph. *Reflections Addressed to the Rev. John Hawkins*. London, 1785.

Berington, Joseph. *The State and Behavior of English Catholics, from the Reformation to the year 1780. Second Edition, Containing . . . a Full Answer to Critics and an Address to Catholics*. London, 1781.

Bernard, John. *The Independents Catechisme*. London, 1645.

Blount, Charles. *A Just Vindication of Learning: Or, An Humble Address to the High Court of Parliament In behalf of the Liberty of the Press*. London, 1679.

Brinsley, John. *A Looking-Glass for Good Women, Held forth by way of Counsell and Advice to such of that Sex and Quality, as in the simplicity of their Hearts, are led away to the imbracing or looking towards any of the dangerous Errors of the Times, especially that of the Separation*. London, 1645.

Brooke, Frances. *The Excursion, A Novel*. 2nd ed. 2 vols. London, 1785.

Brooke, Frances. *The History of Emily Montague*. Edited by Laura Moss. Ottawa: Tecumseh Press, 2001.

Brooke, Frances. *The History of Lady Julia Mandeville*. Edited by Enit Karafill Steiner. London: Pickering and Chatto, 2012.

Brooke, Frances. *The Old Maid. By Mary Singleton, Spinster*. London, 1764.

Burnet, Gilbert. *Some Passages of the Life and Death of the Right Honourable John Earl of Rochester, Who Died the 26th of July, 1680*. London, 1680.

Burton, Henry. *Conformities Deformity: In a Dialogue between Conformity and Conscience*. London, 1646.

Calamy, Benjamin. *A Sermon Preached at St. Lawrence-Jury, upon the 9th of September, being the Day of Thanksgiving for the Deliverance of the King & Kingdom from the late Treasonable Conspiracy*. London, 1683.

Care, George. *A Reply to the Answer of the Man of No Name to His Grace the Duke of Buckingham's Paper of Religion, and Liberty of Conscience*. London, 1685.

Catholic Committee. *To the Catholics of England*. 1789.

Clarke, Samuel. *A Looking-Glass for Good Women, Held forth by way of Counsell and Advice to such of that Sex and Quality, as in the simplicity of their Hearts, are led away to the imbracing or looking towards any of the dangerous Errors of the Times, especially that of the Separation*. London, 1645.

Collyer, Mary. *Letters from Felicia to Charlotte*. 3rd ed. 2 vols. London, 1755.

Cook, E. T., and Alexander Wedderburn, eds. *The Works of John Ruskin*. London: George Allen, 1908.

Cumberland, Richard. *The observer: being a collection of moral, literary and familiar essays . . . The fifth edition, newly arranged . . . In six volumes*. 1798.

Defoe, Daniel. *Religious Courtship*, edited by G. A. Starr. Vol. 4 of *The Religious and Didactic Writings of Daniel Defoe*. London: Pickering & Chatto, 2006.

Defoe, Daniel. *Roxana, the Fortunate Mistress*. Edited by David Blewett. London: Penguin, 1992.

Diderot, Denis. "Éloge de Richardson." In *Contes et romans*, edited by Michel Delon, 895–911. Paris: Gallimard, 2004.

Edgeworth, Maria. *Harrington*. Edited by Susan Manly. Peterborough, ON: Broadview Press, 2004.

Edgeworth, Maria. *Harrington, a Tale; and Ormond, a Tale, in Three Volumes*. London, 1817.

Edwards, Thomas. *The Second Part of Gangraena*. London, 1646.
Encyclical Letter. In *Original Papers, relative to the Present Application to the British Parliament for relief of the Roman Catholics in England*, 39–40. Dublin, 1791.
The Epistle from the Yearly-Meeting. London: Friends Printed Epistles, 1734.
An Expedient to Preserve Peace and Amity Among Dissenting Brethren. London, 1647.
Evelyn, John. *The Diary of John Evelyn*. Vol. 5, *Kalendarium, 1690–1706*, edited by E. S. de Beer. Oxford: Clarendon Press, 1955.
Featley, Daniel. *The Dippers Dipt*. London, 1645.
Female Sensibility; Or, the History of Emma Pomfret, a Novel: Founded on Facts. London, 1783.
"The First Church Book of Rothwell Congregational Church Northamptonshire, 1655–1708." Unpublished typescript of original manuscript volume housed in Rothwell. Dr. Williams's Library, London.
Fownes, Joseph. *An Enquiry into the Principles of Toleration* [1772]. 3rd ed. London, 1790.
Geddes, Alexander. *Cursory Remarks on a Late Fanatical Publication Entitled a Full Detection of Popery, &c*. London, 1783.
Geddes, Alexander. *Letter to a Member of Parliament, on the Case of the Protestant Dissenters and the Expediency of a General Repeal of All Penal Statutes that Regard Religious Opinions*. London, 1787.
Goodwin, John. *Independencies Gods Veritie: or, the Necessitie of Toleration*. London, 1647.
Gouge, William. *Of Domesticall Duties, Eight Treatises*. London, 1634.
Greenham, Richard. "A Treatise of a Contract Before Mariage." In *The Works of the Reverand and Faithfull Servant of Jesus Christ, M. Richard Greenham*, 122–28. London, 1599.
Griffith, Elizabeth. *The Delicate Distress: A novel, in letters, by Frances* [1769]. 2 vols. London, 1788.
Griffith, Elizabeth. *The Story of Juliana Harley*. London, 1776.
Hazlitt, William. *The Complete Works of William Hazlitt*, edited by P. P. Howe, A. R. Waller, Arnold Glover, and James Thornton. London: J. M. Dent and Sons, 1930.
Heads of a Bill, To relieve, Upon Conditions and under Restrictions, Persons called Protesting Catholic Dissenters from certain Penalties and Disabilities to which Papists, or Persons professing the Popish Religion, are by Law subject. London, 1789.
Henry, Matthew. *A Sermon Concerning Family-Religion*. London, 1704.
Heywood, Samuel. *The Right of Protestant Dissenters, to a Compleat Toleration*. London, 1787.
Inchbald, Elizabeth. *The Massacre: Taken from the French; A Tragedy, in Three Acts*. London, 1791.
Inchbald, Elizabeth. *A Simple Story*. Edited by J. M. S. Tompkins. Oxford: Oxford University Press, 1967.
Inchbald, Elizabeth. *Such things are; a play, in five acts. As performed at the Theatre Royal, Covent Garden. By Mrs. Inchbald*. London, 1788.
Jacob, Henry. *An Humble Supplication for Toleration and Libertie*. London, 1609.
The Jerusalem Infirmary, A Farce. Reprinted from the only extant copy (at the Huntington Library) in Richard Barnett. "Dr. Jacob de Castro Sarmento and Sephardim in Medical Practice in 18th-Century London." *Transactions: The Jewish Historical Society of England* 27 (1982): 104–9.
Kirkwood, James. *A New Family-Book; Or, the True Interest of Families* [2nd ed. of *The True Interest of Families*, 1692]. London, 1693.
Lennox, Charlotte. *Henrietta* (1758). Edited by Ruth Perry and Susan Carlile. Lexington: University Press of Kentucky, 2008.
Leslie, Charles. *Concerning marriages in different communions: in a sermon at Chester*. London, 1702.
L'Estrange, Roger. *Toleration Discussed*. London, 1663.
A Letter of the Presbyterian Ministers in the City of London, Presented the First of Jan. 1645, to the Reverend Assembly of Divines Sitting at Westminister . . . Against Toleration. London, 1645.

Letter to a Member of Parliament, on the Case of the Protestant Dissenters and the Expediency of a General Repeal of All Penal Statutes that Regard Religious Opinions. London, 1787.
A Letter to the Minister on the Subject of the East-India Dividend. London, 1767.
Locke, John. *Two Tracts on Government*. Edited by Philip Abrams. London: Cambridge University Press, 1967.
Locke, John. *Two Treatises of Government: And, A Letter Concerning Toleration*. Edited by Ian Shapiro. London: Yale University Press, 2003.
Macaulay, Catharine. *An Address to the People of England, Scotland and Ireland, on the Present Important Crisis of Affairs*. London, 1775.
MacDonald, Edgar E., ed. *The Education of the Heart: The Correspondence of Rachel Mordecai and Maria Edgeworth*. Chapel Hill: University of North Carolina Press, 1977.
Maddox, Isaac. *A sermon preach'd before the House of Lords in the Abbey-Church of Westminster, On Monday, June 11, 1739: Being the Day of His Majesty's happy Accession to the Throne*. London, 1739.
Marriot, Thomas. "The Elder Wesley and the Socinians." *Wesleyan-Methodist Magazine* 20, 3rd ser. (1841): 1019–20.
Marshall, Stephen. *An Expedient to Preserve Peace and Amity Among Dissenting Brethren*. London, 1647.
Milner, John. *Divine Right of the Episcopacy addressed to the Catholic Laity of English*. London, 1791.
Milton, John. *The Complete Prose Works of John Milton*. Vol. 2: *1643–1648*, edited by Ernest Sirluck. New Haven, CT: Yale University Press, 1960.
Milton, John. *De Doctrina Christiana*. Part I. In *The Complete Works of John Milton*, vol. 8, edited by John K. Hale and J. Donald Cullington. Oxford: Oxford University Press, 2012.
Milton, John. *The Divorce Tracts of John Milton: Texts and Contexts*. Edited by Sara J. van den Berg and W. Scott Howard. Pittsburgh, PA: Duquesne University Press, 2010.
Milton, John. *Eikonoklastes*. In *The Complete Works of John Milton*, vol. 6, edited by N. H. Keeble and Nicholas McDowell, Oxford: Oxford University Press, 2013.
North, Brownlow. *A Sermon Preached Before the Incorporated Society for the Propagation of the Gospels in Foreign Parts*. London, 1778.
O'Leary, Arthur. *A Review of the Important Controversy Between Dr. Carroll and the Reverend Messrs. Wharton and Hawkins*. London, 1786.
Owen, John. *Indulgence and Toleration Considered*. London, 1667.
Paget, Thomas. *A Religious Scrutiny Concerning Unequal Marriage, to be Represented to the General Assembly of the Kirk of Scotland*. London, 1649.
Parker, Samuel. *Ecclesiastical Polity*. London, 1670.
Payne, William. *Family Religion: Or, the Duty of taking Care of Religion in Families*. London, 1691.
Pemberton, Henry. *A View of Sir Isaac Newton's Philosophy*. London, 1728.
Plowden, Charles. *Observations on the Oath Proposed by the English Roman Catholics*. London, 1791.
Plumer, Francis. *A Candid Examination of the history of Sir Charles Grandison. In a Letter to a Lady of Distinction*. 3rd ed. London, 1755.
Prynne, William. *The Popish Royall Favorite*. London, 1643.
Richardson, Samuel. *The Correspondence of Samuel Richardson: Primarily on "Sir Charles Grandison" (1750–1754)*. Edited by Betty A. Schellenberg. Cambridge: Cambridge University Press, 2015.
Richardson, Samuel. *The Correspondence of Samuel Richardson: With Lady Echlin and Lady Bradsheigh*. Edited by Peter Sabor. 3 vols. Cambridge: Cambridge University Press, 2016.
Richardson, Samuel. *Selected Letters*. Edited by John Carroll. Oxford: Clarendon, 1964.

Richardson, Samuel. *Sir Charles Grandison*. Edited by E. Derek Taylor, Melvyn New, and Elizabeth Kraft. Vols. 8–11 of *The Cambridge Edition of the Works of Samuel Richardson*, edited by Thomas Keymer and Peter Sabor. Cambridge: Cambridge University Press, 2022.
Rous, Francis. *The Ancient Bounds, Or Liberty of Conscience Tenderly Stated, Modestly Asserted, and Mildly Vindicated*. London, 1645.
Schomberg, Meyer. "Emunat Omen" (The true faith), translated by Harold Levy. In *Dr. Meyer Schomberg's Attack on the Jews of London* (1746), reprinted from the *Transactions of the Jewish Historical Society of England*, edited by Edgar R. Samuel, 101–11. London: Jewish Historical Society of England, 1964.
Scott, Walter. "Prefatory Memoir to Richardson." In *The Novels of Samuel Richardson*, Ballantyne's Novelist's Library, i–xlviii. London: Hurst, Robinson, 1824.
Seaman, Lazarus. *Solomons Choice: or, A President for Kings and Princes, and all that are in Authority*. London, 1644.
Shower, John. *Family Religion, in Three Letters to a Friend*. London, 1694.
Slater, Samuel. *An Earnest Call to Family-Religion*. London, 1694.
Stevenson, George J. *Memorials of the Wesley Family*. London: Partridge, 1876.
Thorowgood, Thomas. *Moderation Justified*. London, 1645.
Throckmorton, John. *A Letter Addressed to the Catholic Clergy of England on the Appointment of Bishops*. London, 1790.
Tillotson, John. *Six Sermons*. London, 1694.
Toland, John. *Reasons for Naturalizing the Jews in Great Britain and Ireland*. London, 1714.
A True Account of the Proceedings Before the Lords; between the Duke and Dutchess of Norfolk, Upon the Duke's Bill, Entituled, An Act to Dissolve the Marriage. London, 1692.
The true and affecting history of Henrietta of Bellgrave; a woman born only for calamities. London, 1799.
The True History of Zoa, the Beautiful Indian, Daughter of Henrietta de Bellgrave. London, 1799.
Tucker, Josiah. *Letters to the Rev. Dr. Kippis, occasioned by his treatise, entituled, "A Vindication of the Protestant Dissenting Ministers," with regard to their late application to Parliament*. Gloucester, 1773.
Underhill, Edward Bean, ed. *Records of the Churches of Christ, Gathered at Fenstanton, Warboys, and Hexham, 1644–1720*. London, 1854.
Walwyn, William. *Toleration Justified, and Persecution Condemned*. London, 1646.
Warburton, William. *Doctrine of Grace*. London, 1763.
Wesley, Samuel. *Life of Our Blessed Lord & Savior Jesus Christ* (1693). London, 1697.
Wesley, Susanna. *Susanna Wesley: The Complete Writings*. Edited by Charles Wallace Jr. Oxford: Oxford University Press, 1997.
West, Moses. *A Treatise Concerning Marriage, Wherein the Unlawfulness of Mix-Marriages is laid open from the Scriptures of Truth*. London, 1707.
Williams, Roger. *The Bloudy Tenent of Persecution: The Complete Writings of Roger Williams*. Vol. 3. Edited by Samuel L. Caldwell. New York: Russell & Russell, 1963.
Wolseley, Charles. *Liberty of Conscience the Magistrate's Interest*. London, 1668.

Secondary Texts

Achinstein, Sharon. "Early Modern Marriage in a Secular Age." In *Milton in the Long Restoration*, edited by Blair Hoxby and Ann Coiro Baynes, 363–78. Oxford: Oxford University Press, 2016.
Achinstein, Sharon, and Elizabeth Sauer, eds. *Milton and Toleration*. New York: Oxford University Press, 2007.

Adelman, Janet. "Her Father's Blood: Race, Conversion, and Nation in *The Merchant of Venice*." *Representations* 81, no. 1 (2003): 4–30.

Anderson, David L. "Abélard and Héloïse: Eighteenth Century Motif." *Studies on Voltaire and the Eighteenth Century* 84 (1971): 7–51.

Anderson, Emily Hodgson. "Revising Theatrical Conventions in *A Simple Story*: Elizabeth Inchbald's Ambiguous Performance." *Journal for Early Modern Cultural Studies* 6, no. 1 (2006): 5–30.

Anderson, Misty G. *Female Playwrights and Eighteenth-Century Comedy: Negotiating Marriage on the London Stage*. New York: Palgrave, 2002.

Anderson, Misty G. *Imagining Methodism in Eighteenth-Century Britain: Enthusiasm, Belief, and the Borders of the Self*. Baltimore: Johns Hopkins University Press, 2012.

Apetrei, Sarah. "'Call No Man Master upon Earth': Mary Astell's Tory Feminism and an Unknown Correspondence." *Eighteenth-Century Studies* 41, no. 4 (2008): 507–23.

Arch, Stephen Carl. "Frances Brooke's 'Circle of Friends': The Limits of Epistolarity in *The History of Emily Montague*." *Early American Literature* 39, no. 3 (2004): 465–85.

Armstrong, Nancy. *Desire and Domestic Fiction: A Political History of the Novel*. Oxford: Oxford University Press, 1987.

Armstrong, Nancy, and Leonard Tennenhouse. "The American Origins of the English Novel." *American Literary History* 4, no. 3 (1992): 386–410.

Asad, Talal. *Formations of the Secular: Christianity, Islam, Modernity*. Stanford, CA: Stanford University Press, 2003.

Aveling, Hugh. "The Marriages of Catholic Recusants, 1559–1642." *Journal of Ecclesiastical History* 14 (1963): 69–71.

Axtell, James. *The Invasion Within: The Contest of Cultures in Colonial North America*. New York: Oxford University Press, 1985.

Bakhtin, Mikhail. *The Dialogic Imagination: Four Essays*. Edited by Michael Holquist. Translated by Caryl Emerson and Michael Holquist. Austin: University of Texas Press, 1998.

Balfour, Ian. "Promises, Promises: Social and Other Contracts in the English Jacobins (Godwin/Inchbald)." In *New Romanticisms: Theory and Practice*, edited by David L. Clark and Donald C. Goellnicht, 225–49. Toronto: University of Toronto Press, 1994.

Banfield, Ann. *Unspeakable Sentences: Narration and Representation in the Language of Fiction*. Boston: Routledge & Kegan Paul, 1982.

Bannet, Eve Tavor. *The Domestic Revolution: Enlightenment Feminisms and the Novel*. Baltimore: Johns Hopkins University Press, 2000.

Barbauld, Anna. "Life of Samuel Richardson." In *The Correspondence of Samuel Richardson, Author of Pamela, Clarissa, and Sir Charles Grandison Selected from the Original Manuscripts, Bequeathed by Him to His Family, to which are Prefixed, a Biographical Account of that Author, and Observations on His Writings.*, 6 vols., 1: vii–ccxii. Printed for Richard Phillips, no. 71, St. Paul's Church-Yard, 1804.

Barlow, Richard Burgess. *Citizenship and Conscience: A Study in the Theory of Practice of Religious Toleration in England during the Eighteenth Century*. Philadelphia: University of Pennsylvania Press, 1963.

Barnett, Richard. "Dr. Jacob de Castro Sarmento and Sephardim in Medical Practice in 18th-Century London." *Transactions (Jewish Historical Society of England)* 27 (1978): 84–114.

Baron, Salo Wittmayer. *A Social and Religious History of the Jews*. Vol. 11, *Citizen or Alien Conjurer*. 2nd ed. New York: Columbia University Press, 1967.

Barr, Rebecca Anne. "Richardson's *Sir Charles Grandison* and the Symptoms of Subjectivity." *Eighteenth-Century Theory and Interpretation* 51, no. 4 (2010): 391–411.

Bartolomeo, Joseph F. "The Sentimental Novel in America: *The History of Emily Montague, Charlotte Temple, The Power of Sympathy, The Coquette*." In *The Sentimental Novel in the*

Eighteenth Century, edited by Albert J. Rivero, 173–90. Cambridge: Cambridge University Press, 2019.

Bejan, Teresa M. *Mere Civility: Disagreement and the Limits of Toleration*. Cambridge, MA: Harvard University Press, 2017.

Bender, John. *Imagining the Penitentiary: Fiction and the Architecture of Mind in Eighteenth-Century England*. Chicago: University of Chicago Press, 1987.

Benedict, Barbara M. "The Margins of Sentiment: Nature, Letter, & Law in Frances Brooke's Epistolary Novels." *Ariel* 23, no. 3 (1992): 7–20.

Benis, Tony. "Spatial Consciousness and Spiritual Practices in Austen's *Mansfield Park*." *Studies in Romanticism* 58, no. 3 (2019): 333–55.

Bilge, Sirma. "Beyond Subordination vs. Resistance: An Intersectional Approach to the Agency of Veiled Muslim Women." *Journal of Intercultural Studies* 31, no. 3 (2010): 9–28.

Binhammer, Katherine. "The Failure of Trade's Empire in *The History of Emily Montague*." *Eighteenth-Century Fiction* 23, no. 2 (2010): 295–319.

Binhammer, Katherine. *The Seduction Narrative in Britain, 1747–1800*. Cambridge: Cambridge University Press, 2009.

Bossy, John. *The English Catholic Community, 1570–1850*. London: Darton, Longman, and Todd, 1975.

Bouma, Gary D. *Australian Soul: Religion and Spirituality in the Twenty-First Century*. Cambridge: Cambridge University Press, 2006.

Boutelle, Anne Edwards. "Frances Brooke's *Emily Montague* (1769): Canada and Women's Rights." *Women's Studies* 12, no. 1 (1968): 7–16.

Bowers, Toni. "Family." In *Samuel Richardson in Context*, edited by Betty A. Schellenberg and Peter Sabor, 231–38. Cambridge: Cambridge University Press, 2017.

Bowers, Toni. *Force or Fraud: British Seduction Stories and the Problem of Resistance, 1660–1760*. Oxford: Oxford University Press, 2011.

Bowers, Toni. *The Politics of Motherhood: British Writing and Culture, 1680–1760*. Cambridge: Cambridge University Press, 2008.

Brown, Gayle K. "'Into the Hands of Papists': New England, Captives in French Canada and the English Anti-Catholic Tradition, 1689–1763." *Maryland Historian* 21 (1990): 1–11.

Brown, Wendy. *Regulating Aversion: Tolerance in the Age of Identity and Empire*. Princeton, NJ: Princeton University Press, 2006.

Brückmann, Patricia. "'Men, Women and Poles': Samuel Richardson and the Romance of a Stuart Princess." *Eighteenth-Century Life* 27, no. 3 (2003): 31–52.

Bulman, William J. *Anglican Enlightenment: Orientalism, Religion and Politics in England and its Empire, 1648–1715*. Cambridge: Cambridge University Press, 2015.

Bumsted, J. M. "The Cultural Landscape of Early Canada." In *Strangers within the Realm: Cultural Margins of the First British Empire*, edited by Bernard Bailyn and Philip D. Morgan, 363–92. Chapel Hill: University of North Carolina Press, 1991.

Butler, Judith, Zeynap Gambetti, and Leticia Sabsay. Introduction to *Vulnerability in Resistance*, edited by Judith Butler, Zeynap Gambetti, and Leticia Sabsay, 1–11. Durham, NC: Duke University Press, 2016.

Butler, Marilyn. *Maria Edgeworth: A Literary Biography*. Oxford: Clarendon, 1972.

Cable, Lana. "Secularizing Conscience in Milton's Republican Community." In *Milton and Toleration*, edited by Sharon Achinstein and Elizabeth Sauer, 268–83. New York: Oxford University Press, 2007.

Cambers, Andrew, and Michelle Wolfe. "Reading, Family Religion, and Evangelical Identity in Late Stuart England." *Historical Journal* 47, no. 4 (2004): 875–96.

Canuel, Mark. "Jane Austen and the Importance of Being Wrong." *Studies in Romanticism* 44, no. 2 (2007): 123–50.

Canuel, Mark. "Joseph Priestley's Romantic Progressivism." In *Imagining Religious Toleration: A Literary History of an Idea, 1600–1830*, edited by Alison Conway and David Alvarez, 216–33. Toronto: University of Toronto Press, 2019.

Canuel, Mark. *Religion, Toleration, and British Writing, 1790–1830*. Cambridge: Cambridge University Press, 2002.

Carnes, Geremy. *The Papist Represented: Literature and the English Catholic Community, 1688–1791*. Newark: University of Delaware Press, 2017.

Castelli, Elizabeth A. "Women, Gender, Religion: Troubling Categories and Transforming Knowledge." In *Women, Gender, Religion: A Reader*, edited by Elizabeth A. Castelli, 3–25. New York: Palgrave, 2001.

Castle, Terry. *Masquerade and Civilization: The Carnivalesque in Eighteenth Century English Culture and Fiction*. Stanford, CA: Stanford University Press, 1986.

Catalogue of Political and Personal Satires in the Department of Prints and Drawings in the British Museum. Vols. 5–11. Edited by Mary Dorothy George. London: British Museum, Department of Prints and Drawings, 1870–1954.

Chaber, Lois A. "'Sufficient to the Day': Anxiety in *Sir Charles Grandison*." In *Passion and Virtue: Essays on the Novels of Samuel Richardson*, edited by David Blewett, 268–94. Toronto: University of Toronto Press, 2001.

Chico, Tita. "Details and Frankness: Affective Relations in *Sir Charles Grandison*." *Studies in Eighteenth-Century Culture* 38, no. 1 (2009): 45–68.

Chinnici, Joseph P. *The English Catholic Enlightenment: John Lingard and the Cisalpine Movement, 1780–1850*. Shepherdstown, WV: Patmos Press, 1980.

Choudhury, Mita. *Interculturalism and Resistance in the London Theatre, 1660–1800: Identity, Performance, Empire*. Lewisburg, PA: Bucknell University Press, 2000.

Colley, Linda. *Britons: Forging the Nation, 1707–1837*. London: Yale University Press, 2009.

Connell, Joan. *The Roman Catholic Church in England, 1780–1850: A Study in Internal Politics*. Philadelphia: American Philosophical Society, 1984.

Conway, Alison. "'As So Many Dead Corpses': Religious Tolerance from beyond the Grave." *Restoration* 45, no. 2 (2021): 41–61.

Conway, Alison. Introduction to *Imagining Religious Toleration: A Literary History of an Idea, 1600–1830*, edited by Alison Conway and David Alvarez, 1–17. Toronto: University of Toronto Press, 2019.

Conway, Alison. *Private Interests: Women, Portraiture, and the Visual Culture of the English Novel, 1709–1791*. Toronto: University of Toronto Press, 2001.

Conway, Alison. *The Protestant Whore: Courtesan Narrative and Religious Controversy in the English Novel, 1680–1750*. Toronto: University of Toronto Press, 2010.

Conway, Alison. "'Uncommon Sentiments': Religious Freedom and the Marriage Plot in Charlotte Lennox's *Henrietta*." *Tulsa Studies in Women's Literature* 34, no. 2 (2015): 231–48.

Conway, Alison. "'Unequally Yoked': Defoe and the Challenge of Mixed Marriage." In *Reflections on Sentiment: Essays in Honor of George Starr*, edited by Alessa Johns, 11–28. Newark: University of Delaware Press, 2016.

Conway, Alison, and Corrine Harol. "Toward a Postsecular Eighteenth Century." *Literature Compass* 12, no.11 (Nov. 2015): 565–74.

Craft-Fairchild, Catherine. "The 'Jewish Question' on Both Sides of the Atlantic: *Harrington* and the Correspondence between Maria Edgeworth and Rachel Mordecai Lazarus." *Eighteenth-Century Literature* 38, no. 3 (2014): 30–63.

Craft-Fairchild, Catherine. *Masquerade and Gender: Disguise and Female Identity in Eighteenth-Century Fictions by Women*. University Park: Pennsylvania State University Press, 1993.

Cranfield, G. A. "The 'London Evening-Post' and the Jew Bill of 1753." *Historical Journal* 8, no. 1 (1965): 16–30.

Crawford, Patricia. *Women and Religion in England, 1500–1720*. London: Routledge, 1993.
Crochunis, Thomas C. "Pre- and Post-realist Dramaturgy: Women Writers, Silence, Speech, and Trauma." In *Teaching British Women Playwrights of the Restoration and Eighteenth Century*, edited by Bonnie Nelson and Catherine Burroughs, 336–47. New York: Modern Language Association, 2010.
Crome, Andrew. "The 1753 'Jew Bill' Controversy: Jewish Restoration to Palestine, Biblical Prophecy and English National Identity." *English Historical Review* 130, no. 547 (2015): 1449–78.
Davidson, Jenny. *Hypocrisy and the Politics of Politeness: Manners and Morals from Locke to Austen*. New York: Cambridge University Press, 2004.
Decker, Sharon L. "The Problem with Binaries: Balancing Reason, Emotion, Body, and Mind in *A Simple Story*." *Studies in the Literary Imagination* 47, no. 2 (2014): 59–82.
Del Bazo, Angelina. "'The Feelings of Others': Sympathy and Anti-Semitism in Maria Edgeworth's *Harrington*." *Eighteenth-Century Fiction* 31, no. 4 (2019): 685–704.
Devereux, Cecily. "'One Firm Body': 'Britishness and Otherness' in *The History of Emily Montague*." In *The History of Emily Montague*, by Frances Brooke, edited by Laura Moss, 459–76. Ottawa: Tecumseh Press, 2001.
Ditchfield, G. M. "'The Right of Private Judgement, with the Case of Public Safety': The Church of England's Perceptions of Protestant Dissent in the Later Eighteenth Century." *Enlightenment and Dissent* 28 (2012): 1–23.
Doerksen, Teri. "*Sir Charles Grandison*: The Anglican Family and the Admirable Roman Catholic." *Eighteenth-Century Fiction* 15, no. 3 (2003): 539–58.
Dolan, Frances E. *Marriage and Violence: The Early Modern Legacy*. Philadelphia: University of Pennsylvania Press, 2008.
Dolan, Frances E. *Whores of Babylon: Catholicism, Gender, and Seventeenth-Century Print Culture*. New York: Cornell University Press, 1999.
Dominique, Lyndon J. *Imoinda's Shade: Marriage and the African Woman in Eighteenth-Century British Literature, 1759–1808*. Columbus: Ohio State University Press, 2012.
Doody, Margaret Anne. *A Natural Passion: A Study of the Novels of Samuel Richardson*. Oxford: Clarendon Press, 1974.
Doody, Margaret Anne. "Richardson's Politics." *Eighteenth-Century Fiction* 2, no. 2 (1990): 113–26.
Doody, Margaret Anne. "Samuel Richardson: Fiction and Knowledge." In *The Cambridge Companion to the Eighteenth-Century Novel*, edited by John Richetti, 90–119. Cambridge: Cambridge University Press, 1996.
Duffy, Eamon. "Ecclesiastical Democracy Detected: 1 (1779–1787)." *Recusant History* 10, no. 4 (1970): 193–209.
Duffy, Eamon. *Peter and Jack: Roman Catholics and Dissent in Eighteenth-Century England*. London: Friends of Dr. William's Library, 1982.
Dussinger, John. "The Negotiations of *Sir Charles Grandison*." In *New Windows on a Woman's World: Essays for Jocelyn Harris*, vol. 1, edited by Colin Gibson and Lisa Marr, 32–50. Dunedin, NZ: University of Otago Press, 2005.
Eagles, Robin. *Francophilia in English Society, 1748–1815*. Houndmills: Macmillan Press, 2000.
Eaves, T. C. Duncan, and Ben D. Kimpel. *Samuel Richardson: A Biography*. Oxford: Clarendon Press, 1971.
Edwards, Mary Jane. "Frances Brooke's Politics and *The History of Emily Montague*." In *The Beginnings: A Critical Anthology*, edited by John Moss, 19–27. Toronto: NC Press, 1980.
Edwards, Mary Jane. Introduction to *The History of Emily Montague*, edited by Mary Jane Edwards, xvii–xxxvi. Ottawa: Carleton University Press, 1991.
"Elizabeth Inchbald." In *Orlando: Women's Writing in the British Isles from the Beginnings to the Present*, edited by Susan Brown, Patricia Clements, and Isobel Grundy. Cambridge:

Cambridge University Press Online, 2006. https://orlando-cambridge-org.eu1.proxy.open athens.net/.

Ellison, Julie. "'There and Back': Transatlantic Novels and the Anglo-American Careers." In *The Past as Prologue: Essays to Celebrate the Twenty-Fifth Anniversary of ASECS*, edited by Carla H. Hay and Sydney M. Conger, 321–71. New York: AMS Press, 1995.

Endelman, Todd M. *The Jews of Georgian England, 1714–1830: Tradition and Change in a Liberal Society.* Philadelphia: Jewish Publication Society of America, 1979.

Felsenstein, Frank. *Anti-Semitic Stereotypes: A Paradigm of Otherness in English Popular Culture, 1660–1830.* Baltimore: Johns Hopkins University Press, 1995.

Ferguson, Moira. *Subject to Others: British Women Writers and Colonial Slavery, 1670–1834.* London: Routledge, 1992.

Field, Clive D. "Counting Religion in England and Wales: The Long Eighteenth Century, c. 1680–1840." *Journal of Ecclesiastical History* 63, no. 4 (2012): 693–720.

Fitzpatrick, Martin Hugh. "From Natural Law to Natural Rights? Protestant Dissent and Toleration in the Late Eighteenth Century." *History of European Ideas* 42, no. 2 (2016): 195–221.

Franke, Wolfgang. "Richardson's *Grandison* as a Novel for Debate." In *Functions of Literature: Essays Presented to Erwinn Wolff on His Sixtieth Birthday*, edited by Ulrich Broich, Theo Stemmler, and Gerd Stratmann, 173–93. Tübingen: Niemeyer, 1984.

Friedman, Jean E. *Ways of Wisdom: Moral Education in the Early National Period.* Athens: University of Georgia Press, 2001.

Friedman, Jerome. "Jewish Conversion, the Spanish Pure Blood Laws and Reformation: A Revisionist View of Racial and Religious Antisemitism." *Sixteenth Century Journal* 13, no. 1 (1987): 3–30.

Friedman, Susan Stanford. "Religion, Intersectionality, and Queer/Feminist Narrative Theory: The Bildungsroman of Ahdaf Soueif, Leila Aboulela, and Randa Jarrar." In *Narrative Theory Unbound: Queer and Feminist Interventions*, edited by Robyn Warhol and Susan S. Lanser, 101–22. Columbus: Ohio State University Press, 2015.

Galgano, Michael. "Out of the Mainstream: Catholic and Quaker Women in the Restoration Northwest." In *The World of William Penn*, edited by Richard S. Dunn and Mary Maples Dunn, 117–38. Philadelphia: University of Pennsylvania Press, 1986.

Gallagher, Catherine. "Embracing the Absolute: Margaret Cavendish and the Politics of the Female Subject in Seventeenth-Century England." *Genders* 1, no. 1 (1988): 24–33.

Gallagher, Catherine. *Nobody's Story: The Vanishing Acts of Women Writers in the Marketplace, 1670–1820.* Berkeley: University of California Press, 1995.

Gerber, Jane S. *The Jews of Spain: A History of the Sephardic Experience.* New York: Free Press, 1992.

Glaser, Elaine. *Religious Tolerance in the Atlantic World: Early Modern and Contemporary Perspectives.* Houndsmills: Palgrave Macmillan, 2014.

Golden, Morris. "Public Context and Imagining Self in *Sir Charles Grandison*." *Eighteenth Century* 29, vol. 1 (1988): 3–18.

Goldie, Mark. "Alexander Geddes (1737–1802): Biblical Criticism, Ecclesiastical Democracy, and Jacobinism." In *Enlightenment and Catholicism in Europe: A Transnational History*, edited by Ulrich Lehner and Jeffrey Burson, 411–30. South Bend, IN: University of Notre Dame Press, 2014.

Gooch, Leopold. "'Chiefly of Low Rank': The Catholics of North-East England, 1705–1814." In *English Catholics of Parish and Town, 1558–1778*, edited by Marie B. Rowlands, 237–57. London: Catholic Record Society, 1999.

Gordon, Albert I. *Intermarriage: Interfaith, Interracial, Interethnic.* Boston: Beacon Press, 1964.

Grant, Ruth. "John Locke on Women and the Family." In *Two Treatises of Government: And a Letter Concerning Religious Toleration*, by John Locke, edited by Ian Shapiro, 286–308. London: Yale University Press, 2008.

Green, Katherine S. "'You Should Be My Master': Imperial Recognition in Elizabeth Inchbald's *Such Things Are*." *Clio* 27, no. 3 (1998): 387–414.
Gregory, Jeremy. "Homo Religious: Masculinity and Religion in the Long Eighteenth Century." In *English Masculinities 1660–1800*, edited by Tim Hitchcock and Michele Cohen, 85–110. London: Longman, 1999.
Grell, Ole Peter, Jonathan Irvine Israel, and Nicholas Tyacke, eds. *From Persecution to Toleration: The Glorious Revolution and Religion in England*. New York: Clarendon Press, 1991.
Grinnell, George. "Timely Responses: Violence and Immediacy in Inchbald's *The Massacre*." ERR 24, no. 6 (2013): 645–63.
Guest, Harriet. *Small Change: Women, Learning, and Patriotism 1750–1810*. Chicago: University of Chicago Press, 2000.
Gwilliam, Tassie. *Samuel Richardson's Fictions of Gender*. Stanford, CA: Stanford University Press, 1993.
Hale, Dorothy. "Aesthetics and the New Ethics." In *American Literature's Aesthetic Dimensions*, edited by Cindy Weinstein and Christopher Looby, 313–27. New York: Columbia University Press, 2012.
Hall, David J. "An Historical Study of the Discipline of the Society of Friends, 1738–1761." MA Thesis, Durham University, Durham, UK, 1972.
Hammill, Faye. "'A Daughter of the Muses': Authorship and Creativity in *The History of Emily Montague*" (1769). In *The History of Emily Montague*, by Frances Brooke, edited by Laura Moss, 437–50. Ottawa: Tecumseh Press, 2001.
Harland-Jacobs, Jessica L. "Incorporating the King's New Subjects: Accommodation and Anti-Catholicism in the British Empire, 1763–1815." *Journal of Religious History* 39, no. 2 (2015): 206–13.
Harris, Jocelyn. *Samuel Richardson*. Cambridge: Cambridge University Press, 1987.
Harrison, Richard S. "'As a Garden Enclosed': the Emergence of Irish Quakers: 1650–1750." In *The Irish Dissenting Tradition, 1650–1750*, edited by Kevin Herlihy, 81–95. Dublin: Four Courts Press, 1995.
Hazlitt, William. *The Complete Works of William Hazlitt* (1931). Vol. 6, edited by P. P. Howe. New York: AMS, 1967.
Hershinow, Stephanie Insley. *Born Yesterday: Inexperience and the Early Realist Novel*. Baltimore: Johns Hopkins University Press, 2019.
Hessayon, Ariel. "Attaway, Mrs (fl. 1645–1646), Baptist preacher." *Oxford Dictionary of National Biography*, September 23, 2004. Accessed Mar. 20, 2022. https://www.oxforddnb.com/view/10.1093/ref:odnb/9780198614128.001.0001/odnb-9780198614128-e-45478.
Hewitt, Regina. "Maria Edgeworth's *Harrington* as a Utopian Novel." *Studies in the Novel* 46, no. 3 (2014): 239–314.
Heydt-Stevenson, Jill, and Charlotte Sussman. "'Launched upon the Sea of Moral and Political Inquiry': The Ethical Experiments of the Romantic Novel." In *Recognizing the Romantic Novel: New Histories of British Fiction, 1780–1830*, edited by Jill Heydt-Stevenson and Charlotte Sussman, 13–48. Liverpool: Liverpool University Press, 2008.
Hirsch, Brett D. "'A Gentle and No Jew': The Difference a Marriage Makes in *The Merchant of Venice*." *Parergon* 23, vol. 1 (2006): 119–29.
Hirshmann, Nancy J., and Kristie M. McClure, eds. *Feminist Interpretations of John Locke*. University Park: Pennsylvania State University Press, 2007.
Hoad, Neville. "Maria Edgeworth's *Harrington*: The Price of Sympathetic Identification." In *British Romanticism and the Jews: History, Culture, Literature*, edited by Sheila A. Spector, 121–37. New York: Palgrave MacMillan, 2002.
Hollander, Rachel. *Narrative Hospitality in Late Victorian Fiction: Novel Ethics*. London: Routledge, 2013.

Horton, John, and Susan Mendus, eds. *John Locke: A Letter Concerning Toleration, in Focus*. London: Routledge, 1991.
Howells, Robin. "Dialogism in Canada's First Novel: *The History of Emily Montague*." *Canadian Review of Comparative Literature* 20, nos. 3/4 (1993): 437–50.
Hunter, J. Paul. *Before Novels: The Cultural Contexts of Eighteenth-Century English Fiction*. New York: Norton, 1990.
Hyamson, Albert M. *The Sephardim of England: A History of the Spanish and Portuguese Jewish Community, 1492–1950*. London: Methuen, 1951.
Jager, Colin. *The Book of God: Secularization and Design in the Romantic Era*. Philadelphia: University of Pennsylvania Press, 2006.
Jager, Colin. "Translating Love in *Prometheus Unbound*." In *Imagining Religious Toleration: A Literary History of an Idea, 1600–1830*, edited by Alison Conway and David Alvarez, 234–58. Toronto: University of Toronto Press, 2019.
Jager, Colin. *Unquiet Things: Secularism in the Romantic Age*. Philadelphia: University of Pennsylvania Press, 2014.
Jensen, Katharine Ann. *Writing Love: Letters, Women, and the Novel in France, 1605–1776*. Carbondale: Southern Illinois University Press, 1995.
Johnson, Claudia. *Jane Austen: Women, Politics, and the Novel*. Chicago: University of Chicago Press, 1988.
Jones, J. R., ed. *Liberty Secured: Britain before and after 1688*. Stanford, CA: Stanford University Press, 1992.
Jones, Wendy. *Consensual Fictions: Women, Liberalism, and the English Novel*. Toronto: University of Toronto Press, 2005.
Jones, Wendy. "The Dialectic of Love in *Sir Charles Grandison*." *Eighteenth-Century Fiction* 8, no. 1 (1995): 15–34.
Jordan, W. K. *The Development of Religious Toleration in England*. London: George Allen & Unwin, 1936.
Judson, Barbara. "The Psychology of Satan: Elizabeth Inchbald's *A Simple Story*." *ELH* 76, no. 3 (2009): 599–619.
Kahn, Victoria. *Wayward Contracts: The Crisis of Political Obligation in England, 1640–1674*. Princeton, NJ: Princeton University Press, 2004.
Kaplan, Benjamin J. *Cunegonde's Kidnapping: A Story of Religious Conflict in the Age of Enlightenment*. New Haven, CT: Yale University Press, 2014.
Kaplan, Benjamin J. *Divided by Faith: Religious Conflict and the Practice of Toleration in Early Modern Europe*. Cambridge, MA: Harvard University Press, 2007.
Katz, David S. *The Jews in the History of England, 1485–1850*. New York: Clarendon Press, 1994.
Katz, David S. *Sabbath and Sectarianism in Seventeenth-Century England*. Leiden: Brill, 1988.
Keane, Angela. *Women Writers and the English Novel in the 1790s: Romantic Belongings*. Cambridge: Cambridge University Press, 2000.
Kebbel, T. E. "Fitzherbert, Maria Anne (1756–1837)." In *Oxford Dictionary of National Biography*, vol. 19, edited by Leslie Stephen, 170–71. London: Smith, Elder, 1889.
Keegan, Bridget. "'Bred a Jesuit': *A Simple Story* and Late Eighteenth-Century Catholic Culture." *Huntington Library Quarterly* 71, no. 4 (2008): 687–706.
Keen, Suzanne. *Empathy and the Novel*. New York: Oxford University Press, 2007.
Kelly, Gary. *The English Jacobin Novel, 1780–1805*. Oxford: Clarendon, 1976.
Kelly, P. J. "Authority, Conscience, and Religious Toleration." In *John Locke: An Essay Concerning Religious Toleration in Focus*, edited by John Horton and Susan Mendus, 125–46. London: Routledge, 1991.
Kessler, Sanford. "John Locke's Legacy of Religious Freedom." *Polity* 17, no. 3 (1985): 484–503.

Kilgour, Maggie. *From Communion to Cannibalism: An Anatomy of Metaphors of Incorporation.* Princeton, NJ: Princeton University Press, 1990.
King, Kathryn R. "Frances Brooke, Editor, and the Making of *The Old Maid*." In *Women's Periodicals and Print Culture in Britain, 1690–1820s,* edited by Jennie Batchelor and Manushag N. Powell, 342–45. Edinburgh: Edinburgh University Press, 2018.
Kirk, Silvia. *Many Tender Ties: Women in Fur-Trade Society, 1670–1870.* Tulsa: University of Oklahoma Press, 1980.
Knott, Sarah, and Barbara Taylor, eds. *Women, Gender, and Enlightenment.* New York: Palgrave Macmillan, 2005.
Kramer, Kaley. "Rethinking Surrender: Elizabeth Inchbald and the 'Catholic Novel.'" In *British Women and the Intellectual World in the Long Eighteenth Century,* edited by Teresa Bernard, 87–105. London: Routledge, 2016.
Kraynak, Robert P. "John Locke: From Absolutism to Toleration." *American Political Science Review* 74, no. 1 (1980): 53–69.
Lanser, Susan. "Second-Sex Economies: Race, Rescue, and the Heroine's Plot." *Eighteenth Century: Theory and Interpretation* 61, no. 2 (2020): 227–44.
Latimer, Bonnie. "Samuel Richardson and the 'Jew Bill' of 1753: A New Political Context for *Sir Charles Grandison*." *Review of English Studies* 66, no. 275 (2015): 520–39.
Lee, Hye-Soo. "Women, Comedy, and *A Simple Story*." *Eighteenth-Century Fiction* 20, no. 2 (2007–8): 197–217.
Lee, Yoon Sun. "Bad Plots and Objectivity in Maria Edgeworth." *Representations* 139, no. 1 (2017): 34–59.
Levy, Martin J. "Fitzherbert [née Smythe; other married name Weld], Maria Anne (1756–1837), unlawful wife of George IV by a marriage invalid under the Royal Marriages Act of 1772." In *Oxford Dictionary of National Biography.* September 23, 2004. Accessed Mar. 20, 2022. https://www.oxforddnb.com/view/10.1093/ref:odnb/9780198614128.001.0001/odnb-9780198614128-e-9603.
Little, Ann M. *The Many Captivities of Esther Wheelwright.* New Haven, CT: Yale University Press, 2016.
Lloyd, David. *Anomalous States: Irish Writing and the Post-colonial Moment.* Dublin: Lilliput, 1993.
Logan, Peter Melville. "Harrington's Last Shudder: Maria Edgeworth and the Popular Fear of the Nervous Body." In *Nerves and Narratives: A Cultural History of Hysteria in Nineteenth-Century English Prose,* 109–13. Berkeley: University of California Press, 1997.
Lott, Anna. Introduction to *A Simple Story,* by Elizabeth Inchbald, edited by Anna Lott, 13–46. Peterborough, ON: Broadview Press, 2007.
Lupton, Christina. "Contingency, Codex, the Eighteenth-Century Novel," *ELH* 81, no. 4 (2014): 1173–92.
MacDonald, Edgar E., ed. *The Education of the Heart: The Correspondence of Rachel Mordecai and Maria Edgeworth.* Chapel Hill: University of North Carolina Press, 1977.
Mack, Phyllis. *Heart Religion in the British Enlightenment: Gender and Emotion in Early Methodism.* Cambridge: Cambridge University Press, 2008.
Macleitch, Gail D. "'Your Women Are of No Small Consequence': Native American Women, Gender, and Early American History." In *The Practice of U.S. Women's History: Narratives, Intersections, and Dialogues,* edited by S. Jay Kleinberg, Vicki L. Ruiz, and Eileen Boris, 30–49. New Brunswick, NJ: Rutgers University Press, 2007.
Mahmood, Saba. *Politics of Piety: The Islamic Revival and the Feminist Subject.* Princeton, NJ: Princeton University Press, 2012. First published 2005.
Maltzahn, Nicholas von. "Milton, Marvell, and Toleration." In *Milton and Toleration,* edited by Sharon Achinstein and Elizabeth Sauer, 86–106. New York: Oxford University Press, 2007.

Mandell, Laura. "Bad Marriages, Bad Novels: The 'Philosophical Romance.'" In *Recognizing the Romantic Novel: New Histories of British Fiction, 1780–1830*, edited by Jillian Heydt-Stevenson and Charlotte Sussman, 49–77. Liverpool: Liverpool University Press, 2008.

Manly, Susan. "Burke, Toland, Toleration." In *Edmund Burke's Reflections on the Revolution in France: New Interdisciplinary Essays*, edited by John C. Whale, 145–67. Manchester: Manchester University Press, 2000.

Manly, Susan. "*Harrington* and Anti-Semitism: Mendelssohn's Invisible Agency." In *An Uncomfortable Authority: Maria Edgeworth and Her Contexts*, edited by Heidi Kaufman and Christopher J. Fauske, 235–49. Newark, NJ: Associated University Presses, 2004.

Manvell, Roger. *Elizabeth Inchbald: England's Principal Woman Dramatist and Independent Woman of Letters in 18th Century London*. Lanham, MD: University Press of America, 1987.

Marshall, John. *John Locke: Resistance, Religion, and Responsibility*. Cambridge: Cambridge University Press, 1994.

Marshall, John. *John Locke, Toleration and Early Enlightenment Culture*. Cambridge: Cambridge University Press, 2006.

McCarthy, Dermot. "Sisters under the Mink: The Correspondent Fear in *The History of Emily Montague*." *Essays on Canadian Writing* 51–52 (1993–94): 340–57.

McClure, Kirstie M. "Difference, Diversity, and the Limits of Toleration." *Political Theory* 18, no. 3 (1990): 361–91.

McDonagh, Josephine. *Literature in a Time of Migration: British Fiction and the Movement of People, 1815–1870*. Oxford: Oxford University Press, 2021.

McDowell, Paula. *Elinor James: The Early Modern Englishwoman*. Series 2. Part 3. Vol. 11. Farnham, UK: Ashgate, 2005.

McDowell, Paula. *The Women of Grubstreet: Press, Politics, and Gender in the Literary Marketplace, 1678–1730*. Oxford: Clarendon Press, 1998.

McInelly, Brett. *Textual Warfare and the Making of Methodism*. Oxford: Oxford University Press, 2014.

McMullen, Lorraine, and W. H. New. *An Odd Attempt in a Woman: The Literary Life of Frances Brooke*. Vancouver: University of British Columbia Press, 1983.

McMurran, Mary Helen. *The Spread of Novels: Translation and Prose Fiction in the Eighteenth Century*. Princeton, NJ: Princeton University Press, 2009.

McNeff, Heather. "Finding Happiness: Interfaith Marriage in British Literature, 1745–1836." PhD diss., University of Minnesota, 2013.

Meer, Nasar. "Racialization and Religion: Race, Culture and Difference in the Study of Antisemitism and Islamophobia." *Ethnic and Racial Studies* 36, no. 3 (2013): 385–98.

Mello, Patrick. "'Piety and Popishness': Tolerance and the Epistolary Reaction to Richardson's *Sir Charles Grandison*." *Eighteenth-Century Fiction* 25, no. 3 (2013): 511–31.

Mellor, Anne K. "Embodied Cosmopolitanism and the British Romantic Writer." *European Romantic Review* 17, no. 3 (2006): 289–300.

Merrett, Robert. "The Politics of Romance in *The History of Emily Montague*." *Canadian Literature* 133 (1992): 92–108.

Messenger, Ann. "Arabella Fermor, 1714 and 1769: Alexander Pope and Frances Moore Brooke." In *His and Hers: Essays in Restoration and Eighteenth-Century Literature*, 148–71. Lexington: University Press of Kentucky, 1986.

Metzger, Mary Janell. "'Now by My Hood, a Gentle and No Jew': Jessica, *The Merchant of Venice*, and the Discourse of Early Modern English Identity." *PMLA* 113, no. 1 (1998): 52–63.

Miller, D. A. *Jane Austen, or The Secret of Style*. Princeton, NJ: Princeton University Press, 2003.

Milligan, Edward H. *Quaker Marriage*. Kendal, UK: Quaker Tapestry Booklets, 1994.

Mills, Charles W. *Black Rights/White Wrongs: The Critique of Racial Liberalism*. Oxford: Oxford University Press, 2017.

Min, Eun Kyung. "Giving Promises in Elizabeth Inchbald's *A Simple Story*." ELH 77, no. 1 (2010): 105–27.
Morvan, Alain. *La tolérance dans le roman anglais de 1726 à 1771*. Paris: Didier, 1984.
Moss, Laura. "Colonialism and Postcolonialism in *The History of Emily Montague*." In *The History of Emily Montague*, by Frances Brooke, edited by Laura Moss, 451–59. Ottawa: Tecumseh Press, 2001. First published 1769.
Moss, Laura, ed. *Is Canada Postcolonial? Unsettling Canadian Literature*. Waterloo, ON: Wilfred Laurier University Press, 2003.
Munson, James. *Maria Fitzherbert: Secret Wife of George IV*. New York: Carroll and Graff, 2001.
Neuman, Justin. *Fiction beyond Secularism*. Chicago: Northwestern University Press, 2014.
Neumann, Anne Waldron. "Free Indirect Discourse in the Eighteenth-Century Novel: Speakable or Unspeakable? The Example of *Sir Charles Grandison*." In *Language, Text, Context: Essays in Contextualized Stylistics*, edited by Michael Toolan, 113–35. London: Routledge, 1992.
New, W. H. "The Old Maid: Frances Brooke's Apprentice Feminism." *Journal of Canadian Fiction* 2, no. 3 (1973): 9–12.
Newman, Aubrey. "Anglo-Jewry in the 18th Century." *Transactions of the Jewish Historical Society of England* 27 (1982): 1–10.
Ng, Su Fang. *Literature and the Politics of the Family*. Cambridge: Cambridge University Press, 2007.
Nichols, Robert. *Theft Is Property*. Durham, NC: Duke University Press, 2020.
Nielsen, Wendy C. "A Tragic Farce: Revolutionary Women in Elizabeth Inchbald's *The Massacre* and European Drama." *ERR* 17, no. 3 (July 2006): 275–88.
Nirenberg, David. *Anti-Judaism: The History of a Way of Thinking*. New York: Norton, 2013.
Noel, Jan. "'Fertile with Fine Talk': Ungoverned Tongues among Haudenosaunee Women and Their Neighbors." *Ethnohistory* 57, no. 2 (2010): 201–23.
Nussbaum, Felicity. *Torrid Zones: Maternity, Sexuality, and Empire in Eighteenth-Century English Narratives*. Baltimore: John Hopkins University Press, 1995.
O'Brien, Karen. *Women and Enlightenment in Eighteenth-Century Britain*. Cambridge: Cambridge University Press, 2009.
O'Connell, Lisa. *The Origins of the English Marriage Plot: Literature, Politics and Religion in the Eighteenth Century*. Cambridge: Cambridge University Press, 2019.
O'Quinn, Daniel. *Staging Governance: Theatrical Imperialism in London, 1770–1800*. Baltimore: Johns Hopkins University Press, 2005.
Osland, Dianne. "Heart-Picking in *A Simple Story*." *Eighteenth-Century Fiction* 16, no. 1 (2003): 79–101.
Page, Judith. *Imperfect Sympathies: Jews and Judaism in British Romantic Literature*. New York: Palgrave Macmillan, 2004.
Parker, Jo Alyson. "Complicating *A Simple Story*: Inchbald's Two Versions of Female Power." *Eighteenth-Century Studies* 30, no. 3 (1997): 255–70.
Pateman, Carole. *The Sexual Contract*. Stanford, CA: Stanford University Press, 1988.
Patterson, Annabel. "Milton, Marriage, and Divorce." In *A Companion to Milton*, edited by Thomas N. Corns, 279–93. Oxford: Blackwell, 2001.
Patterson, Annabel. "Parliament and the Control of Religion, 1661–1674." In *The Long Parliament of Charles II*, 145–162. New Haven, CT: Yale University Press, 2008.
Pawl, Amy. "Only a Girl? Miss Milner, Matilda, and the Consolations of Filial Piety in *A Simple Story*." In *Reflections on Sentiment: Essays in Honor of George Starr*, edited by Alessa Johns, 105–34. Newark: University of Delaware Press, 2016.
Perkins, Pam. "Frances Brooke, Emily Montague, and Other Travellers: Representing Eighteenth-Century North America." In *The History of Emily Montague*, by Frances Brooke, edited by Laura Moss, 421–36. Ottawa: Tecumseh Press, 2001. First published 1769.

Perkins, Pam. "Imagining 18th Century Quebec: British Literature and Colonial Rhetoric." In *Is Canada Postcolonial? Unsettling Canadian Literature*, edited by Laura Moss, 151–61. Waterloo, ON: Wilfred Laurier University Press, 2003.

Perry, Ruth. "Colonizing the Breast: Sexuality and Maternity in Eighteenth-Century England." *Journal of the History of Sexuality* 2, no. 2 (1991): 204–34.

Perry, Ruth. *Novel Relations: The Transformation of Kinship in English Literature and Culture, 1748–1818*. Cambridge: Cambridge University Press, 2004.

Perry, Thomas W. *Public Opinion, Propaganda, and Politics in Eighteenth-Century England: A Study of the Jew Bill of 1753*. Cambridge, MA: Harvard University Press, 1965.

Peterson, Jacqueline. "Women Dreaming: The Religiopsychology of Indian-White Marriages and the Rise of a Metis Culture." In *Western Women: Their Lands, Their Lives*, edited by Lillian Schlessel, Vicki L. Ruiz, and Janice Monk, 49–68. Albuquerque: University of New Mexico Press, 1988.

Pinto, Samantha. *Infamous Bodies: Early Black Women's Celebrity and the Afterlives of Rights*. Durham, NC: Duke University Press, 2020.

Plotz, John. *The Absentee in the Crowd: British Literature and Public Politics*. Berkeley: University of California Press, 2000.

Pollak, Ellen. "Introduction: Modernity, Incest, and Eighteenth-Century Narrative." In *Incest and the English Novel, 1684–1814*, 1–26. Baltimore: Johns Hopkins University Press, 2003.

Popkin, Richard H., and Mark Goldie. "Scepticism, Priestcraft, and Toleration." In *The Cambridge History of Eighteenth-Century Political Thought*, edited by Mark Goldie and Richard Wokler, 79–109. Cambridge: Cambridge University Press, 2006.

Pritchard, Elizabeth A. *Religion in Public: Locke's Political Theology*. Stanford, CA: Stanford University Press, 2013.

Probert, Rebecca. *Marriage Law and Practice in the Long Eighteenth Century: A Reassessment*. Cambridge: Cambridge University Press, 2009.

Probert, Rebecca, and Liam D'Arcy Brown. "Catholics and the Clandestine Marriages Act of 1753." *Local Population Studies* 78 (2008): 78–82.

Purves, Maria. *The Gothic and Catholicism: Religion, Cultural Exchange and the Popular Novel, 1785–1829*. Cardiff: University of Wales, 2009.

Rabin, Dana. "The Jew Bill of 1753: Masculinity, Virility, and the Nation." *Eighteenth-Century Studies* 39, no. 2 (2006): 157–71.

Ragussis, Michael. *Figures of Conversion: "The Jewish Question" and English National Identity*. Durham, NC: Duke University Press. 1995.

Ragussis, Michael. *Theatrical Nations: Jews and Other Outlandish Englishmen in Georgian Britain*. Philadelphia: University of Pennsylvania Press, 2010.

Richardson, Robbie. *The Savage and Modern Self: North American Indians in Eighteenth-Century British Literature and Culture*. Toronto: University of Toronto Press, 2018.

Riley, Naomi Schaefer. *'Til Faith Do Us Part: How Interfaith Marriage Is Transforming America*. Oxford: Oxford University Press, 2014.

Rivero, Albert J. "Representing Clementina: 'Unnatural' Romance and the Ending of *Sir Charles Grandison*." In *New Essays on Samuel Richardson*, edited by Albert J. Rivero, 209–25. New York: St. Martin's Press, 1996.

Robbins, John. "Documenting Terror in Elizabeth Inchbald's *The Massacre*." *SEL* 57, no. 3 (2017): 605–19.

Rogers, Hannah Lee. "Philosophy in Austen's Pump Room: How Enlightened Tolerance Became Disgust." *Eighteenth-Century Fiction* 32, no. 2 (2019–20): 317–40.

Rogers, Katharine M. "Elizabeth Inchbald: Not Such a Simple Story." In *Living by the Pen: Early British Women Writers*, edited by Dale Spender, 82–90. New York: Teachers College Press, 1992.

Rogers, Katharine M. "Sensibility and Feminism: The Novels of Frances Brooke." *Genre* 11 (1978): 159–70.
Ruskin, John. *The Works of John Ruskin*. Vol. 35. Edited by E. T. Cook and Alexander Wedderburn. London: George Allen; New York: Longmans, Green, 1908.
Ryan, Robert M. *The Romantic Reformation: Religious Politics in English Literature, 1788–1824*. Cambridge: Cambridge University Press, 1997.
Sabor, Peter. "'A Safe Bridge over the Narrow Seas': Crossing the Channel with Samuel Richardson." In *English Literature and the Wider World*, vol. 1, *All before Them: Attitudes to Abroad in English Literature, 1660–1780*, edited by John McVeagh, 159–70. London: Ashfield Press, 1990.
Sainsbury, John. *Disaffected Patriots: London Supporters of Revolutionary America, 1769–1782*. Kingston, ON: McGill-Queen's University Press, 1987.
Samuel, Edgar. "Gideon, Samson (1699–1762), financier." In *Oxford Dictionary of National Biography*. September 23, 2004. Accessed Mar. 20, 2022. https://www.oxforddnb.com/view/10.1093/ref:odnb/9780198614128.001.0001/odnb-9780198614128-e-10645.
Samuel, Edgar. "Sarmento, Jacob De Castro [Formerly Henrique De Castro]." In *Oxford Dictionary of National Biography*. January 8, 2015. Accessed Mar. 20, 2022. https://www.oxforddnb.com/view/10.1093/ref:odnb/9780198614128.001.0001/odnb-9780198614128-e-24670.
Schaffer, Talia. *Romance's Rival: Familiar Marriage in Victorian Fiction*. Oxford: Oxford University Press, 2016.
Schellenberg, Betty A. *The Professionalization of Women Writers in Eighteenth-Century Britain*. Cambridge: Cambridge University Press, 2005.
Schochet, Gordon. "From Persecution to 'Toleration.'" in *Liberty Secured? Britain before and after 1688*, edited by J. R. Jones. 122–56. Stanford, CA: Stanford University Press, 1992.
Schulkins, Rachel. "Imagining the Other: The Jew in Maria Edgeworth's *Harrington*." *European Romanticism Review* 22, no. 4 (2011): 477–99.
Scott, Joan Wallach. *The Politics of the Veil*. Princeton, NJ: Princeton University Press, 2007.
Scott, Joan Wallach. "Secularism and Gender Equality." In *Religion, the Secular, and the Politics of Sexual Difference*, edited by Linell Cady and Tracy Fessenden, 25–43. New York: Columbia University Press, 2013.
Scott, Walter. "Prefatory Memoir to Richardson." In *The Novels of Samuel Richardson*, Ballantyne's Novelist's Library, 6: i–xlviii. London: Hurst, Robinson, 1824.
Scrivener, Michael Henry. *Jewish Representation in British Literature 1780–1840: After Shylock*. New York: Palgrave Macmillan, 2011.
Seeton, A. A. *The Theory of Toleration under the Late Stuarts*. Cambridge: Cambridge University Press, 1911.
Shapiro, James. *Shakespeare and the Jews*. New York: Columbia University Press, 1996.
Shore, Daniel. "Was Milton White?" *Milton Studies* 62, no. 2 (2020): 252–65.
Simpson, Audra. "The Sovereignty of Critique." *South Atlantic Quarterly* 119, no. 4 (2020): 685–99.
Singer, Alan H. "Great Britain or Judea Nova? National Identity, Property, and the Jewish Naturalization Controversy of 1752." In *British Romanticism and the Jews: History, Culture, Literature*, edited by Sheila A. Spector, 19–36. New York: Palgrave Macmillan, 2002.
Sitter, John E. *Literary Loneliness in Mid-eighteenth-century England*. Ithaca, NY: Cornell University Press, 1982.
Sleeper-Smith, Susan. "Women Kin and Catholicism: New Perspectives on the Fur Trade." *Ethnohistory* 47, no. 2 (2000): 423–52.
Smith, Nigel. "Milton and the European Contexts of Toleration." In *Milton and Toleration*, edited by Sharon Achinstein and Elizabeth Sauer, 23–44. New York: Oxford University Press, 2007.

Snead, Jennifer. "Religion and Eighteenth-Century Literature." *Literature Compass* 15, no. 4 (2008): 707–20.
Solkin, David. "The Excessive Jew in *A Harlot's Progress.*" In *Hogarth: Representing Nature's Machines*, edited by Frederic Ogée, David Bindman, and Peter Wagner, 219–35. Manchester: Manchester University Press, 2001.
Song, Eric B. "Love against Substitution: John Milton, Aphra Behn, and the Political Theology of Conjugal Narratives." *ELH* 80, no. 3 (2013): 681–714.
Soni, Vivasvan. *Mourning Happiness: Narrative and the Politics of Modernity*. Ithaca, NY: Cornell University Press, 2010.
Sowerby, Scott. *Making Toleration: The Repealers and the Glorious Revolution*. Vol. 181. Cambridge, MA: Harvard University Press, 2013.
Spencer, Jane. Introduction to *A Simple Story*, by Elizabeth Inchbald, edited by J. M. S. Tompkins, vii–xx. Oxford: Oxford University Press, 2009. First published 1967.
Stanbridge, Karen. *Toleration and State Institutions: British Policy toward Catholics in Eighteenth-Century Ireland and Quebec*. London: Lexington Press, 2003.
Starr, George. Introduction to *Religious Courtship*, by Daniel Defoe, edited by G. A. Starr, vol. 4 of *The Religious and Didactic Writings of Daniel Defoe*, 1–26. London: Pickering & Chatto, 2006.
Staves, Susan. *A Literary History of Women's Writing in Britain, 1660–1789*. Cambridge: Cambridge University Press, 2006.
Stevens, Ralph. *Protestant Pluralism: The Reception of the Toleration Act, 1689–1720*. Cambridge: Boydell and Brewer, 2019.
Stevenson, Bill. "The Social Integration of Post-Restoration Dissenters, 1660–1775." In *The World of Rural Dissenters 1520–1725*, edited by Margaret Spufford, 360–87. Cambridge: Cambridge University Press, 1995.
Stevenson, George J. *Memorials of the Wesley Family*. London: Partridge, 1876.
Stevenson, John Allen. "'A Geometry of His Own': Richardson and the Marriage-Ending." *SEL* 26, no. 3 (1986): 469–83.
Stow, Kenneth R. *Jewish Dogs: An Image and Its Interpreters: Continuity in the Catholic-Jewish Encounter*. Stanford, CA: Stanford University Press, 2006.
Suzuki, Shigeo. "Marriage and Divorce." In *Milton in Context*, edited by Stephen B. Dobranski, 386–90. Cambridge: Cambridge University Press, 2010.
Taylor, Charles. "Porous and Buffered Selves." *The Immanent Frame: Secularism, Religion, and the Public Sphere*, September 2, 2008. https://tif.ssrc.org/2008/09/02/buffered-and-porous-selves/.
Taylor, Charles. *A Secular Age*. Cambridge, MA: Harvard University Press, 2007.
Temple, Kathryn. "Printing like a Post-colonialist: The Irish Piracy of *Sir Charles Grandison.*" *Novel: A Forum on Fiction* 33, no. 2 (2002): 157–74.
Tessone, Natasha. "Homage to Empty Armor: Maria Edgeworth's *Harrington* and the Pathology of National Inheritance." *ELH* 75, no. 2 (2008): 439–69.
Thackery, William. "Richardson's Novels," *Cornhill Magazine* 17 (Jan.–June 1868): 48–69.
Thomas, J. M. "The Racial Formation of Medieval Jews: A Challenge to the Field." *Ethnic & Racial Studies* 33, no. 10 (2010): 1737–55.
Thomas, Keith V. "Women and the Civil War of Sects." *Past & Present*, no. 13 (Apr. 1958): 42–62.
Thompson, Helen. *Ingenuous Subjection: Compliance and Power in the Eighteenth-Century Domestic Novel*. Philadelphia: University of Pennsylvania Press, 2005.
Todd, Janet. *The Sign of Angellica: Women, Writing and Fiction, 1660–1800*. New York: Columbia University Press, 1989.
Tomko, Michael. "'All the World Have Heard of the Devil and the Pope': Elizabeth Inchbald's *The Mogul Tale* and English Catholic Satire." *Tulsa Studies in Women's Literature* 31, no. 1 (2012): 117–36.

Tomko, Michael. "Between Revolutionary Jacobins and English Catholic Cisalpines: The Roles of Elizabeth Inchbald (1753–1821) in the Age of Enlightenment." In *Women, Enlightenment and Catholicism*, edited by Ulrich L. Lehner, 189–201. London: Routledge, 2017.

Tomko, Michael. *British Romanticism and the Catholic Question: Religion, History and National Identity, 1778–1829*. Houndsmill: Palgrave Macmillan, 2011.

Tomko, Michael. "Remembering Elizabeth Inchbald's *The Massacre*: Romantic Cosmopolitanism, Sectarian History, and Religious Difference." *European Romantic Review* 19 (2008): 1–18.

Tønder, Lars. *Tolerance: A Sensorial Orientation to Politics*. New York: Oxford University Press, 2013.

Trilling, Lionel. *Sincerity and Authenticity*. Cambridge, MA: Harvard University Press, 1972.

Turner, James Grantham. "The Aesthetics of Divorce: 'Masculinism,' Idolatry, and Poetic Authority." In *Milton and Gender*, edited by Catherine Gimelli Martin, 34–52. Cambridge: Cambridge University Press, 2005.

Turner, James Grantham. "Libertinism and Toleration: Milton, Bruno, Aretino." In *Milton and Toleration*, edited by Sharon Achinstein and Elizabeth Sauer, 107–25. New York: Oxford University Press, 2007.

Turner, James Grantham. "Sexuality." In *Samuel Richardson in Context*, edited by Betty A. Schellenberg and Peter Sabor, 247–54. Cambridge: Cambridge University Press, 2017.

Van den Berg, Sara J., and W. Scott Howard. Introduction to *The Divorce Tracts of John Milton: Texts and Contexts*, edited by Sara J. Van den Berg and W. Scott Howard, 1–35. Pittsburgh, PA: Dusquesne University Press, 2010.

Vanneste, Tijl. *Global Trade and Commercial Networks: Eighteenth-Century Diamond Merchants*. London: Pickering and Chatto, 2011.

Vernon, Richard. "Further Reading." In *Locke on Toleration*, edited by Richard Vernon, xxxvi–xxxviii. Cambridge: Cambridge University Press, 2010.

Vernon, Richard. Introduction to *Locke on Toleration*, edited by Richard Vernon, viii–xxxii. Cambridge: Cambridge University Press, 2010.

Vesselova, Natalia. "'The Strongest Tie to Unity and Obedience': Paradoxes of Freethinking, Religion and Colonialism in Frances Brooke's *The History of Emily Montague*." *Lumen* 30 (2011): 171–80.

Vickery, Amanda. *The Gentleman's Daughter: Women's Lives in Georgian England*. New Haven, CT: Yale University Press, 2003.

Viswanathan, Gauri. *Outside the Fold: Conversion, Modernity, and Belief*. Princeton, NJ: Princeton University Press, 1998.

Von Maltzahn, Nicholas. "Milton, Marvell and Toleration." In *Milton and Toleration*, edited by Sharon Achinstein and Elizabeth Sauer, 86–106. New York: Oxford University Press, 2007.

Waldron, Jeremy. "Locke, Adam, and Eve." In *Feminist Interpretations of John Locke*, edited by Nancy J. Hirschmann and Kirstie Morna McClure, 241–68. University Park: Pennsylvania State University Press, 2007.

Waldron, Mary. "The Frailties of Fanny: *Mansfield Park* and the Evangelical Movement." *Eighteenth-Century Fiction* 6, no. 3 (1994): 259–82.

Wallace, Miriam. "Wit and Revolution: Cultural Resistance in Elizabeth Inchbald's *A Simple Story*." *European Romantic Review* 12, no. 1 (2001): 92–121.

Walsh, John, Colin Haydon, and Stephen Tayler, eds. *The Church of England c.1689–c.1833: From Toleration to Tractarianism*. Cambridge: Cambridge University Press, 1993.

Walsham, Alexandra. *Charitable Hatred: Tolerance and Intolerance in England, 1500–1700*. Manchester: Manchester University Press, 2006.

Wanhalla, Angela. "Indigenous Women, Marriage, and Colonial Mobility." In *Indigenous Mobilities: Across and beyond the Antipodes*, edited by Rachel Standfield, 209–32. Acton: Australian National University Press, 2018.

Wanklyn, Malcolm. "Catholics in the Village Community: Madeley, Shropshire, 1630–1770." In *English Catholics of Parish and Town, 1558–1778*, edited by Marie B. Rowlands, 210–36. London: Catholic Record Society, 1999.

Watt, Ian. *Rise of the Novel: Studies in Defoe, Richardson, and Fielding*. 2nd ed. Berkeley: University of California Press, 2001. First published 1957.

Webb, R. K. "From Toleration to Religious Liberty," in *Liberty Secured? Britain before and after 1688*, ed. J. R. Jones. 158–98. Stanford, CA: Stanford University Press, 1992.

Weil, Rachel. "Howard, Henry, Seventh Duke of Norfolk (1655–1701), Politician." *Oxford Dictionary of National Biography*. Last modified September 23, 2004. Accessed Mar. 20, 2022. https://www.oxforddnb.com/view/10.1093/ref:odnb/9780198614128.001.0001/odnb-9780198614128-e-13908.

Weil, Rachel. *A Plague of Informers: Conspiracy and Political Trust in William III's England*. New Haven, CT: Yale University Press, 2013.

Weil, Rachel. *Political Passions: Gender, the Family, and Political Argument in England, 1680–1714*. Manchester: Manchester University Press, 1999.

Welland, Heather Mary Alice. "Interest Politics and the Shaping of the British Empire, ca. 1720–1791." PhD diss., University of Chicago, Chicago, IL, 2011.

Whale, John C, ed. *Edmund Burke's Reflections on the Revolution in France: New Interdisciplinary Essays*. Manchester: Manchester University Press, 2000.

White, Daniel. *Early Romanticism and Religious Dissent*. Cambridge: Cambridge University Press, 2006.

Windstrup, George. "Freedom and Authority: The Ancient Faith of Locke's *Letter on Toleration*." *Review of Politics* 44, no. 2 (1982): 242–65.

Winter, Sarah. "The Novel and Prejudice." *Comparative Literature Studies* 46, no. 1 (2009): 76–102.

Wolper, Roy S. "Circumcision as Polemic in the Jew Bill of 1753: The Cutter Cut?" *Eighteenth-Century Life* 7, no. 3 (1982): 28–36.

Woolf, Maurice. "Joseph Salvador, 1716–1786." *Transactions (Jewish Historical Society of England)* 23, no. 5 (1962): 104–37.

Worden, Blair. "Toleration and the Cromwellian Protectorate." In *Persecution and Toleration*, edited by W. J. Shields, 218–27. Oxford: Oxford University Press, 1984.

Wyett, Jodi L. "'No Place Where Women Are of Such Importance': Female Friendship, Empire, and Utopia in *The History of Emily Montague*." *Eighteenth Century Fiction* 16, no. 1 (2003): 33–57.

Yeazell, Ruth. *Fictions of Modesty: Women and Courtship in the English Novel*. Chicago: University of Chicago Press, 1991.

Young, Francis. "Elizabeth Inchbald's 'Catholic Novel' and Its Local Background." *Recusant History* 31, no. 4 (2013): 573–92.

Yovel, Yirmiyahu. *The Other Within: The Marranos; Split Identity and Emerging Modernity*. Princeton, NJ: Princeton University Press, 2009.

Zagorin, Perez. *How the Idea of Religious Toleration Came to the West*. Princeton, NJ: Princeton University Press, 2003.

INDEX

Act of Settlement, 16
Act of Toleration, 35, 41, 177n55
Adelman, Janet, 161, 172n20
adolescents, 130–31, 135
adoption, 97, 129, 180n21
adultery, 26, 40–41, 77, 102, 179n15
Almon, John, 108
alterity, religious, 9–10, 60, 100, 114, 141, 163, 164, 169; racial and gendered, 5, 6, 16–17, 93, 141
American colonies, 92–94, 95, 106, 107–8
Ames, William, 25
Anderson, Emily Hodgson, 120
Anderson, Misty, 45, 116, 178n1
Anglican clergy, 14, 16, 42–45, 96, 165, 166, 167, 193n6
Anglicanism, 8, 14, 22–23, 31, 35, 36, 165, 168, 184n35, 187n8; conversion to, 52–53; hegemony, 29, 31, 95, 185n38; in *The History of Emily Montague* (Brooke), 82, 84, 92, 94, 95, 99, 100, 185n38; in *Mansfield Park* (Austen), 164, 165, 166, 168. *See also* Church of England
Anglo-Irish, 138, 154, 157, 161, 192n39
Anglo-Jews. *See* Richardson, Samuel, *Sir Charles Grandison*
Answer to a Book, intituled, The Doctrine and Discipline of Divorce . . . , 27–29
anti-Catholicism, 8, 11, 39, 40, 45–46, 76, 83, 101, 111, 117, 138, 156, 157, 188n47
antinomianism, 13, 27
anti-Semitism, 4, 13, 17, 150, 172n21; in art, 52–53, 54–55, 142–48; in *Harrington* (Edgeworth), 15, 138, 140–42, 144, 145–48, 153, 156–60, 162; in *Merchant of Venice*, 15, 140, 142–43, 151–52, 154–55, 160–61, 162; oral metaphors, 144–47; in *Sir Charles Grandison* (Richardson), 56, 58, 60, 78, 138; suffering caused by, 140–42, 145, 154–55

Arch, Stephen Carl, 83, 103, 106
Armstrong, Nancy, 14, 98, 183n6
art: anti-Semitism portrayed in, 52–53, 54–55, 142–48, 179n12, 191n20; as objects of exchange, 148–53, 159, 191n20
Asad, Talal, 6, 172n35
Ashkenazim, 52, 154
Athenian Mercury, 37–38, 174n4
Austen, Jane, 8; *Emma*, 164–65; *Mansfield Park*, 164, 165–68; *Persuasion*, 164; *Pride and Prejudice*, 168; *Sense and Sensibility*, 168
authority: Catholics' submission to, 114; civil, 75; of husbands, 21–22, 34, 36, 40, 61, 83–84, 175n11; of Indigenous women, 90–91, 97; masculine, 6, 44; monarchical, 93–94; paternalistic/patriarchal, 28, 29, 36, 49, 79, 83, 87–88, 108, 111, 126–27, 168, 181n47; of women, 28, 91, 104; women's spiritual, 49, 78–79, 181
autonomy, 108; of conscience, 12, 49, 62–63; religious, 14, 31–32, 34, 42–43, 49, 78, 118; sexual, 14, 102

Bakhtin, Mikhail, 9
Balfour, Ian, 116–17
baptism, 52–53
Baptists, 3, 8, 20–21, 23, 27–28, 82
Barbauld, Anna Laetitia, 67, 181n52
Barnett, Richard, 180n28
Bartolomeo, Joseph F., 106
Bejan, Teresa, 6, 12, 17, 177n53
Bender, John, *Imagining the Penitentiary*, 9
Benedict, Barbara, 89
Berington, Joseph, 110, 111, 118–19, 123–25, 187n5, 187n10; *The State and Behaviour of English Catholics*, 112, 113, 114
Bernard, John, 28
Bildung/bildungsroman, 60, 103, 111, 130, 141, 142

Index

Binhammer, Katherine, 90, 107, 182n54, 184n25
Black laws, 127
blended identities, 97, 161–62
Bowers, Toni, 13, 78, 181n47
Brinsley, John, *A Looking-Glass for Good Women*, 21–22, 23
British colonialism/imperialism, 4–5, 14, 84, 93, 107–9, 164, 183n6, 185n51, 186n67. *See also* American colonies; French Canada
Brooke, Frances, 83; *The History of Lady Julia Mandeville*, 82, 83, 85–88; *The Old Maid*, 83, 84–85, 86, 94, 100–101, 109
Brooke, Frances, *The History of Emily Montague*, 4–5, 14, 15–16, 82–84, 88–91, 98–100, 101–3; epistolary form, 88–89, 101, 103, 183n6n9; influence of *Sir Charles Grandison* (Richardson) on, 82, 83, 84; unequal marriage plot, 83–84, 89–90, 107
Brown, Gayle K., 98, 185n49
Brown, Henry, 21
Brown, Liam D'Arcy, 171n11
Brown, Wendy, 10, 182n59
Bumsted, J. M., 97, 185n42
Burnet, Gilbert (Archbishop of Canterbury), 56–57
Burney, Frances, 8
Burton, Henry, 29

Cable, Lana, 25
Calvinism, 2, 22
Cambers, Andrew, 36
Cano, Alonzo, 143–44, 147, 159, 162
Canuel, Mark, 96, 172n27, 174n66
captivity narrative, 14, 48, 98–99, 100, 107, 183n7, 185n49
Carnes, Geremy, 80, 119–20, 122, 127, 188n32
Caroline of Brunswick, 17
Carter, Elizabeth, 79
castration, 58–59, 180n37
Catholic Church, 33, 62, 64, 76, 92, 98, 118, 181n47, 187n5, 187n12
Catholic Committee, 112–13, 117, 118, 187n5, 187n12, 189n52
Catholic Emancipation Act, 168
Catholic identity, 56, 75–76, 101, 110, 115
Catholic Relief Acts, 111, 112–13, 117–18, 123–24
Catholic women authors. *See* Inchbald, Elizabeth
Charles I, King of England, 20, 26, 28–29
Chico, Tita, 48, 63, 72, 73, 171n4, 181n43
Chinnici, Joseph P., 135–36
Christianity, 33, 56, 74, 94, 96, 99, 111, 115–16, 190n1

Church of England, 12, 25–26, 95, 96; relations with Protestant Dissenters, 35–36, 45, 95, 185n7n12, 1857n
circumcision, 58, 60, 180n36n37
Cisalpines, 111–16, 117, 118–19, 125, 134–35, 136, 186n4, 188n32
civility, 19, 30, 34, 50, 57, 64, 74, 90; gentlemanly expression of, 137–39; race and, 49, 90, 97, 185n38; religious tolerance and, 6–7, 12–14, 34, 60
Civil War (English), 12, 20, 112, 175n11, 176n28
class, 6, 14, 52, 53, 84, 87, 152, 184n27
Colley, Linda, 92; *Britons*, 101
Collyer, Mary, *Letters from Felicia to Charlotte*, 2, 173n60
colonial-settler culture, 88, 89, 92–93, 96–97, 184n27, 185n38, 185n40. *See also* British colonialism/imperialism
companionate marriage, 14, 15, 153, 172n33n36, 174n2; *Harrington* (Edgeworth), 137, 139, 141, 143, 162, 164, 191n9; *The History of Emily Montague* (Brooke), 100, 106–7, 109; inequalities, 136; literary criticism, 172n36; *Mansfield Park* (Austen), 164, 167, 168; *The Massacre* (Inchbald), 136; Milton and, 24–25, 175n12; Protestant support, 19; religious sameness principle, 18–19; scapegoat creation, 60; *Sir Charles Grandison*, 50, 67, 70, 78, 79, 182n55
congregationalism, Catholic, 113–14
Congregationalists, 3, 8, 21, 23
conversion, 2, 97; assimilation through, 52–53; as *Bildung* plot, 60; against husband's wishes, 21–22; of Indigenous people, 84; to Judaism, 58, 152; of libertines, 56–57; Pauline doctrine, 24, 30, 49, 175n15; racial purity and, 4; to "true religion," 56–57; of wives, 21–22, 35
conversion, of Jews, 150; *conversos*, 53–54, 150–51, 161, 191n24; in *Harrington* (Edgeworth), 140, 142, 149, 150–51, 152–53, 160, 161; in *The Merchant of Venice* (Shakespeare), 139, 140, 160–61; in *Sir Charles Grandison* (Richardson), 56–57, 58, 60, 78
cosmopolitanism, 54, 60, 62, 73, 79–80, 100, 164, 172n26, 182n53
Critical Review, 82, 88, 183n2
Crome, Andrew, 53, 179n20
cultural assimilation: French Canadians, 14, 84, 91–92, 94, 96–97, 185n44; Indigenous people, 96–97; Jews, 52–53, 58, 141, 142, 151, 168, 179n20, 180n21
Cumberland, Richard, 151

Declaration for Liberty of Conscience, 41
Defoe, Daniel: *A Journal of the Plague Year*, 173n56; *Religious Courtship*, 1–2, 171n1; *Roxana, the Fortunate Mistress*, 181n41
Derrida, Jacques, 9
Devereux, Cecily, 96, 185n44
divorce, 19, 39–41, 40–41, 167, 177n72. *See also* Milton, *Doctrine and Discipline of Divorce*
Doody, Margaret, 74, 78
dueling, 57, 88, 127
Duffy, Eamon, 124, 188n32, 189n52

Eagles, Robin, 101
Earl of Rochester, 56–57, 180n35
Eaves, T. C. Duncan, 73, 182n66
Edgeworth, Maria, *Harrington*, 15–16, 124, 137–62, 163, 164; alternative model of marriage, 139; anti-Semitic culture in, 15, 138, 140–43, 144, 145–49, 153, 156–61, 162, 192n43; companionate marriage plot, 137, 139–48; conversion plot, 15, 140, 142, 149, 150–51, 152–53, 160, 161; influence of *Sir Charles Grandison* (Richardson) on, 137–39; *The Merchant of Venice* in, 15, 140, 142–43, 160–61, 192n43
Edgeworth, Maria, *Ormond*, 138
Edwards, Thomas, *Gangraena*, 27–28, 176n28
Endelman, Todd, 53, 154, 191n31
English Catholicism, 2, 13, 15–16, 22, 45–46, 56, 74, 113–14; independence from papal authority, 111–12, 114, 117–19; of royal wives, 16–17, 20. *See also* Cisalpines
English Catholics, 3, 13–14, 41; educational practices, 123–27; emancipation, 18, 112–13, 163, 168
Enlightenment, 8, 54, 91, 99, 100, 176n46; British, 2, 101, 163, 173n40, 184n30, 184n35; Catholic, 110, 111, 112; Christian, 17n46, 162, 176n38; Jewish, 137, 153, 154, 155–56, 162, 192n35
evangelism, 13, 45–46, 94, 165, 166
Evelyn, John, 41
excommunication, 20–21, 117
Expedient to Preserve Peace and Amity Among Dissenting Brethren, An, 25

family religion, 1–2, 31, 35–39, 165; in Austen's novels, 165, 166; Catholicism's perspective, 113–14, 165; interfaith marriage as threat to, 37–39; marital conflict and, 39–45; religious toleration and, 11, 28
Farrakhan, Louis, *The Secret Relationship between Blacks and Jews*, 17
Featley, Daniel, 26–27

feminism and feminists, 7, 17, 83, 85, 87, 173n38, 183n8
Fielding, Henry, 8
Fitzherbert, Maria, 16–17
Fownes, Joseph, 82
French Canada: acquisition by Britain, 91–92; Anglican assimilation in, 94, 95–96; fur trade, 88, 97; Indigenous people, 4–5, 14, 90–91, 92, 96, 97–98, 108, 184n22, 185n48; religious toleration in, 95, 106, 107–8. *See also* Brooke, Frances, *The History of Emily Montague*
French Catholicism, 109
French culture, 100–102
French Revolution, 129, 136
Friedman, Jerome, 150
Friedman, Susan Stanford, 7

Gallagher, Catherine, 85, 154, 161, 191n20, 192n3, 192n39, 192n40
Geddes, Alexander, 112, 113–14, 117, 124, 187n5
George, Prince of Wales, 16–17
George III, King of England, 127
George IV, King of England, 16–17
Gerber, Jane S., 53, 179n20
Gideon, Samson, *The Grand Conference or the Jews Predominate*, 54–55, 179n13
Godwin, William, 110, 116, 136
Goodwin, John, 25, 29
Gordon Riots of 1780, 8, 11, 83, 138, 156, 157
gothic novels and tropes, 127–28, 130–31, 133, 168, 172n27, 181n42, 187n8, 189n60
Gouge, William, 19–20, 24
Greenham, Richard, 22–23, 175n11
Guest, Harriet, 101
Gwilliam, Tassie, 73

Hale, Dorothy J., 9–10
Hall, David J., 3
Hammill, Faye, 101–2
Hardwicke Marriage Act, 4, 127
Harland-Jacobs, Jessica L., 99–100, 185n51
Harris, Jocelyn, 73
Hawkins, John, 118–19, 187n5
Hazlitt, William, 67
Héloise-Abelard story, Richardson's recasting of, 60–67, 181n40, 181n41, 181n46
Henrietta Maria, Queen of England, 28–29
Hershinow, Stephanie Insley, *Born Yesterday: Inexperience and the Early Realist Novel*, 130–32

Hewitt, Regina, 139, 161
Heywood, Samuel, 112
Hickes, George, 43, 44–45, 177n81, 178n87
Hindus, 5
Hirsch, Brett, 161
Hobbes, Thomas, 26, 40
Hogarth, William, *The Rake's Progress*, 51, 179n12
Hollander, Rachel, *Narrative Hospitality in Late Victorian Fiction*, 9, 10, 11
hospitality, 9, 164–65; English Catholic principles of, 15, 111–16, 125, 135–36
Howard, Henry and Mary, Duke and Duchess of Norfolk, 19, 39, 40–41, 177n72
Hunter, J. Paul, 35

Inchbald, Elizabeth: *The Massacre*, 136, 189n79; *Such Things Are*, 115–16, 188n25
Inchbald, Elizabeth, *A Simple Story*, 110–36; Cisalpine movement and, 111–16, 135–36, 186n32, 188n32; feminist critiques, 111, 123; gothic elements, 126–28, 130–31, 133; oaths and vow making question, 119–23
incorporation, metaphors of, 145
India, 107–8, 186n67, 188n26
Indigenous people, 89, 92, 93, 96–98, 184n22, 185n48
Indigenous women, 4–5, 82; freedom of movement, 84, 88, 91, 92, 108, 184n22; mixed (interracial) marriages, 14, 84, 88, 97, 98, 108, 185n40; political authority, 90–91, 97
inheritance practices, 40, 41, 74, 89, 107, 121–22
Inquisitions, 53, 54, 144, 147, 148–49, 150–51, 152
interfaith marriage: biblical references, 19–20, 21, 24; in contemporary America, 169; Protestant antipathy to, 19–23; rates, 3, 13
interfaith marriage plot, 2, 11
Interregnum, 12, 26
interregnum, as metaphor, 83
Italian Catholics. *See* Richardson, Samuel, *Sir Charles Grandison*, Clementina della Porretta plot

Jacobins, 110, 116, 123, 186n4
Jacobite Rebellions, 45–46, 62, 112
Jager, Colin, 129, 165, 173n43
James, Henry, 10
James II, King of England, 41
Jerusalem Infirmary, The, 52
Jesuits, 96–97, 99, 119, 123, 124, 186n1, 188n41
Jewish Naturalization Act, 4, 11, 13, 48, 54–55, 59, 79
Jews, 17; Anglo-Jewish libertinism, 49, 50–60, 62, 75, 78; emancipation, 163; expulsion from Spain, 53; naturalization, 4, 11, 13, 18, 180n21; as percentage of British population, 3. *See also* anti-Semitism; Ashkenazim; Sephardim
John II, King of England, 53, 145, 180n21
John II, King of Portugal, 53
Johnson, Claudia, 168, 193n11
Johnson, Jane, 20–21, 23
Jones, Wendy, 70, 182n55, 182n60
Judson, Barbara, 111

Kant, Immanuel, 164
Keegan, Bridget, 123, 186n1, 188n41
Kelly, Gary, 123, 186n1, 188n50
Kemble, John, 115
Kemble, Roger, 115
Kessler, Sanford, 33
kidnappings, 54, 134, 180n21. *See also* captivity narrative
Kilgour, Maggie, 145
Kimpel, Ben D., 73, 182n66
Kramer, Kaley, 126

Lanser, Susan, 83–84
Lee, Yoon Sun, 137
Lennox, Charlotte, *Henrietta*, 47–48, 178n2
Leslie, Charles, 34–35, 38
Levinas, Emmanuel, 9
liberalism, 5–6, 7, 15, 17, 50, 79, 90, 136
libertines/libertinism, 98; Anglo-Jewish, 49, 50–60, 62, 75, 78
liberty of conscience, 12, 14, 18, 19, 28, 79–80, 94; Church of England's authority and, 25–26, 94–95; Cisalpines' defense of, 112, 114, 117; colonialism and, 94–95; in English Puritan discourse, 25; evangelical Christians' position, 13; of French Canadians, 95; during the Interregnum, 26; Locke's model, 19, 33–34, 176n47; of marginalized groups, 93; Milton's divorce tracts and, 18–19, 26–28, 175n17; monarchical prerogative and, 94; patriarchal authority and, 21–22, 36, 61; Protestant Dissent's commitment to, 35–36, 112; women's claims for, 27, 40, 42–43, 61, 79–80, 163, 178n83
linguistic skills, 49, 62–64, 65, 66, 67, 101, 169, 181n45
Little, Ann M., 97
Locke, John, 6, 11, 18, 26, 31–37, 48–49, 125; *A Letter Concerning Toleration*, 2–3, 12–13, 31–32, 33, 34, 53, 155–56; *Second Treatise on Government*, 31–32, 33–34; *Some Thoughts Concerning Education*, 34, 35

Logan, Peter, 143, 158, 190n6, 192n36
Louis XIV, King of France, 103
love: between father and daughter, 126–27, 130–31, 130–32, 131, 133; idealistic, 67–72; moderate, 128, 135–36; obsessive, 116, 128–29, 130; paternal oversight and, 86; "queer," 111, 135; romantic, 1, 39, 70, 103, 128, 135, 148; zealotry of, 68, 69, 72, 75, 104, 135, 182n66

Macaulay, Catherine, 109
Maile, Edmond, 21
Mallory, Tamika, 17, 174n72
Mandell, Laura, 15, 110
Manly, Susan, 161, 191n34, 192n37
Manuel I, King of Portugal, 53
marriage: arranged, 50, 86, 87–88, 132; of convenience, 71; as sacrifice, 78; unequal, 14, 83, 86–87, 89–90
Marriage Act of 1772, 16
Marriot, Thomas, 44, 178n85
Mary, Queen of England, 35, 41
masculinity, 58, 60, 78, 90, 102
maternity, 71, 72, 76, 182n61
McCarthy, Dermot, 103
McDonagh, Josephine, 168, 193n12
McMullen, Lorraine, 87, 183n2
McMurran, Mary Helen, *The Spread of Novels*, 100, 101, 185n38
Meer, Nasar, 4, 172n21
Mellor, Anne K., 5, 172n26
Mendelssohn, Moses, 153, 155–56, 191n34, 192n35
Merleau-Ponty, Maurice, 10
Methodism, 13, 18, 45, 47, 86, 94, 178n1, 193n6; founders, 41–42, 44, 45, 47, 178n85
Milligan, Edward H., 3–4
Mills, Charles W., 5–6
Milner, John, 118
Milton, John, 20, 26, 27, 30, 31, 174n4, 175n12–n17, 175n15; *Doctrine and Discipline of Divorce*, 8, 12, 18–19, 23–25, 26–29, 30, 164, 174n12; *Paradise Lost*, 5
Min, Eun Kyung, 122, 134, 188n31
Morgan, Sydney, 5
Murillo, Bartolomeo Esteban, 147, 149–50, 162
Muslims, 5, 6, 17, 47

natural law, 90, 93
Neuman, Justin, 8
Neumann, Mary Waldron, 165, 181n45, 193n7
Nielsen, Wendy C., 136, 189n78

nonjurors, 34–35, 38–39, 40–41, 42, 189n83
North, Roger, 40–41
novel, interfaith marriage plot (1750–1820), 1–17; hermeneutic challenges of, 8–9; secularization thesis of, 6–8, 111, 165; women novelists' contributions to, 14–17. *See also titles of specific novels*
nuns, 14, 48, 97, 98–100, 104, 124
Nussbaum, Felicity, 108–9

oaths and vows, 116–24
objectification, of women, 66, 87, 152, 153
O'Connell, Lisa, 8
O'Leary, Arthur, 114
O'Quinn, Daniel, 127
Oracle, The (Dixon), 92, 93
Osland, Dianne, 120

Pateman, Carole, 5–6, 172n33, 176n48
Payne, William, 36
Pelham, Henry, 55, 180n32
Pelham, Thomas, 55
Penha, Mordecai da la, 52
Perez, Carmen, 17
Pharepoint, Anne, 21, 23
Pitt, William, 112–13, 117
Plotz, John, 147, 152, 190n7
Plowdon, Charles, 117
Pollak, Ellen, 106
Pope, "Rape of the Lock," 101–2
Powell, Mary, 27, 31
Presbyterians, 3, 8, 12, 28, 29–30, 184n34
priests, 20, 48, 79, 98, 111, 121–22, 151, 181n47
Pritchard, Elizabeth, 34, 177n53
Probert, Rebecca, 4, 5, 171n11
Protestant Dissent/Dissenters, 3, 5, 14–15, 35–36, 37, 39, 45, 116–17, 166, 174n66, 193n6; in the American colonies and French Canada, 92, 93–94, 95, 96; relations with Catholics, 111–12, 187n6, 187n8, 187n13
Protestantism, 10, 15–16, 19–23, 73–74. *See also individual sects*
Prynne, William, 20
Puritans, 9, 20, 25, 29, 31, 54, 175n22

Quakers, 3–4, 8, 38–39, 43, 171n12, 177n70
Quebec Act of 1774, 92, 108

race and racism, 4–5, 84, 172n20
Radcliffe, Ann, 127
rape, 13, 50, 63, 101, 134, 180n39

Rawls, John, 10
realist novels and narrative, 8, 13, 15, 45, 83, 111.
  See also Austen, Jane, *Mansfield Park;* Brooke,
  Frances, *The History of Emily Montague;*
  Edgeworth, Maria, *Harrington;* Inchbald,
  Elizabeth, *A Simple Story*
Reformation, 25, 26, 114, 118, 123, 136, 175n11
religiosity, 2, 6, 7, 8, 45
religious activism, 7, 15, 93–94
religious conformity, 12–13, 36, 163, 168; companionate marriage and, 168; interfaith marriage and, 39, 67, 163; liberty of conscience and, 25–27; as moral contract, 12; patriarchal authority and, 28, 36; relation to love and attachment, 18–19
religious difference, 31, 153, 163; in *Harrington* (Edgeworth), 137, 139, 140, 141–42, 153, 158, 162; in *The History of Emily Montague* (Brooke), 88; Locke's perspective, 32, 34–35; love and, 34–35; as marital conflict cause, 2, 23, 24–26, 28, 30, 42–45; Milton's perspective, 12, 23, 24–26, 28, 30, 31; in post-Austen novels, 168–69; privatization of, 142; in *A Simple Story* (Inchbald), 121; in *Sir Charles Grandison* (Richardson), 13, 48, 58, 60, 66, 71, 74–75, 76, 79, 179n19; storytelling as conduit for, 9
religious integrity, 22–23, 28
religious minorities, 8; in Hanoverian England, 154; as percentage of British population, 3; as political subjects, 163; rights of, 15. See also *individual religious denominations*
religious pluralism, 2, 5, 7, 8, 12, 19, 30–31, 169, 189n52; as discursive practice, 49–50; Milton's perspective, 28; as threat to communal/familial bonds, 11, 29, 114
religious toleration, 2, 5–6, 9, 17, 18, 24, 26–27, 173n44; 1640s, 18–31; 1690-1745, 31–46; in the American colonies and French Canada, 93–94, 106, 107–8; Cisalpine model, 111–16, 117, 118–19, 125, 134–35, 136, 186n4, 188n32; conflation with secularism, 6–7; evolution of, 5, 174n1; in *Harrington* (Edgeworth), 138; in *The History of Emily Montague* (Brooke), 82–83, 93–94, 106, 107–8, 110; Locke's perspective, 11, 12–13, 31–37, 80; in *The Massacre* (Inchbald), 136; Milton's perspective, 24, 28; opposition to, 26, 28, 30; politics of, 9–10, 41, 136, 164, 174n1; private-public sphere relationship, 6–7, 6–8, 10, 12–13, 18–19, 25, 29, 31–32, 34, 49, 57, 162; religious precedent against, 28–29; in *A Simple Story* (Inchbald), 110–11, 121; in *Sir Charles Grandison* (Richardson), 47–48, 54, 110, 138, 178n1; in *Such Things Are* (Inchbald), 115

religious vocation, 64, 65, 66, 76, 99–100, 121–22
Restoration, 39–40
Richardson, Samuel, 8, 78–79; *Clarissa*, 13, 48–49, 50, 63, 65, 72, 74, 88, 103; *Pamela*, 11, 14, 98
Richardson, Samuel, *Sir Charles Grandison*, 11–12, 15–16, 47–81, 88, 108, 135, 164; anti-Catholic sentiment, 76; anti-Semitism, 58, 60, 138; Austen's admiration for, 164, 167; Clementina della Porretta's story, 13–14, 48, 49–50, 60–67, 69, 72, 73–78, 79, 80–81, 104, 105, 138, 168, 180n39; conversion plots, 49, 61, 76, 78; converso libertinism and, 49, 50–60, 78, 79–80; Harriet Byron's story, 49–50, 60, 66, 67–72, 75–80, 102, 104, 135, 182n54, 182n66; idealist love portrayed, 67–72, 76; influence on Frances Brooke, 82; influence on Jane Austen, 164, 167–68; influence on Maria Edgeworth, 137–39; Methodism in, 47; parody, 47–48; plots of refusal, 49–50, 65; as recasting of Heloise-Abelard story, 60–67; religious toleration theme, 13–14, 47–49, 70–71, 73–74, 181n41–48, 181n41–52; Sir Charles' character, 73–81; women's spiritual authority theme, 49, 60–67
Richardson, Samuel, *Sir Charles Grandison*, women authors' rewritings of: See Austen, Jane, *Mansfield Park;* Brooke, Frances, *The History of Emily Montague;* Edgeworth, Maria, *Harrington;* Inchbald, Elizabeth, *A Simple Story*
riots, 8, 11, 83, 138, 156–57, 159
Rogers, Hannah Lee, 164–65
Romanticism, 110
Rowlandson, Thomas, *Transplanting of Teeth,* 146–47
royal marriages, interfaith, 16–17, 20, 28–29
Royal Proclamation Act, 91–92
Royal Society, 51–52, 54
Ruskin, John, 67

Sabor, Peter, 77
salvation, 22, 29, 32, 38, 73
Sarmento, Jacob de Castro, 51–52, 53, 54, 180n28
Schaffer, Talia, 168–69
Schellenberg, Betty, 85, 87, 96, 182n67
Schochet, Gordon J., 26
Scott, Joan Wallach, 6–7, 172n33
Scott, Walter, 67
Scrivener, Michael, 161
Seaman, Lazarus, 28–29
secularism, 1, 11, 39, 53, 127, 130, 133–34, 165, 175n17, 176n46; evolution of, 6–8, 172n35; secularization thesis, 6–8, 111, 165
self-sovereignty, of women, 85, 100, 109

sentimentalism, 82, 89, 101–2, 135, 182n55, 185n49, 192n43
Sephardim, 154, 179n15; cultural alliance and assimilation, 50–54, 139, 153. *See also* Edgeworth, Maria, *Harrington;* Richardson, Samuel, *Sir Charles Grandison*
servants, 29, 37, 52–53, 54, 55, 61, 65, 74, 79, 127–28, 132, 148
Seven Years' War, 91
sexual difference, religious toleration relationship, 6, 79–80, 100, 109, 111, 168, 182n61; companionate marriage and, 77, 79–80, 172n33; relation to sexual attraction and desire, 139–40, 152
sexual intimacy, 24–25
Shakespeare, William, 63, 149–50; *The Merchant of Venice,* 15, 140, 142–43, 144, 151–52, 160–61, 162, 192n43
Shapiro, James, 151–52
Shore, Daniel, 5
Shower, John, 36
Siddons, Sarah, 115
single women, 83, 84–85, 87–88, 109, 115
Slater, Samuel, 36–37
slavery, 4, 14, 84
Smith, Charlotte, *Desmond,* 5
sociability, religious, 2, 11, 13, 18, 25, 33, 39, 169, 171n4; Brooke's narratives, 83, 84, 111; Christian, 33; Edgeworth's narratives, 137, 154, 162; Inchbald's narratives, 111, 113, 116, 130, 135; Richardson's narratives, 13, 56, 70, 77–78, 80, 83, 84, 87, 108, 111, 137; secularism *versus,* 53; storytelling as conduit for, 19, 45
social contract theory, 116, 188n31
speech, women's right of, 13, 39, 66, 119–20, 165, 168
Staves, Susan, 2
Stevenson, John Allen, 78
storytelling, 9, 19, 44–45, 131, 154, 158, 159
Stuarts, 13, 35, 174n4

Taylor, Charles, 73, 172n35
teeth, extraction or transplanting of, 145–46, 158–59
Tennenhouse, Leonard, 14, 98, 183n6
Test and Corporation Acts, 45, 91–92, 108, 116–17
Thorowgood, Thomas, 29
Throckmorton, John, *A Letter addressed to the Catholic Clergy of England . . . ,* 118
Tillotson, John, 35–36
Toleration Act of 1689, 2, 11
Tomko, Michael, 114–15, 127, 136, 186n1, 186n4, 187n21, 188n24, 189n79

Tønder, Lars, 173n56; *Tolerance: A Sensorial Orientation to Politics,* 10, 138
Tories, 13, 85
Turner, James Grantham, 54, 175n12

Uffington, Sarah, 3

Vanneste, Tijl, 53, 179n13, 180n21
Vernon, Richard, 32, 176n38
Victorian novel, 168–69

Wabanaki people, 97
Waldron, Mary, 165, 193n7
Walsham, Alexandra, 154, 174n61
Walwyn, William, 30, 31
Ward, Sarah, 115
Webb, R. K., 46
Welbourne, Robert, 40
Welland, Heather, 94, 107, 184n34, 186n67
Wesley, Charles, 41–42, 44, 45, 47
Wesley, John, 41–42, 44, 45, 47
Wesley, Samuel, 39–45, 178n82; *The Life of Our Blessed Lord & Saviour Jesus Christ,* 42, 178n82
Wesley, Susanna, 19, 39, 41–45, 178n84; "A Religious Conference," 44
West, Moses, 38–39
Wheelwright, Esther, 97, 98
Whigs, 11, 13, 94
whiteness, as racial category, 5, 49, 52
widows, 14, 78–79, 85–86, 100, 102–6
William III, King of England, 35, 40, 41, 43
Williams, Roger, 30–31; *The Bloudy Tenant,* 26–27
Windstrup, George, 32
Winter, Sarah, 156–57
Wolfe, Michelle, 36
women authors, British, 161–62; British-French competition, 101; independence as writers, 49; support for Protestant imperialism, 108–9
women's movement, global, 17
Wruble, Vanessa, 17

xenophobia, 13, 18, 40, 46, 54, 145, 152, 156

Young, Francis, 115, 187n23
Yovel, Yirmiyahu, 150, 191n21

zealotry: affective, 68, 69, 72, 75, 104, 135, 182n66; religious, 2, 7, 12, 24–25, 33, 34–35t, 35, 76, 78–80, 122, 165

www.ingramcontent.com/pod-product-compliance
Lightning Source LLC
Chambersburg PA
CBHW030648230426
43665CB00011B/1002